FROM KANT TO WEBER

Freedom and Culture in Classical German Social Theory

Edited by
Thomas M. Powers and Paul Kamolnick

OPEN FORUM SERIES

KRIEGER PUBLISHING COMPANY
MALABAR, FLORIDA
1999

Original Edition 1999

Printed and published by
KRIEGER PUBLISHING COMPANY
KRIEGER DRIVE
MALABAR, FLORIDA 32950

Library of Congress Cataloging-in-Publication Data

From Kant to Weber : freedom and culture in classical German social
  theory / edited by Thomas M. Powers and Paul Kamolnick.
     p. cm.—(Open forum series)
  Includes bibliographical references and index.
  ISBN 0-89464-992-2 (alk. paper)
    1. Sociology—Germany—History. 2. Culture. 3. Liberty.
  I. Powers, Thomas M., 1965– . II. Kamolnick, Paul. III. Series.
HM22.G2F776 1999
301'.0943—dc21
                                    98-34309
                                       CIP

10 9 8 7 6 5 4 3 2

CONTENTS

FOREWORD

Freedom and Culture in Classical German Social Theory

Beginning with Immanuel Kant, a notable succession of German thinkers produced a complex tradition of thought which has had enormous repercussions on twentieth-century social science and philosophy. Originating in pointed contrast to varieties of naturalism represented by British utilitarianism and French organicism, and developing in continuous tension with later forms of naturalism, including Marxian materialism and American pragmatism, the creators of the German tradition developed a rich array of analyses and projects centered on the special status of human subjectivity. Their transgenerational efforts to protect the dignity and autonomy of the human subject against what they perceived as insidious intellectual and moral threats posed by hegemonic positive natural science produced an outpouring of creativity that restructured or gave birth to a number of modern disciplines. Interpretive cultural anthropology, phenomenological sociology, comparative religious and legal history, sociology of knowledge, experimental and psychoanalytic psychology, philosophic anthropology, and "critical" social theory represent some of the contemporary intellectual venues they have inspired.

With these words I opened a proposal to the National Endowment for the Humanities to offer a summer seminar at the University of Chicago in 1995. It was my great good fortune to be asked to direct that seminar and thus to have the opportunity to explore some of the contours of this tradition with a group of colleagues from several academic fields—education, law, literature, philosophy, political science, and sociology.

At the time my proposal was submitted, the Endowment was being threatened by efforts to cut its budget drastically and even to terminate it altogether. Undeterred by such assaults, the NEH staff maintained the extraordinarily high level of professional administration that I had come to know through dealing with them over many years. They understood their mission very well indeed and pursued it with energy and integrity, even to the extent of ensuring that the composition of my seminar was rounded up to a full dozen with participants of the highest quality.

But what they may not have planned—what sociologists call an

unintended consequence or latent function—was that those semi-
nars offer especially congenial conditions for nourishing what has
been called "the life of the mind." What might that mean?

One of the fairest flowers of Western civilization, the life of the
mind is also one of the rarest; there are times I want to call it an en-
dangered species. As I understand it here, the life of the mind involves a communal experience wherein persons exchange views with
no other goal than the clarification of opinion and the pursuit of
truth, but the persons so engaged are expected to have paid certain
dues in order to participate—to have mastered certain basic intellectual skills through hard work, devotion, and self-discipline.

The NEH Seminar that produced this volume exhibited a rare
specimen of that rare species. Its members ventured forth into new
terrain, always respectful of one another and respectful no less of the
great tradition of thought we were examining and one of the endur-
ingly important questions it has addressed. With this volume, the
process turns full circle; a number of talented and devoted college
teachers, selected for their performance as undergraduate teachers
as well as their intellectual qualifications, now return the gift of participating in a rare banquet in the life of the mind, by producing a
splendid collection of essays for use in undergraduate teaching. I
hope you find it at least a fraction as rewarding as we all found the
dialogues that stimulated and inspired it.

Donald N. Levine
Peter B. Ritzma Professor
The University of Chicago

CONTRIBUTORS

Gary Backhaus received his Ph.D. from American University and currently teaches at Morgan State University. His special interests concern phenomenology and social philosophy. Some recently published and forthcoming articles include, "The Phenomenology of Telephone Space," "Georg Simmel as an Eidetic Social Scientist," "The Death of a Significant Other," and "The Phenomenology of the Experience of Enchantment."

Ingeborg Baumgartner is professor of foreign language at Albion College in Michigan, where she teaches the German and Russian languages and their literature. She studied at the Free University of Berlin and received an M.A. from the University of Wisconsin and a Ph.D. from the University of Michigan. She has published on the works of Georg Buechner, Thomas Mann, and Christian Wagner.

Felecia M. Briscoe has an M.S. in psychology from the University of Nevada, Las Vegas, and a Ph.D. in the social foundations of education from the University of Cincinnati. She is assistant professor of education at Concord College in Athens, West Virginia.

David W. Felder has a Ph.D. and is professor of philosophy and peace studies and a long-time student of peace and conflict. He is the author of *How to Work for Peace* (University Press of Florida), as well as numerous articles in social philosophy. He teaches at Florida A&M University and Florida State University.

Paul Gomberg is professor of philosophy at Chicago State University in the Department of Sociology and Philosophy. He received his Ph.D. from Harvard University and his recent work has focused on political philosophy and on the problems of racial separation and racial inequality. He is writing a book on a conception of morality as decentralized social control.

Randall Halle received his Ph.D. in German studies from the University of Wisconsin. He has worked on the relation of social theory to nationalism and has published articles on the Frankfurt School, social psychology, and the women's movement. He teaches at the University of Rochester.

Nathan W. Harter, J.D. has been a practicing attorney and is currently associate professor of organizational leadership at Purdue University. He works in the areas of conflict theory and arbitration and mediation.

Paul Kamolnick is associate professor of sociology at East Tennessee State University. He received his Ph.D. from Florida State University and teaches social theory and critical theory. His publications include *Classes: A Marxist Critique* (General Hall) and articles in *The Review of Radical Political Economy, Current Perspectives in Social Theory, and Philosophy of the Social Sciences.*

David L. McNaron has a Ph.D. in philosophy from the University of Miami and is assistant professor of philosophy at NOVA University in Florida. His main area of research is the philosophy of mind, and he also teaches and writes in the areas of the philosophy of law and ethics.

Thomas M. Powers received a Ph.D. in philosophy from the University of Texas at Austin. He studied German philosophy, particularly the ethical theory of Immanuel Kant, as a DAAD-Fulbright Fellow at the University of Munich. He teaches philosophy at Santa Clara University in California.

Ronald L. Schultz, received his Ph.D. in sociology from The Graduate Center of The City University of New York. He has taught at Queens College and The University of Wisconsin at Milwaukee. He has also completed a qualitative study on the post-Fordist phenomenon of temporary work.

INTRODUCTION
Thomas M. Powers
and Paul Kamolnick

The chief goal of this volume is to provide students and scholars with a richer understanding of the philosophical underpinnings of classical German social theory. It is not intended for experts in the field of German studies, nor does it provide the advanced scholar with reconstructions of classic works. Rather, our mission as editors has been to craft a sophisticated but accessible text geared toward advanced undergraduate or graduate students in the fields of social theory, philosophy of the social sciences, and intellectual history. We hope that the contributions to this volume present a coherent account of the main contours and issues animating the German tradition in social thought from the late eighteenth to early twentieth centuries. Specifically, we wish to tell a certain story about the development of social theory that runs through the works of Kant, Herder, Hegel, Dilthey, the neo-Kantians, Simmel, and Weber.

CONTEMPORARY SIGNIFICANCE

Though the point of departure of these essays is primarily historical, the reader would be mistaken to think that our subject matter has little currency in philosophical and sociological circles. There are two reasons for the contemporary significance of classical German social theory. First, it has had a remarkable impact on interpretivist and critical-theoretic approaches to methodology, which comprise two of the three chief forms of contemporary philosophy of social science; second, it poses questions that have yet to be met fully in contemporary debates over the nature and proper method of the social sciences.

As background for the first reason above, let us consider the view that is most often cast opposite the German tradition: naturalistic positivism. Naturalistic positivism claims that a science of the social ought be modeled on the methodology of the physical. It holds that society is analogous to a natural organism and is therefore determined by causal laws. These laws are invariant and binding on social phenomena, and on this view the laws also determine the functional and structural relations of all of society's members. The positivist orientation in social theory is best represented by the French tradition—particularly Auguste Comte and Emile Durkheim—but can also be found in the works of Herbert Spencer and John Stuart Mill. This tradition is what is often thought of as "scientific sociology" and has been the critical foil against which much of the German tradition has defined itself.

Though it is the authoritative norm of much of scientific research, naturalistic positivism has had to compete in this century with two rival traditions in the philosophy and methodology of the social sciences: Interpretivism and Critical Theory. These challenges to naturalistic positivism came primarily from the founders of classical German social theory.

The interpretivist approach to the philosophy and methodology of the social sciences argues, in opposition to positivism, that a science of the social cannot be modeled on the natural sciences. Social phenomena are embedded with intentions and meaning and hence must be *understood* and not merely explained. The critical-theoretic tradition offers a second distinct alternative to naturalistic positivism. In opposition to the ideal of complete scientific objectivity and neutrality, critical-theoretic approaches point to the inevitable influence of the practical and historical conditions of a given society's way of doing scientific "labor." Critical-theoretic approaches in sociology developed later than the interpretivist approaches and are also indebted to the same Kantian and Hegelian roots. Further, Critical Theory owes some intellectual debts to the intellectual progeny of Kant and Hegel— namely, to Georg Simmel and Max Weber. Indeed, many members of the Frankfurt School—as well as Lukács—had intellectual and personal contact with the "mainstream" of German social theory.

Interpretivist and critical-theoretic approaches to the philosophy of social science ramify into wider intellectual discussions and become important to a number of contemporary debates. The theoretical grounding of Cultural Studies, for example, turns on the claim that questions of value, meaning, and social identity fundamentally shape one's patterns of participation in social life. Whether Cultural Studies will survive in the academy may depend in part on the truth of that claim. The contributions of Weber, Dilthey, and Alfred Schutz to an interpretive sociological conception of human action have become central to debates within the sociology of science and knowledge; they have also given rise to debates pitting social constructionists against anti-constructionists in the arena of social problems

theory. Georg Simmel's rich philosophical and sociological legacy has
found expression in the path-breaking contributions of Erving Goff-
man, as well as in the social interactionist tradition more generally.
The appreciation of Simmel has also found expression in current debates over modernity and postmodernity. In the philosophy of law,
the movement known as Critical Legal Studies has gone to the well
of both interpretivist and critical-theoretic viewpoints in order to
elucidate the concepts of action, intention, and judgment. Finally,
various insurgent or radical perspectives have also been deeply influenced by Interpretivism and Critical Theory.

Interest remains of course in the roots of the German tradition.
Contemporary developments such as Jürgen Habermas's theory of
communicative action, Norbert Elias's theory of "figurational sociology," and Charles Taylor's writings on the nature of the self, to name
a few, incorporate key elements drawn from various classical German theorists. Even the American political philosopher John Rawls
has been drawn recently to the dialogue begun, over 100 years ago,
by German social theorists.

FREEDOM AND CULTURE

The general rubric of analysis in these essays focuses on human
freedom and the influence of culture. Freedom becomes the pivotal
concept in Kant's resolution of the crisis in metaphysics brought
about by Hume. Without an argument for human freedom, morality—and eventually faith—is lost at the hands of a rigid determinism.
The philosophy of culture, on the other hand, is literally rescued from
Kant's Enlightenment neglect by Herder and is then historicized by
Hegel. In the interplay of these two concepts, the major theses of German Romanticism are forged. The conceptual dialectic of freedom and
culture in Enlightenment and Romantic writings gave birth to several other movements in nineteenth- and early twentieth-century
Germany. Indeed, historicism, organicism, individualism, aestheticism, vitalism, and cultural criticism are all offspring of a sort. By focusing on freedom and culture, then, these essays hope to illuminate
several generations of intellectual movements in philosophy and social theory.

INTRODUCTION TO THE ESSAYS

This collection opens with essays on several strands in the tradition of social thought inaugurated by three important figures of eigh-

teenth- to early nineteenth-century German philosophy: Immanuel Kant, J. G. Herder, and G. W. F. Hegel. Kant's philosophy is especially important to the German tradition, since all subsequent contributors to the German tradition were compelled to develop their own positions in a dialogue with Kant's metaphysical worldview. In "Kant's Legacy for German Social Theory," Thomas Powers provides a succinct account of Kant's critical philosophy and the relations therein between science, ethics, freedom, and objectivity. He shows how Kant's "Copernican Revolution" in philosophy yields a difficult but rich conception of the person, one committed to a kind of individuality and also to a competing "universalism" of moral and social obligation. In addition, Kant's moral theory provides a foundation for thinking that humans possess a kind of dignity—a central thesis of Enlightenment morality.

In "Johann Gottfried Herder and German Romanticism," Ingeborg Baumgartner explicates the profound significance of Herder and Romanticism for the development of the German tradition. Her essay features a discussion of several of the aforementioned movements of the tradition—cultural relativism, organicism, historicism, aestheticism, nationalism, individualism, and vitalism—which can be traced directly to Herder's influence. Baumgartner focuses especially on Romanticism's role in recovering ancient and medieval legends, myths, folk tales, and fairy tales. What emerges from her essay is a sense of the lasting influence of that tradition on the cultural sensibilities of modernity generally. In "Hegel on History and Freedom: An Exposition and Marxist Assessment," Paul Gomberg explains why Hegel's conception of history and freedom represents a powerful but problematic attempt to synthesize the universalist thrust of Kantian ethics with the historicist and relativist conceptions of Romanticism. Gomberg also demonstrates how Hegel's vision of a purposeful universe is vulnerable to certain objections which confront his apparent uncritical indebtedness to some classical liberal assumptions. Contrary to what Hegel may have thought, liberal capitalist market society is not likely to be the last form of organized social life. Gomberg provides the rudiments of a radical, Marxian-inspired scheme of postcapitalist possibilities.

The next three essays focus on different aspects of the *Methodenstreit*—the dispute within Germany over the proper methodology of the human sciences. In "The Neo-Kantian Predicament," Gary Backhaus first identifies the assumptions undergirding the reconstructive efforts of a broad movement collectively known as neo-Kantianism. This movement arose because many philosophers in the mid 1800s had become disillusioned with the direction of German Idealism and the philosophies of Fichte, Schelling, and Hegel. There was a cry to go "back to Kant," but several interim developments in science and epistemology made such a return quite difficult. As Backhaus shows, there was a growing rift between Kantian Transcendental Idealism and Empirical Realism. Backhaus describes how, in the formulations of their various schools, the neo-Kantians tried to come to terms with this rift through various forms of naturalism, materialism, psychologism, and biologism. Having described the philosophical landscape, Backhaus then introduces some of the central neo-Kantians and their contributions to the *Methodenstreit*.

Wilhelm Dilthey was perhaps the most formidable figure to have shaped the terms of debate over method, and his contributions are the subject of Ronald Schultz's essay "Dilthey's Hermeneutics: Between Idealism and Realism." Dilthey imagined himself to be grounding a revolutionary conception of the *Geisteswissenschaften,* the "human sciences." His conception is based on the claim that human beings are unique in that they project meaning, value, and purpose into the world, and hence that a science of humans cannot operate by means of the deterministic laws otherwise applicable to nature. Though Dilthey's project remained incomplete, his labors started a fecund program in philosophy and social science, as David McNaron argues in his essay, "Social Science and the *Verstehen* Thesis." This program is the *"verstehen"* tradition that can be seen from the classic works of Dilthey and Max Weber to the contemporary attempts of more radical *verstehen* theorists such as Charles Taylor and Paul Ricouer. After describing several versions of the tradition, McNaron explains why attempts to defend the *verstehen* thesis are unsuccessful. Nonetheless, McNaron argues, the anti-*verstehen* theorists or *naturalists* also face daunting problems in trying to explain human action. Their theories cannot easily rid philosophical analysis of the concept of meaning.

The remaining five essays of the volume are dedicated to exploring various aspects of the social thought of Germany's two most original social theorists: Georg Simmel and Max Weber. In "Simmel's Theory of Conflict," David Felder introduces Simmel's notion of a social form and reveals why, for Simmel, conflict is a part of our social life. He discusses the function of conflict, the rise of individuality, and the Simmelian picture of conflict and modernity. By comparing Simmel's views with those of Hobbes and Marx, Felder argues that Simmel's views offer a creative and promising approach to conflict. Next, Nathan Harter takes us "From Simmel's Conception of Society to the

Function and Form of Legal Conflict." Harter explains why, for Simmel, conflict is by no means incidental to social structure, nor is it
merely destructive. Rather, conflict is essential to social life; it assumes diverse manifestations from the private to the organized social life and is also a dynamic agent in human social interaction. Harter illustrates in the second half of the essay the specific form that
conflict assumes when dominated by its legal form.

Paul Kamolnick provides a second window into Simmel's doctrines
in "Central Themes in Simmel's *Philosophy of Money.*" The *Philosophy of Money* was considered by Simmel to be his greatest achievement; it is a book that captures the fundamental motifs of his mature conception of society and history. The contemporary consensus
in Simmel scholarship bears out Simmel's own sense of its importance. Kamolnick elaborates the theory of value in and other aspects
of Simmel's great work.

The final section comprises two essays on various aspects of Max
Weber's social thought. Like many who had contributed to the German tradition that preceded him, Max Weber was immersed in the
high-stakes politics of his era, often in fierce rivalry over the political direction that post-Wilhelmian Germany ought to follow. As Randall Halle points out in his essay "The Historical and Biographical
Context of Max Weber's Methodology," Weber's well-known doctrine
of value-neutrality was by no means motivated by a nihilism about
values, nor was Weber detached from the issues facing German aca-
demics. Weber's stance was precisely the opposite, in fact, and that
led him to demand full responsibility from persons wielding political
or academic authority. Halle explains the German historical context
from 1870 through the early 1920s with the intention of encouraging
a higher regard for Weber's predicament and a greater appreciation
for the role of historical and political factors in the shaping of
methodological orientations.

In the final essay, "Max Weber: On Freedom, Rationality, and
Value Judgments in Educational Discourse," Felecia Briscoe identifies the "value-contingency dilemma" that Weber faced in his politics
and philosophy of education. She spells out Weber's resolution of this
dilemma and draws a comparison between Weber's intellectual situation and that faced by writers on postmodernity, including Richard
Rorty and Michel Foucault. Briscoe offers an interpretation of contemporary convictions about value contingency that promises a Weberian solution.

The contributions to this volume were inspired by a National Endowment for the Humanities Summer Seminar held at the Univer-

sity of Chicago during the summer of 1995. We are thankful to the NEH and to the "philosophy of education" which inspires governments to provide for scholars and thereby to benefit the common good. We also greatly appreciate Gordon Patterson, history professor at Florida Institute of Technology and editor of The Open Forum Series for Krieger Publishing, for his guidance. Most of all, though, these essays are indebted to Professor Donald N. Levine of the University of Chicago, our director for the seminar. What Wallace Stevens said of the poet is surely true of Don: He fulfills himself as he sees his imagination become the light in the minds of others.

1

KANT'S LEGACY FOR GERMAN SOCIAL THEORY

Thomas M. Powers

INTRODUCTION

Among the great philosophers of the modern period, Immanuel Kant (1724–1804) left a peculiar legacy for German thinkers. As the intellectual "Moses" of the German nation,[1] Kant came to influence all German intellectuals of the ensuing century. But Kant's "gift"— the Kantian picture of the world—is replete with troublesome dualisms. These dualisms range from benign dichotomies to seeming contradictions—or what Kant tried to pass off as *antinomies*. The Kantian world-image contains, for instance, a division of reality into noumena (things-in-themselves) and phenomena (appearances); a belief in the objective validity of scientific laws *governing* experience, which laws are constructed by knowing subjects *independently* of all experience; a rational faith in God and immortality, coupled with an attack on all philosophical theology; and finally—and most important for social theory—a picture of human agency as rigidly determined yet capable of a transcendental and dignifying freedom. It was within this *Weltanschauung* of metaphysical splits that the social theorists of the nineteenth and early twentieth centuries came to develop the views that would dominate social theory.

This essay will unpack some of the Kantian dualisms that are important for an understanding of the development of German social theory. A focal point will be Kant's multilayered constructions of the individual and society. Though none of the later social theorists accepted this picture in its entirety, Heinrich Rickert, Wilhelm Windelband, Georg Simmel, and Max Weber all work from different aspects of the Kantian world-image (Martindale 1981, 377–380; cf. Levine 1995). Since the views of these figures are treated extensively in the upcoming essays, it will be our goal here to lay the groundwork for those discussions.

1

The reader must keep in mind that Kant was not a social theorist. He ignored Aristotle's claim (*Politics* 1253a) that the essence of humanity includes *zoon politikon* (political animal), which derives from its defining status as *zoon noetikon* (rational animal). He neglected as well the influence of *die Sittlichkeit* (the ethical community) on rational beings, which was a serious error in the eyes of Hegel. Kant preferred to understand each person as a moral agent and each moral agent as an incarnation of 'Rational Being,' immune to the influences of history or society. Like Plato and Aristotle, Kant did believe that there is a nonrational part of a human agency, but he thought that it would admit only of scientific and not of philosophic treatment.

According to Kant, rationality or Pure Reason is that which is the same in us all, and this sameness makes knowledge of the world of appearances (phenomena) possible. Since the categories of knowing—Kant thought that there were twelve in all—are the same for everyone, we all have access to the same truths of science, mathematics, and metaphysics. Pure Reason also stipulates that the laws which constitute this knowledge are necessary and unchanging. But these "truths," it ends up, just apply to the world of appearances. Since human social interactions take place in this world, it follows on Kant's view that they too are bound by necessary and unchanging causal laws. Kant declined to enumerate these laws, leaving that work for coming generations who would fill in the Critical philosophy[2]—the philosophy in the spirit of Kant's *Critique of Pure Reason* (1781).

The road Kant took in the development of the Critical philosophy quite often strayed into an intellectual cul-de-sac. But those seeming missteps were crucial in Kant's resolution of the rift between the two main strands of early modern philosophy, Rationalism and Empiricism. In moral theory, these two strands were characterized by what we will call the "*A Priori* Theory" and the "*A Posteriori* Theory," respectively.

The *A Priori* Theory

Kant began his philosophical career in the camp of Leibnizian rationalists, a group of thinkers with a penchant for immodest *a priori* claims about metaphysics. In declaring that ours is "the best of all possible worlds," G. W. Leibniz (1646–1716) fathered a moral optimism that the modern period has rarely encountered since. In Leibniz's disciples, this general metaphysical view was translated into the moral theory of perfectionism.

Discussions of perfectionism in ethics were abundant in the works of Leibniz's successors; during Kant's university education in Königsberg, Christian Wolff (1679–1754) and Christian August Crusius (1715–75) were at the forefront of this movement.[3] Kant's *eventual* position in ethical theory was opposed to the doctrines of Wolff, A. G. Baumgarten (1714–62), and Crusius (Höffe 1994, 20). Initially, though, Kant had embraced Wolff's formal criterion of good action,[4] one that called for the harmony of social action based in "a universal point of view" (*in einer allgemeinen Absicht*).[5] According to Wolff, one's moral perfection would consist in the striving for absolute harmony amongst disparate wills. The universal point of view was to help one achieve the harmony. Success in this impersonal endeavor, according to Wolff, could somehow be measured. His view, then, is a formalist type of perfectionism. Generally, formalism in ethical theory is the view that obligation can be calculated by a formula or algorithm which gives a decisive answer.

Wolff's view suffers from a calculation problem similar to that which plagues modern utilitarianism. It turns out to be quite difficult to calculate the harmony among wills which any act produces, just as it is virtually impossible to give a cardinal measure of utility which follows upon any action. Kant recognizes as much in his Berlin Academy Prize Essay of 1764.[6] In this essay Kant agrees with Crusius's criticism of Wolff, wherein Crusius complains that Wolff's principle of human perfection takes refuge in formal obscurity and is no help whatsoever in determining obligation.[7]

In turn, Kant also criticizes Crusius's view that moral obligation is an obligation of a law relating human and divine will—a law which is "written" by a divine legislator (Prize Essay, 300). Crusius has merely replaced Wolffian perfection (*Vollkommenheit*) with the notion of a law ordering one's will to the will of God (*Gesetzmäßigkeit*). In the end, Kant sees that the views of both Wolff and Crusius are fatally tethered to unprovable theological assumptions about perfection, harmony, and divine will. Moreover, these assumptions run afoul of one of Kant's principal doctrines of his Critical philosophy: concepts which apply in the sphere of human experience cannot meaningfully apply to the nonexperienced world of the divine (Diss. § 24). Kant brandishes here for the first time the arguments which he would use so effectively in his mature Critical philosophy against religious ethics. With Kant's emancipation of philosophical ethics from religious dogma, the Enlightenment had gained one of its central intellectual triumphs.

The *A Posteriori* Theory

The second of Kant's early positions is an experiential or *a posteriori* theory of value. This view—value phenomenalism—comes from the psychological doctrine that Kant learned from Francis Hutcheson (1694–1746) and later admired in Adam Smith (1723–90).[8] It is also present in the moral theory of David Hume (1711–76). Basically, the view allows that each individual senses or intuits goodness or value, and that these psychological or phenomenal data lead to right judgment or action. This kind of position is typical of British moral sense theory—as the view has come to be called—and does not pretend to offer moral absolutes. In value phenomenalism, there is no guarantee that every person will sense the same goodness or value in an act. Therefore, the moral obligation which is concomitant with the sensing of value would be a contingent matter, as it can vary among persons. For this reason, Kant's acceptance of value phenomenalism leads him to skepticism about a philosophical treatment of morality, since it leads to no theory at all. But rather than bemoan a lack of success in his search for a theory, Kant momentarily embraces the skeptical conclusions of the doctrine. He writes that "since many simple sensations of the good are certainly in us, there are many simple unanalyzable conceptions of the good (Prize Essay 299).[9] By the mid 1770s, it is clear that the doctrine of value phenomenalism has seduced Kant away from Leibnizian optimism.

THE CRITICAL TURN

Kant's "silent decade" from 1771–81 came to a resounding end with the publication of the first *Critique*. Schopenhauer's claim that Kant's *Critique of Pure Reason* was "the most important book ever written in Europe" (Höffe 1994, 21) is a telling (if hyperbolic) estimation of its importance. Surely, the publication of Kant's Critical masterpiece was the watershed of eighteenth-century philosophy.

On the surface, one might think that the first *Critique* has little to do with moral theory. But a closer look reveals two clear and competing moral views. The first of these is an astonishing moral Platonism which remains hidden until the latter part of the work (Seung 1994, 59–94). This Platonism is expressed in Kant's enthusiasm for the Ideas of the virtuous person and the perfect constitution or republic (KrV A313–320/B370–377; A569/B597). The second position, which comes to dominate Kant's mature ethical views in the *Grounding for the Metaphysics of Morals* (1785) and *Critique of Practical Reason* (1788), is a type of ethical formalism. Kant puts forth an ethic based on the logical universality in the mere notion of law—on the logical property that a law as such quantifies over *all* phenomena. At the same time, Kant fails to spell out what the moral law would be, saying only that it "borrows" this property of universality from law as such. Later on, we will pursue the second tendency, since it is the formalist or "universalist" doctrine that later philosophers and social theorists take to be distinctively Kantian.

The significance of the first *Critique* for Kant's moral theory might be seen more clearly with an analogy to science, one which connects two notions of law. For Kant, a moral law is a law of obligation; it tells us how certain phenomena (human beings) *ought* to act. Natural or scientific laws tell us how phenomena *do* act. Moral laws, if there are to be any, must be universally valid and necessary, which is to say, they must command categorically. A scientific law is also universally valid and necessary, at least for the phenomena it governs.[10] Let us concentrate on this shared feature of *necessity*.

Philosophers in both the Rationalist and early-Empiricist traditions wanted for the most part to defend the necessity of both moral and scientific law. In the wake of these traditions, Hume presented the following problem: How are we to know of the necessity of the scientific law from the mere repetition of phenomena? The traditional (unsatisfactory) response, found already in Descartes' *Meditations* (1641), points to the necessary connection between cause and effect and employs an assumption about the behavior of tokens or instances of *types*. This assumption—call it causal equivalence—is that events of the same type will give rise to the same effects. An actual scientific law of the form "A follows B" allegedly *must* hold for all instances because B-type things are the cause of A-type things.

Hume saw that this traditional answer is merely a restatement of the original question, only replacing the necessity of the law with the necessity of the causal nexus between types. So Hume reformulates the question. The defender of causation needs to know either (1) how the mere concept of a cause brings with it its own necessity—for Hume, this would be a "relation of ideas"; or (2) how *this* object that we experienced as a cause—a Humean "matter of fact"—contains the guarantee that it must always cause the selfsame effect.

In answering Hume, Kant sees that we must focus not on the scientific object (the actual phenomena, observable, or "token" in some experiment, let us say) but on the concept which makes possible the knowledge of the lawlike behavior of that object. That is, we must investigate how the *a priori* concept of cause *can* be synthetic, or how it can provide "objectively valid" knowledge *of* experience while not being derived *from* experience. Kant's theoretical philosophy tries to find out what is behind the metaphysics of causal equivalence in types.

This problem about causation is considerably more difficult than the problem usually associated with Kant's critical project: How is a synthetic *a priori* concept possible? Paul Guyer has called this the "Problem of Objective Validity" (Guyer 1987, 23):

> The problem is that these pure concepts furnish "axioms of pure reason concerning" their objects, that the understanding "construct[s] for itself entirely *a priori* concepts of things, with which the things are necessarily in agreement" (10:130–1). That is, because its principles are known to be true *a priori,* the understanding must draw them up, out of its own resources, independently of experience, yet the objects *necessarily,* rather than accidentally, agree with these principles.[11]

With respect to the issue of scientific law, the problem can be put as follows: How can laws come *a priori* from the understanding but describe the ordering of objects which are entirely independent of the understanding, even though the cognition of that ordering is not independent of understanding or sensibility? Kant's answer comes in one of his famous "transcendental" arguments: the laws of the understanding correspond to the conditions of the possibility of knowing anything whatsoever in the realm of experience.

Likewise, in the sphere of practical philosophy Kant repeats a form of the transcendental argument. He wants us to focus our attention not on the moral phenomena such as good and bad people[12] or even on their feelings about the good. Rather, we must attend to the very conditions for the possibility of moral action. That is, we must investigate the conditions for the possibility of a universally valid and necessary normative obligation. So the analogy with science delivers the following research problem for Critical philosophy. For science: how does the concept of a type of cause bring with it necessity?; and for ethics: how does the concept of obligation—a duty to do a type of action—bring with it necessity of the "moral" kind? The key to the solution, Kant believes, is that a *necessary* moral obligation would come from a moral law that was *objectively valid*—one that held for all moral agents.

The Problem of Objectivity

Kant's earlier preoccupation with necessity in moral obligation is carried over to the Critical metaphysics, only now the problem must be approached from an entirely new direction. This "revolution" in perspective requires a new notion of objectivity. The old notion of objectivity—connoting what "exists independently" of human cognition—simply would not do. Kant thinks of his revolution on the model of Copernicus' and describes it accordingly.

> Up till now, we assumed that all of our knowledge must conform to objects. But all of our attempts to find out something about [objects] *a priori,* through concepts, whereby our knowledge would be extended, have gone—under this prerequisite—for nought. We should therefore see whether we will not have more success in the tasks of metaphysics by assuming that the objects must conform to our knowledge . . . Our explanation would then match the primary thoughts [or "opening moves"] of Copernicus. When he assumed that the heavens revolved around the spectator, he failed to explain celestial movement. He then tried to see if he might be more successful by revolving the spectator and leaving the stars at rest . . . (KrV Bxvi, my trans.)

The objects to which scientific and moral propositions refer can no longer be seen as simply "out there." Neither can they be, for Kant, entirely "in us." The elusive truth-maker of allegedly necessary scientific and moral propositions, Hume had shown, was neither where the Rationalists nor Empiricists thought it would be found; it could be found neither in the relations of ideas nor in matters of fact. To answer Hume, Kant believed, we would need a new understanding of the very problem of objectivity.[13]

One side of Kant's answer is a view that he calls transcendental idealism. Unlike other forms of idealism, Kant's view does not deny that there is an objective world. The objective world of experience is not just the mind, nor is it a world created entirely by mind. The Objective is neither the world "out there" nor the forms or concepts "in us." It is a cooperative project of both. The world *that* we know is known only *through* us; "In the practical sphere, as in the theoretical, objectivity is only possible through the subject" (Höffe 1994, 135). So objectivity in the Critical philosophy is not the contrary of subjectivity. Subjectivity for Kant is connected with the mind but cannot be understood merely as that which is mentally "private." Objectivity is a property of our representations only when we constrain the domain of objects to appearance. When Kant speaks of *objective validity,* he means a property of knowledge that holds for all experiential objects.

The other side of Kant's answer to Hume's skepticism is the doctrine of empirical realism. Kant is a realist in the following sense: he believes our mental representations of objects can have objective validity, provided that we keep in mind that the object is an object of experience and not a "thing in itself." Kant's "realism" is only half-hearted, for it is a realism about objects of experience and not about "ultimate reality." This central dualism in the first *Critique* lays the foundation for the rest of the Critical project.

Science and Freedom

The long-running analogy between science and morality in Kant's philosophy connects the theoretical doctrines of the first *Critique* to the formalism of his later ethical position by means of the notion of lawfulness. Science consists of our understanding of nature, and nature is seen by Kant in the first *Critique* as a system of laws about sensible-world experience. For Kant, this is the only kind of experience there is. But how do morality and experience link up? Morality is a *possible* system of behavior according to lawful maxims. We do not have experience of morality *per se.* The moral law is not an empirical or *a posteriori* law.

This division between morality and the rest of our experience can be seen if we attend once again to the crucial difference between moral phenomena and scientific phenomena. The causal determination of scientific phenomena—indeed their very cognition—takes place under one unified set of laws, given by the understanding. The determination of moral phenomena (human actions) through the will takes place in one of *two* ways, which Kant calls the causality of natural necessity and the causality of freedom, respectively (KrV A532/B560).

The first kind of determination of moral phenomena, through natural necessity, is that which is shared in common with natural phenomena. Natural necessity here operates through the appetitive connection between objects of inclination and the actual inclination in the subject. This is Kant's garden-variety rendition of moral determinism, the modern strains of which can be seen in Freudianism, Behaviorism, Social Darwinism, and other deterministic reductions of moral phenomena. In Kant's rendition, a causal law describes the connection of inclination and object as an instance of "A follows B," such as "John lusts for chocolate after John sees chocolate." The further effect in this case might be that John is compelled to do almost anything—including killing Maria—to get the chocolate. We have a science of such causal determinations of humans (as animals) in the phenomenal world which Kant calls anthropology (KrV A550/B578).

The second kind of determination, and the kind which exclusively can be called moral, applies a different type of law to a different type of subject. The law is not an empirical causal law but an *a priori* normative one, and the subject of the law is the human as both noumenal rational agent *and* phenomenal effect.[14] The phenomenal determination of John in the first instance, the "scientific" determination, is actual, whereas the noumenal determination of any rational being is merely possible, according to Kant. Humans as phenomenal beings can "think" this possibility by acknowledging that John could have done otherwise than to kill Maria; he could have acted in accordance with the moral law as opposed to the causal law determining the effect—his crime. When the agent frees himself from the first kind of scientific determination by willing his actions—or indeed himself—into the realm *created by his idea of normative determination,* he thus gains his freedom.

The metaphor of some sort of moral journey, of the agent entering into the noumenal realm in virtue of his willing, comes readily in to view. Kant sketches this journey as an outline of an argument in which the chain of stages leads from everyday moral experience to the noumenal world. Unfortunately, this chain of stages passes through the infamous muddle created by Kant's two-part doctrine of freedom, practical freedom and transcendental freedom.[15] Kant's followers would expend great energy in trying to clear up this difficulty.

Kant's practical philosophy—his doctrines on ethics and law—tries to exploit his central contribution to theoretical philosophy: the establishment of synthetic *a priori* knowledge. Only by establishing a species of knowledge which is *informative* of experience (synthetic) yet nonetheless *necessary* (*a priori*) could Kant defeat Hume's challenge to causation and metaphysics in general. On one side of that challenge lies the Scylla of tautologous relations of ideas, and on the other side awaits the Charybdis of contingent matters of fact. Once awakened by Hume from his famous "dogmatic slumber," Kant wastes little philosophical energy in attacking the problem of necessity in moral obligation with the same weapon he uses against the problem of causal necessity in scientific laws. For just as a defense of causation requires a notion of scientific necessity which holds for objects of experience while not being derived from experience, so too must moral necessity hold for human agents without being derived from the phenomenal laws of agency, that is, empirical anthropology and psychology. Kant's practical philosophy must be a *pure* undertaking, for he is not interested in an empirical or descriptive ethic. He wants to show that the conditions for the possibility of morals are those very transcendental conditions which allow for human freedom.

Likewise, adherents to Kantianism who wanted to extend the transcendental method to the social sciences were not interested in mere "fact gathering." Georg Simmel, for instance, would argue for conceptions of sociology and history that looked toward the conditions of the possibility of those disciplines *a priori* (Simmel 1971, 3 ff., 23 ff.).

The Critical Ethics

Kant's transcendental ethic the issues in the *Grounding for the Metaphysics of Morals* (1785) and famous "moral law" that Kant had failed to deliver in the first *Critique*. This moral law is the categorical imperative. There are several formulations of the imperative, but the two main ones we shall call C1 and C2. They are (C1) "Act only according to that maxim whereby you can at the same time will that it should become a universal law"; and (C2) "Act in such a way that you treat humanity, whether in your own person or in the person of another, always at the same time as an end and never simply as a means" (Gr. 421, 429). Although the first formulation is an outcome of Kant's resolution of the *a priori* and *a posteriori* theories of morality, the second formulation introduces non-formal or substantive elements of morality which were new to Kant's approach to moral theory. Since this non-formal part of the ethics is also influential for later social theory, its argumentation and terminology deserves some unpacking.

The Non-Formal Ethic

The notion of the *person* occupies a central position in Kant's non-formal theory of value.[16] This notion is for him an explicitly normative concept, not a biological one. "A person," he tells us, "is a being who has rights of which he can become conscious." The human tendency to follow inclination creates duties for the person, and in the course of moral development the person is supposed to become conscious of them (OP, 203). Kant's categorical imperative is proposed as an aid to the consciousness of rights and duties. Such consciousness is a function of *practial reason*.

The outcome of the moral project of practical reason is *dignity* in the person, a sign that an individual has transcended the brute animality of nature. This type of moral success connects a category of being with a way of acting. Namely, an agent's

> ... dignity (prerogative) of being above all the mere things of nature implies that his maxims must be taken from the viewpoint that regards himself, as well as every other rational being, as being legislative beings (and hence are they called persons). (Gr., 438)

Dignity, then, is a term of success for moral action, which for Kant—in the language of C1—is action on maxims which are universalizable. Hence persons are *legislative* beings, for their maxims could serve as universal laws of action. Beings without the opportunity for dignity are just those beings that cannot make their own laws of action but must follow slavishly the laws set for them by nature. Sensuous impulse is their master, and they cannot escape the world of causally determined phenomena.

Kant's view on human dignity has been inspiring for many enlightenment and modern thinkers. But the view has also suffered from some ambiguities. Some commentators have read Kant to be saying that the dignity of a person is unconditional and constitutes the "absolute value" of persons.[17] On this interpretation, no rights and duties would follow from such an automatic and unconditional notion. A more plausible view, one which connects moral success to dignity, would hold that dignity is defeasible. Much rides on this dispute for philosophical ethics.

It is important to recognize that, under any interpretation, the Kantian notion of human dignity is not just a metaphysical notion with which to separate humans from animals. Kant's view is that there is a peculiar way in which we distinguish ourselves from animals, one which makes a difference for our moral status. Besides our technological and social differences with animals, and the fact that we have knowledge of our own mortality, we would seem to be, at bottom, animals. But of course the only morally relevant difference is our potential for practical rationality free from the determination of sensuous nature. Since potentiality without actuality would not be enough for Kant, we actually have to carry through on practical rationality in order to create, in some sense, the notion of the normative. For Kant, actions manifesting dignity are what do this; they actually bring value into a world of fact.

Not only does dignity connect a way of being (person) with a way of acting (morality). It also serves to explain the status alluded to in the second formulation of the categorical imperative: that persons are ends-in-themselves and not mere means. The status of a person as an end-in-himself simply reiterates the fact of his moral success, for as Kant says "just this very fitness of his maxims for the legislation of universal law distinguishes him as an end-in-himself."[18] The explanation that dignity provides tells us why the restriction on the treatment of persons is a "supreme limiting condition" for actions that affect persons. On Kant's view, nonpersons are allowed to be used as means for the satisfaction of human preferences. Since persons are ends-in-themselves, they are separated from the realm of "usable" objects and things. This status denies that authorities external to the self, for example, society, the church, the state, and others, can command morally the ends which an agent chooses. The upshot of Kant's view is that a person's dignity provides the conditions for her to transcend sensuous animality, and her status as an end-in-herself delivers the person from the realm in which objects and things can be used.

We can now give a synopsis of Kant's ethics in its formal and nonformal elements. This combination of elements might be thought of as a synthesis of C1 and C2, what we can call the "thick" conception of the categorical imperative. It is the version of the categorical imperative with the universality condition and all of the non-formal elements of his ethics included, that is, the fullest possible conception of *the* categorical imperative. This version Kant refers to as the supreme principle of morality—the principle of autonomy. This "thick," categorical imperative commits Kant to the following comprehensive ethic:

1. Agents are restricted in what they can universalize by the rule governing the treatment of persons. Persons must be afforded a kind of reverential status because they have dignity.
2. Persons gain dignity not through some static "existential" position as ends but as self-legislating beings, that is, as persons whose maxims are fit to be universal laws.
3. The making of universal law takes place in an ideal context— that is, one which surveys not the actual world of nature and imperfect society but a merely possible community of like-minded self-legislators in an analogous "kingdom of nature." The normative laws in this ideal world would function just like descriptive causal laws in the actual world.

In this synthesis Kant comes full circle to rejuvenate some ideas which dominate his earlier ethical writings. The universalization procedure in C1 captures the purpose of Rousseau's Universal Will in the context of a community of Rousseauan citizens. That purpose is to further a hypothetical communal good of the kingdom of ends. More important, in this comprehensive view the obscurity of the doctrine of freedom gives way to the relative clarity of the doctrine of self-legislation. Practical autonomy in *Grounding* spells out the steps one must take in order to *achieve* freedom. By the time the agent achieves this freedom, she does so under the direction of a thick categorical imperative, one which contains formal and non-formal elements of morality.

It should be apparent that Kant's moral philosophy is ambitious to a fault. In the first two *Critiques* and *Grounding* he carved out a space for human freedom from difficult metaphysical territory. He then situated the free human agent in an abstract, two-part ethic. Unfortunately, the "popular" Kant gets watered down and assimilated to the major developments of enlightenment thought, humanism and individualism.[19] While surely there is an attenuated sense in which his views are "humanistic" and "individualistic," Kant would likely not give a blanket endorsement for either view. He believed in the dignity of human agents who were rational and successful in the project of practical reason—moral consciousness. But Kant also advocated the death penalty and slavery for crimes (MM § 49). Kant did advocate "thinking for oneself," and his formal ethics offer a kind of moral self-determination in the C1's procedure of self-legislation. But as Max Scheler argues (1973 [1913–16], 370 ff.), Kant's "individualism" extends only to the de-personalized agent who wills nothing other than universalizable maxims—the individual who wills just what any other rational being would will. For later German moral theoists like Scheler and Nicolai Hartmann, Kant's doctrine seemed *anti-individualistic*.

The Kantian Citizen

In Kant's *Metaphysics of Morals* (1797), consisting of the *Rechtslehre* or Doctrine of Right and the *Tugendlehre* or Doctrine of Virtue, he finally cashes out the import of his moral theory for the would-be virtuous individual and for the organization of the state.

One of Kant's goals in the *Rechtslehre* is to derive a principle of justice—a principle ordering external freedom—from the categorical imperative and connect it to traditional (but subsidiary) political

concepts such as right and equality. This principle of justice, which
is often called the universal principle of right (Reiss 1991, 23) is the
following:

> Each action is just (*Recht*) which, through it or its maxim, allows the free-
> dom of the will of each with everyone, according to a universal law, to co-
> exist. (MM 230)

The principle of justice is used to establish substantive claims of
right from the vacuum of the state of nature. Once this conclusion is
reached, the rest of Kant's political theory falls out as a necessary
construction in order to secure the freedom of all. A civil constitution,
the authority to use coercion, a system of retributive justice, and the
rights of property, equality before the law, and suffrage are all seen
as necessary for justice in the Kantian sense. Like Hobbes, then,
Kant believes that the civil state will emerge from the state of nature through the dictates of reason. Unlike Hobbes, Kant did not give
unrestricted power to the sovereign, and he seems generally more
concerned with the welfare of the citizen in the state. As in the first
Critique, Kant again connects his concepts to several Platonic ideas,
viz., the social contract, the ideal constitution, and a peaceful universal community of all nations (Seung 1994, 131–32). This last idea
resurfaces from two of Kant's essays that made him a famous pro-
ponent of the Enlightenment, *Idea for a Universal History with a
Cosmopolitan Purpose* (1784) and *Perpetual Peace* (1795). The latter
was often the first selection of Kant's opus to be translated for foreign readers (Höffe 1994, 239–40).

CONCLUSION

Heine and Marx, among others, have attested to the significance
of Kant's moral and political philosophy for justifying (if not inspiring) the French and American revolutions (Reiss 1991, 3) The aforementioned "institutions" of liberal and modern political structures—
rights, equality, property, etc.—can be grounded, perhaps, not *only*
through Kantian doctrines, but arguably best through them. Kant's
attention to the rule of law, universality, freedom, and dignity left for
the coming social theorists a multifaceted notion of the person as a
building block for their theories. Later commentators would com-
plain of course that the Kantian 'person' was austerely rational, de-
void of human emotion, and too much of an abstraction to be of use.
But they nonetheless took up a picture of the world and of individuals in it that was Kantian in outline and origin.

NOTES

1. It was the poet and writer Hölderlin, no less, who said that Kant was "the Moses of our nation." See Höffe (1994), 233.

2. The term 'Critical philosophy' was often used by Kant to indicate (what he took to be) his major contributions to philosophical thought: a defense of empirical realism and transcendental idealism, prefaced with an investigation into the limits of human reason. 'Critical', in the Kantian sense, is not to be confused with the 20th century 'Critical Theory'.

3. There are regrettably few historical expositions available in English of the philosophical climate surrounding Kant in his pre-Critical period. The most complete is Cassirer (1981) especially chapters 2 and 5. For a focus on ethics, see Paul A. Schilpp, *Kant's Pre-Critical Ethics* (Evanston: 1938). For those with German, Dieter Henrich's "Über Kants früheste Ethik" in *Kant-Studien,* vol. 54, 1963, is perhaps the best source for Kant's ethical views in this period.

4. Kant's early deference to the views of Wolff and Baumgarten surely had something to do with his tenuous position as a *Privatdozent* charged with teaching the neo-Leibnizian party line. This deference is clear in the 1759 essay "Versuch einiger Betrachtungen über den Optimismus." Viggo Rossvaer carefully expounds Kant's early position with respect to Wolff. See his *Kant's Moral Philosophy,* (Universitetsforlaget, Oslo: 1979), 24 f.

5. The quote is from Wolff's *Vernünftige Gedanken von Gott, der Welt, und der Seele des Menschen,* vol. 1 (Halle: 1725), p. 79 ("Rational Thoughts about God, the World, and the Soul of Man"). Though Kant was compelled to teach the ethics of Baumgarten and not Wolff, the latter was still influential for the young Kant in his earliest encounters with formalism in ethics.

6. Kant's essay, *Untersuchung über die Deutlichkeit der Grundsätze der natürlichen Theologie und der Moral,* was actually awarded the second prize from the Berlin Academy in 1763, with first prize going to Moses Mendelssohn.

7. It is not obvious in the Prize Essay that Kant wants to embrace Crusius' position. Kant praises Crusius for having understood the problem with empty ethical formalism and criticizes his doctrine of obligation for being likewise an empty formalism. See Prize Essay 294, 300.

8. Kant cites approvingly the attempts by "Hutcheson and others" to develop a theory of moral feeling (*Untersuchung,* 300). In the announcement of his lectures for the winter semester 1765–66, Kant says that they will include the ethical theories of Hutcheson, Hume, and Shaftesbury. By 1771, Kant seems to have adopted Smith as his "favorite" amongst the British moralists, according to the July 9 letter from Marcus Herz. There are approving references to Smith in the *Rechtslehre* (289), *Anthropologie* (209), and in *Reflexionen* (1355).

9. See also the discussion of this passage in Cassirer (1981), 234.

10. For Kant, a scientific law governs phenomena in a very strong and unusual sense. The law represents the function by means of which the concepts of the understanding order the given intuitions and allow them to be cognized. In Kantian terminology:

> Thus the order and regularity in the appearances, which we entitle *nature,* we ourselves introduce. We could never find them in appearances, had not we ourselves, or the nature of our mind, originally set

them there . . . We may now characterize [the understanding] as the *faculty of rules* . . . Rules, so far as they are objective, and therefore necessarily depend upon the knowledge of the object, are called laws . . . They are not borrowed from experience; on the contrary, they have to confer upon appearances their conformity to law, and so to make experience possible. Thus the understanding is something more than a power of formulating rules through comparison of appearances; it is itself the lawgiver of nature. (KrV A125–26)

11. Guyer's references are to the famous Letter to Marcus Herz of February 1772, as found in volume 10 of the *Akademie* edition of Kant's works.

12. In the type-token way of speaking, the particular good and bad persons are tokens of types 'Good Person' and 'Bad Person', respectively.

13. For the history of Kant's views on objectivity, see Cassirer (1981), 131 f).

14. This dual-aspect theory of the self requires one to think of oneself both as a puppet being controlled by the forces which control all other phenomena *and* at the same time as the controller of the puppet, the spontaneous causality which itself as reason is uncaused and lies outside of the time-order of determinations. This "subtle and obscure" distinction is the heart of Kant's solution to the Third Antinomy (KrV A532–558/ B560–586).

15. Not all commentators believe the two-part doctrine of freedom to be so problematic. For a sympathetic exposition, see Bernard Carnois' *The Coherence of Kant's Doctrine of Freedom,* trans. David Booth (Chicago: 1987).

16. For a more in-depth discussion of the Kantian notions of person and dignity, see my essay "The Integrity of Body: Kantian Moral Constraints on the Physical Self," in *Persons and their Bodies: Rights, Relationships, and Responsibilities,* ed. Mark J. Cherry and Thomas Bole III (Dordrecht: [forthcoming]).

17. Another way to view this controversy is to ask whether *human beings* have dignity automatically, that is, regardless of successful moral performance or status as persons. There is disagreement amongst Kant scholars. I am defending the view that they do not; that while individual agents should be *presumed* to have dignity on the basis that we generally have no evidence of their moral failures, dignity is defeasible and indeed *is* forfeited in acts of egregious immorality. I believe that, among other positions, Kant's supportive position on capital punishment in the *Rechtslehre* is evidence for my view. For the view that dignity is unconditional, see Thomas E. Hill, Jr.'s *Dignity and Practical Reason in Kant's Moral Theory* (Cornell: 1992), pp. 50, 204–205.

18. Gr., 438. See also Kant's long discussion of means and ends. (LOE, 120f). Here he states quite precisely that "man is not free to dispose of his person as a means."

19. Hence Martindale (1981), 37:

Humanism locates ultimate value in the fullest self-realization of the human personality. This aspect of its theory was never more brilliantly formulated than by Kant in his various formulations of the categorical imperative: so act that one's action can become a universal law. This meant, for Kant, that a type of individuality was the ultimate good.

REFERENCES

Cassirer, Ernst. 1981. *Kant's Life and Thought,* trans. James Haden. New Haven, CT: Yale University Press.

Höffe, Otfried. 1994. *Immanuel Kant,* trans. Marshall Farrier. Albany, NY: SUNY Press.

Guyer, Paul. 1987. *Kant and the Claims of Knowledge.* Cambridge: Cambridge University Press.

Kant, Immanuel. 1922. *Kants gesammelte Schriften,* ed. Königliche Preußische Akademie der Wissenschaften. Berlin: Walter de Gruyter, hereafter KgS. Other works cited as follows:

Diss.   *De mundi sensibilis atque intelligibilis forma et principiis* [1770]. (Kant's Inaugural Dissertation) trans. John Handyside, as it appears in *Kant's Latin Writings,* ed. Lewis White Beck. New York: Peter Lang, 1986.

Gr.   *Grounding for the Metaphysics of Morals* [1785]. trans. James W. Ellington Indianapolis: Hackett Publishing, 1983, with the pagination of the KgS.

KrV   *Critique of Pure Reason* [1781]. trans. N. Kemp Smith. New York: St. Martins' Press, 1965. KgS pagination.

LOE   *Lectures On Ethics* [posthumous]. trans. Louis Infield. Indianapolis: Hackett Publishing, 1963.

MM   *Metaphysics of Morals* [1797]. trans. James W. Ellington. Indianapolis: Hackett Publishing, 1983.

OP   *Opus Postumum* [posthumous]. ed. Eckart Förster. Cambridge, England: Cambridge University Press, 1993.

Prize Essay   *Untersuchung über die Deutlichkeit der Grundsätze der natürlichen Theologie und der Moral* [1764]. KgS pagination.

Levine, Donald N. 1995. *Visions of the Sociological Tradition.* Chicago: The University of Chicago Press.

Martindale, Don. 1981. *The Nature and Types of Sociological Theory,* 2nd ed. New York: Harper & Row.

Powers, Thomas M. (forthcoming). "The Integrity of Body: Kantian Moral Constraints on the Physical Self," in *Persons and their*

Bodies: Rights, Relationships, and Responsibilities, ed. Mark J. Cherry and Thomas Bole III. Dordrecht, Kluwer Academic Publishing.

Reiss, Hans. (ed.) 1991. *Kant: Political Writings.* trans. H. B. Nisbet, 2nd ed. Cambridge, England: Cambridge University Press.

Scheler, Max. 1973. *Formalism in Ethics and Non-Formal Ethics of Value.* trans. Manfred S.Frings and Roger L. Funk. Evanston: Northwestern University Press. from *Der Formalismus in der Ethik und die Materiale Wertethik.* 1966 [1913–16], 5th ed.

Seung, T. K. 1994. *Kant's Platonic Revolutions in Moral and Political Philosophy.* Baltimore: Johns Hopkins University Press.

Simmel, Georg. 1977. *Problems of the Philosophy of History.* trans. Guy Oakes. New York: The Free Press, from *Die Probleme der Geschichtsphilosophie.* 1905 [1892], 2nd ed.

———. 1971. *On Individuality and Social Forms.* ed. Donald N. Levine. Chicago: University of Chicago Press.

2

JOHANN GOTTFRIED HERDER AND GERMAN ROMANTICISM

Ingeborg Baumgartner

INTRODUCTION

A knowledge of Herder and German Romanticism[1] is essential for fully comprehending key elements of classical German social thought. Indeed, a line may be drawn from Kant to Herder and to the various literary movements that dominated German intellectual life during the late eighteenth and the nineteenth centuries, one that eventually reaches to "life philosophers" (*Lebensphilosophen*) such as Wilhelm Dilthey and Georg Simmel. Steeped in the writings of German poets, classical German theorists drew from their predecessors' ideas about human personality, individuality, culture, language, and history. They did not create in a vacuum, but had their roots in the works of Hamann and Herder whose ideas offered critical tools for exploring social relationships, the role of language, poetry, and native history. Moreover, Herder's seminal ideas have invigorated and inspired interdisciplinary investigations that combine philosophy, history, literature, sociology, psychology, and anthropology. My contribution to this collection of essays intends to offer a brief overview of Herder's life and principal works, of his profound effect on German literary movements, focusing on concepts that link Herder to the German Romanticists, and to conclude with some observations about the implication such ideas may have on subsequent social theory.

Herder's Life and Works

Johann Gottfried Herder was born on August 25, 1744, in the small East Prussian town of Mohrungen (today Morag, Poland). Educated in the town grammar school, he was befriended by a learned minister, and later by a Russian army surgeon who employed him to trans-

late a treatise into Latin and took him from Mohrungen to Königsberg (today Kaliningrad). Coming from a simple, pietistic home,
Herder enrolled at the university in Königsberg to study theology. His
teacher, Immanuel Kant, impressed by Herder's brilliance, allowed
him to register for courses in philosophy, mathematics, and physical
geography. Later, Herder met Johann Georg Hamann (1730–1788), a
mystic, knowledgeable in European literature, who introduced
Herder to the English language and to the works of English writers
such as Shakespeare, Shaftesbury, and Sterne. From Kant, Herder
learned to probe basic principles, from Hamann he learned about the
primacy of feelings over reason and about the origin of language and
poetry. Having completed his university training for the Lutheran
ministry, Herder in 1764 was appointed teacher at the cathedral
school in Riga (Latvia), where three years later, he published anony-
mously *Fragments. Concerning Recent German Literature* (*Frag-
mente. Über die neuere deutsche Literatur*). These review essays on
the current literary scene in Germany foreshadow ideas concerning
the totality of the human personality on which Herder later elaborated. Reflecting Hamann's teaching, these essays suggest a shift in
emphasis from rationalism to emotionalism, from conscious design to
spontaneous art, and from art justified in terms of imitation of non-
indigenous traditions to art justified in terms of its own criteria
(Gillies 1945, 36 f.).

In 1769 Herder resigned his post in Riga and set out on a sea journey to France. The record of this voyage, *Diary of My Journey in the
Year 1769* (*Journal meiner Reise im Jahre 1769,* published posthu-
mously in 1846) is a compendium of personal notes on his plans for
the future. Herder soon left France, returning to Germany. Travel-
ing through different cities and getting acquainted with literary
luminaries, Herder met in Darmstadt (Germany) Caroline Flachs-
land, the woman he would later marry. Having suffered eye trouble
since he was young, Herder interrupted his journey in Strassburg
(France) and underwent an eye operation. It was there in Septem-
ber 1770 that he encountered the young Johann Wolfgang Goethe
(1749–1832), who was then enrolled as a student of law at the university. Herder directed Goethe's attention away from French literature, introduced him to Shakespeare, opened his eyes to Ossian and
the folk song, and made him aware of indigenous figures like Luther
and Faust as possible subjects for literary treatment.

Moving from Strassburg, Herder accepted a post as chief pastor in
Bückeburg (southwest of Hannover). Despite the oppressive atmosphere in Bückeburg due to disagreements with bureaucrats and his

own distaste for practical life, Herder devoted himself to writing. He produced theological works (e.g., *Oldest Documents of the Human Race* [*Älteste Urkunde des Menschengeschlechts*], 1774–76), but especially, significant literary essays: *Treatise on the Origin of Language* (*Abhandlung über den Ursprung der Sprache*, 1772), *Of German Kind and Art* (*Von deutscher Art und Kunst*, 1773), and *Another Philosophy of History for the Education of Humankind* (*Auch eine Philosophie der Geschichte zur Bildung der Menschheit*, 1774). In 1776 Herder accepted an invitation to Weimar, where Goethe had secured a post for him as chief of the clergy and where a new phase of productivity set in. In 1778 Herder compiled the collection of folk songs, later published as *Voices of Peoples in Song*, (*Stimmen der Völker in Liedern*, 1807). But his major achievement at this time, though it remained incomplete, was *Ideas for the Philosophy of the History of Humankind* (*Ideen zur Philosophie der Geschichte der Menschheit*, 1784–1791). It is in this work that Herder developed his cyclical, organic conception of the birth, growth, and death of civilizations, suggesting that history is not to be perceived in terms of progressive linear development.

In 1788 Herder began a tour of Italy staying one year, returning to Weimar in the summer of 1789, the year of the French Revolution. In his *Letters for the Advancement of Humanity* (*Briefe zur Beförderung der Humanität*, 1793–97), appearing after but only indirectly alluding to the French Revolution, Herder touches upon several themes. He tries to explain his understanding of the word *humanity* (*Humanität*) as the essence of all that is human, a characteristic that must be nurtured by means of education, or *Bildung*, and suggests the perfectibility of humankind; he also speaks about the Republic of Europe as a federation of nations, and he discusses the social and moral function of literature. Eclectic in their outlook, these letters reflect a fighter for causes in which he believed (Koepke 1987, 86). Herder was a complex individual and alternated throughout his life between rapturous enthusiasm and melancholy hypochondria. Fearful of criticism, he was liberal in criticizing others, often seeming harsh and arrogant (Pascal 1953, 16 f.). In Herder's last years he was overcome by an oppressive sense of failure; these years are marked by illness, financial difficulties, unpleasant official duties, and an estrangement from Goethe and Friedrich Schiller (1759–1805). In his last works, *Metacritique* (*Metakritik zur Kritik der reinen Vernunft*) and *Kalligone* Herder waged a bitter battle against Kant. "Enduring happiness was never Herder's lot" (Gillies 1945, 24). Herder died on 18 December, 1803, at age fifty-nine.

German Romanticism

German literature blossomed between 1775–1800, during which several distinct schools can be identified. Though neither strictly coincident nor sequential, the Enlightenment, Storm and Stress, and Romantic movements seem to have evolved in an almost dialectical process. The proponents of these movements held different views of the creative process, purpose of literature, the role of the poet, and their subject matter. (1) The *Enlightenment,* represented by writers such as Gotthold Ephraim Lessing (1729–1781), a friend of Moses Mendelssohn (1729–1786), and Christoph Martin Wieland (1733–1813), was a movement marked by tolerance, the idea of world citizenship (*Weltbürgertum*), an emphasis on the rational capacities of human beings and the rationality of history (Behler 1993, 3). The artist, according to Enlightenment criteria, could learn rules from the established canon such as those in French classicism, Greek literature or Roman literature, apply them, and thereby create works of beauty and usefulness. The period of the Enlightenment did not separate aesthetics from ethics (Todorov 1982, 153).

The movement called *Storm and Stress* (*Sturm und Drang*), dates from the meeting between Herder and Goethe in Strassburg in 1770 when Herder's radical ideas concerning the importance of feeling and imagination in poetry and his emphasis on creative genius left an indelible impression on the younger Goethe. Also known as the "period of genius" (*Geniezeit*), the Storm and Stress group includes poets who rebelled against what they claimed to be prescriptive notions of art and advocated instead a notion of creative genius: the individual artist who rejects rules, relies upon innate feeling, and produces original works whose purpose no longer resides in their usefulness but in their ability to give pleasure. Representatives of Storm and Stress sought out the irrational and reveled in an exuberant intoxication of feeling that glorified a communion with nature and the natural. This movement also exhibits the first stirrings of nationalist thinking (Barnard 1965,29). Such ideas clearly had their source in the writings of Hamann and Herder. Rejecting French influences, the young Goethe, foremost representative of Storm and Stress, chose the works of Shakespeare and the Bible as his models, since they epitomize nationalist literature. Like Shakespeare's relation to British history, like the Jews' relation to the Old Testament, German poets also were directed to Germany's national past, its history, in order to take from it native forms such as the doggerel (*Knittelvers*) that Goethe used in *Faust Part 1,* and its subjects such as Faust, Götz von Berlichingen, or Clavigo. Indeed, Goethe's *Faust* became the principal symbol, theme, and representative work of the Storm and Stress movement. Above all, Herder's elevation of folk song to the rank of poetry and holding it up as a model worthy of emulation, awakened a fresh, dynamic lyric voice. Under Herder's spell in Strassburg, Goethe began to trust his own imagination, to write unconventional lyric poetry expressing bold emotions and personal feelings. Storm and Stress was dominated by the youthful Goethe and Schiller. In time, these writers were tamed by new inspiration drawn from the Greeks (for Goethe) and from German idealistic philosophy (for Schiller); the movement had run its course, being replaced by "Weimar Classicism" (Goethe and Schiller) and Romanticism.

Goethe and Schiller, living near one another in Weimar, enjoyed a decade-long (1794–1805) fruitful collaboration. In the same period, and a short distance away, the university city of Jena became *the* hotbed of the German Romantic movement. The circle of Romanticists gathered at Jena forged, in a creative burst of energy, a program for a new kind of modern literature. "Jena soon became the centre for a group of young critics who promoted a new style of thinking and judging in matters of literature and taste, and created an attitude that, for lack of a better name, received the designation 'romantic'" (Behler 1993, 24). In 1794 Johann Gottlieb Fichte (1762–1814) was appointed professor at the university in Jena. He delivered a series of popular lectures on man's place in society and on the vocation of the scholar (Ziolkowski 1990, 240 passim). In 1799 Fichte was replaced by Friedrich Wilhelm Schelling (1775–1854) who lectured and wrote on the nature of science, knowledge, and the philosophy of the modern university. At this time, August Wilhelm Schlegel (1767–1845) moved to Jena, coming upon the urging of Schiller, who had invited Schlegel to contribute essays to Schiller's publication *Horae* (1795–1797). Such journals assumed great importance, as they furnished writers with an immediate public forum. Also appearing in Jena at that time was the *Allgemeine Literaturzeitung,* a paper for reviews of the most important publications in the humanities to which Schlegel contributed several hundred (Behler 1993, 16). Another publication, *Philosophical Journal of a Society of German Scholars,* founded by Friedrich Immanuel Niethammer, published the major works of Fichte and Schelling. Finally, the Schlegel brothers founded *Athenäum* in 1798; it later became the most significant journal of the Romantic movement.

Though the origins of German Romanticism are easy to place, its evolution is multifaceted. Characterized by kaleidoscopic change, it never actually constituted a homogeneous "school." Its membership was in constant flux as adherents moved from Jena to Berlin, from Berlin to Heidelberg, or from Jena to Vienna. Subject to new interests and new influences, its creative works are marked by manifest diversity. Because of its heterogeneity, sheer number of adherents, and the extensive distribution throughout German cities and principalities, the movement may be divided into three phases, each characterized by dominant features. The emergence of the first phase, early Romanticism, can be dated quite precisely because of publication dates: 1797, when Wilhelm Heinrich Wackenroder (1773–1798) published *Outpourings of an Art-Loving Monk* (*Herzensergießungen eines kunstliebenden Klosterbruders*) and 1798, when A. W. Schlegel and his brother Friedrich Schlegel (1772–1829) founded the literary journal *Athenäum*. Members of this early group included persons who also lived for a time at least in Jena: Novalis, a pseudonym for Friedrich von Hardenberg (1771–1801), Ludwig Tieck (1773–1853), Friedrich Schleiermacher (1768–1834), Friedrich Wilhelm Schelling (1775–1854), and Friedrich Hölderlin (1770–1843). These participants specialized in different areas: theory and history are represented by the brothers Schlegel, poetry by Novalis and Hölderlin, novel and drama by Tieck, and the visual arts by Wackenroder. Schelling's interest lay in problems of philosophy, nature, religion, ethics, politics, and literary history.

The second phase of the Romantic movement is called the "Heidelberg School." Important figures representing this phase studied at the university in Heidelberg and include Achim von Arnim (1781–1831), Clemens Brentano (1778–1842), and Joseph Görres (1776–1848). For this group, philosophy and aesthetics were demoted and replaced by a preoccupation with Germany's medieval past. Collections of anthologies, especially of folk songs, notably *The Youth's Magic Horn* (*Des Knaben Wunderhorn*), published in three volumes from 1805 to 1808 by Arnim and Brentano, and of national epics such as *The German Chapbooks* (*Die Teutschen Volksbücher*) published by Görres in 1807, were the most important legacy of these Heidelberg Romantics.

The third phase of German Romanticism included reconstituted groupings in Berlin or in cities such as Dresden or Vienna. Arnim, Brentano, Görres, as well as G. H. Schubert (1780–1860), Caspar David Friedrich (1774–1840), Heinrich von Kleist (1777–1811), and a number of regional representatives from the South (Swabia) and the East (Silesia) belong to this third phase. Interest in religion (a turn to Catholicism) and history, along with fascination with the natural sciences and music dominated this group. Moreover, the mania for restoring and preserving folk art and medieval literature continued. Familiar are the collections of fairy tales by the brothers Grimm, Jakob (1785–1863) and Wilhelm (1786–1859). The enduring achievements of this later phase of the Romantic movement lie in their conceptualization of linguistics, history, natural science, regard for nature (suggesting a precursor of the ecology movement), political allegiances (anticipating German nationalism), thoughts about creativity, and perspectives on the role of the artist. In their achievements, members of this phase of Romanticism pay homage to Herder's seminal ideas about indigenous folk art, native language, and national history. Whereas Herder had brought together a collection of folk songs from diverse foreign nations, his followers exhibited more parochial tastes: they focused on their own native lands. While Herder accorded equal ranking to all nationalities, later collectors underscored their own national achievements.

Herder's Spheres of Influence

Some of the concepts characteristic in the works of Herder and of German Romanticism intersect at several points. Herder generated not only the ideas, but also created the language of Romanticism, imbuing words with new meanings that continue to exert influence on contemporary thought. Herder's neologisms like *Volkslied* (folk song), his unique interpretation of existing terms such as *Bildung, Humanität, Geist, Seele* (education, humanity, spirit/intellect, soul), have become common coin. Above all, Herder contributed a new understanding to concepts such as culture, historical consciousness, nation, and poetry: concepts that reach beyond the German Romantic School. Herder's ideas of historical continuity, of nationality, and of the value of literature serve as the key to understanding of the human condition (Gillies 1945, 77). In the literature about Herder and about the Romanticists, distinctions among people, state, nation, fatherland, history and religion (*Volk, Staat, Nation, Vaterland, Geschichte, Religion*) are often blurred; on occasion, combinations such as people-state, history-state or history-religion, serve as distinct concepts, at other times they may be interrelated. Herder's writings, like fabric woven of different intersecting threads, form patterns that carry different messages to diverse generations and disciplines. Social sciences tend to focus on state, nationality, and folk; literature concentrates on folk, language, and art. The following sections of this essay discuss those themes that assume particular significance for German Romanticists. By absorbing and modifying them, the Romanticists altered not only Germans' way of thinking, they affected not only the literary canon, but also paved Germany's road to disaster in the middle of the twentieth century.

Historicism and History

Representatives of the French and German Enlightenment, for example Voltaire (1694–1778), Christian Thomasius (1655–1728), A. L. Schlözer (1735–1809) or Lessing, are not known for "thinking historically"; when they do, their writing is imbued by faith in the unconditional progress of history and humankind. The Enlightenment neglected its own historical location and adopted a vantage point of superiority, looking down, for example, on the "dark Middle Ages." Historians of this time wrote for the "world citizen," they compiled comprehensive chronologies that recorded the actions of heads of state. Such summaries refer to the state as being like a machine (Barnard 1965, 20). Herder, however, was of a different turn of mind. By means of his fertile imagination he sought to immerse himself in the concrete, specific time and nature of distinct national peoples. Herder thought one had to evaluate history from an emotional attachment to one's nation (*Nationalgefühl*). Moreover, he regarded even this evaluation or judgment to be conditioned by history. Kant's suggestion in his treatise that humans, too, are subject to a natural history and explicable in naturalistic terms became the guiding assumption behind Herder's *Ideas for the Philosophy of the History of Humankind*. The aim of the *Ideas* was to apply Kant's naturalism to the sphere of history itself. The *Ideas* were to be a natural history of humans. Herder repeated Kant's central teaching: "that what appears to be given and eternal—whether language, art, law, or religion—is in fact the product of history" (Beiser 1992, 194). With this, Herder developed a new historical consciousness which in itself was historical: that which develops historically can only be understood historically. Herder learned that nature has a history, and that to understand its structure is to understand its genesis. Initially, Herder imagined history to be analogous to the stages of an individual's cultural development: each nationality was supposed to manifest a pattern of growth, namely the youthful period characterized as undeveloped and "barbaric," then a middle period, characterized by a balance of courage and feeling, and a third stage displaying restraint and courtly conventions. In later writings, Herder replaces the image of the human being with that of a tree that symbolizes all of humanity; this is especially evident in Book VII of the *Ideas* (1989, vol. vi, 251). It can be called the foundation of Herder's "genetic method." Herder begins his *Ideas* with the motto: "What God's purpose is with you, wherever you are placed in this world, learn it through the deed," and he begins the first book with the title: "Our Earth is a star among stars," in other words, this world is one among many, and by analogy, each *Volk* or ethnic group is one among many.

Because of Herder's *Ideas* and its later appropriation, for example, by the brothers Schlegel, the manner in which Germans regarded the historical past underwent a radical change. For Friedrich Schlegel in his *History of Greek and Roman Poetry* (*Geschichte der Poesie der Griechen und Römer,* 1789), the total variety of life and education became important, especially in his attempt to understand the *Zeitgeist* (literally, the "spirit of the age"), of the unique character of cultures at a given historical time. He wanted to recognize the unity of historical development (Kluckhohn 1966, 107). In contrast to representatives of Enlightenment who claimed similarity among peoples of different nations, the Romanticists believed that in the course of history there exists the possibility of psychological change (*seelische Wandlungen*) which brought about the different periods and peoples (*Völker*). Out of this emerged the need to understand foreign cultures from within their own particular vantage point.

This model called up a historical consciousness that envisioned an organic progress according to laws or principles that are peculiar to the individual peoples. The aim of this historical method was to trace all material down to its roots in order to discover the organic principle. For example, Schelling's work, *Ideas for a Philosophy of Nature* (*Ideen zu einer Philosophie der Natur,* 1797), owes its very title to Herder and consists of broad-ranging speculations about the relationship of nature and philosophy. While Schelling recognizes scientific theories and discoveries of his time, he desires to penetrate secrets of nature believing that nature (i.e., the irrational) and spirit (*Geist,* or the rational) form a unity. Nature is visible spirit, the spirit is invisible nature. Another example for such historical thinking as influenced by Herder is Friedrich Hölderlin. With his friends Hegel and Schelling, Hölderlin read Herder's philosophy of history and his demands for cultural revival. In 1796 Hölderlin planned a periodical called *Iduna* (the "goddess of rejuvenation,") after the title of Herder's dialogue published in Schiller's *Horae;* Hölderlin's imitation of Herder's apotheosis of Greek civilization is evident in his lyrical novel *Hyperion,* in which the character of Adamas, who sets off to Asia to discover a people of rare excellence, may well represent

Herder. Hölderlin was acquainted with Herder's doctrine of *Volks-geist* or "spirit of the people" and shared Herder's view of language. The oneness of man, nature, and the divine was fundamental to Hölderlin's work, and he regarded himself as being in the service of *Humanität* (Gillies 1945, 117).

People (*Volk*), State, and Nation

According to Herder, the principle which unites language, creativity, laws, customs, beliefs and traditions is the *Volk*. Herder's concept of the *Volk* and its meaning for German Romanticists must be separated from its more sinister significance given this concept during the Nazi era. "By the word *Volk* as [Herder] used it in connection with literature he did not intend to designate the uncultured masses or the crowd. '*Volk*,' he wrote, 'does not mean the rabble of the streets, which never sings and creates, but roars and mutilates'" (Ergang 1966, 195 f.). *Volk* was to Herder the "body of the nationality," that part of the group which had remained on its national foundations as opposed to those who attempted to build a culture on foreign acquisitions (Ergang 1966, 195 f). It was that part of the nationality which was working in harmony with the national soul. The literature by means of which the national soul expresses itself is folk literature. Although Herder used only the word *Volk,* the Romanticists (Grimm, Görres, Arnim) combined it with *Geist* (spirit, intellect) to form *Volks-geist*. For them, *Volksgeist* meant the peculiar character of a people, its unique intellectual achievements, a collective power, a community speaking in one language. For example, German professors at a meeting in the middle of the nineteenth century answered the question, "What is a *Volk*?" this way: "A *Volk* is the quintessence of humankind which speaks the same language" (Kluckhohn 1966, 101). In times of oppression, it is language that decides allegiances; Germans speak German, those who speak the German language are German. Grimm went so far as to derive from their language the essential features of the people themselves.

Volk and state or nation are not necessarily identical. Having transferred Herder's genetic thinking to the state, Romanticists looked upon the state as an organic, living totality. Schelling, drawing on medieval Christian corporate views of the state, compares it to a physical body, to a living being, an individual, a *microanthropos* (Kluckhohn 1966, 84). Such a body has unique qualities; it is governed by its own laws, customs and traditions, and thus the idea that one constitution would fit all states is rejected. Görres, for example, went so far as to demand that the German constitution not be constructed according to general, commonly accepted (e.g., Enlightenment) principles, but that it should be based on the traditions of the German people (Kluckhohn 1966, 110). An amalgamation like the Austrian empire—with its collection of ethnic groups speaking different languages such as German, Czech, Slovak, Croatian, Slovenian, Italian or Hungarian—was anathema to Romanticists' conception of the *Volksstaat*. Adherence to Romantic notions of an organic, volkish state (*Volksstaat*) was quite contrary to Enlightenment-based notions of social equality, a liberal constitutional order, and abstract citizenship. The Enlightenment was based on a vision of universal government, rational progress, natural law, a social contract, and the notion of a state as a rational collection of interests. Romanticism was otherwise, however. Dominated by the pietistic movement that advocated a rejection of reason and rationality in favor of the glorification of feeling and inwardness (*Innerlichkeit*), Romanticists claimed that their language and rural life styles provided a deeper capacity of emotional bonding and communal life. The belief in human nature as part of a great chain of being, the recognition of national uniqueness, and the view of the state as a living organism helped to reduce interest in the state *per se* as representative of civilization. From the Romanticists' view point, only individual peoples (*Völker* may be roughly equivalent to "ethnic groups") held validity. For Romanticists, each nation-state that speaks one language and shares a common past stands independently on its own, is its own master, maintains its own unique character, and governs itself according to its own laws. This unique national identity is rooted in its own past and has its own memory.

Poetry, Language, Folk Song

Less interested in the actions of heads of state, Romanticists turned their attention to other sources for understanding the past, namely literature, and particularly in this case, poetry. Not only was poetry regarded as a monument to a nation's past, since it represented "grand old national memories" (Ergang 1966, 236 f.), it was also important for future development and the entire spiritual existence of a nation. Romanticists felt that the development and the difference among peoples can best be learned by studying their poetry. To know and understand such cultures in the best possible way is to have empathy with them. Naturally, these notions led them to study the past of their own nation, Germany, because in their opinion, such history revealed the sub-

stance of their own being. This turn to the history of one's own peoples
is demonstrated especially by the Heidelberg Romanticists, those with
the urge to uncover the past, to preserve it in collections of folk songs,
fairy tales and epics. They maintained that such knowledge of one's
past created a historical consciousness, it awakened in everyone, it
seemed to them, an awareness of the greatness of one's own people, its
uniqueness and special qualities. Thus history, from this point of view,
became not simply a compendium of battles, a list of names and dates,
but rather the "only" path to the "true" recognition of one's own unique
place among nations.

Herder and the Romanticists were also preoccupied with the origin
of language. Herder's treatise *On the Origin of Language* (*Abhandlung über den Ursprung der Sprache,* 1772) was the most important
impulse for the early Romantic theory of language, especially in the
case of A. W. Schlegel. Herder rejected the supernatural theory of an
origin of language as a divine gift, an instantaneous communication
from God, and he also rejected naturalistic explanations of language
as a long process of merely physiological development by way of habit
and repetition originating in animal cries and terminating in human
articulation. Herder developed an expressive theory of language
whereby words have meaning because they express a certain kind of
consciousness of ourselves. Herder equates language with humanity:
human beings and language are coexistent since language is a human possession only, and since its existence is possible because of the
power of reflection (*Besonnenheit*), a specifically *human* gift. Stressing the close association of speech and culture, language and art,
Herder recognized the historical importance of primitive literatures,
calling them keys to the understanding of phases to which they be-
longed, and ultimately to understanding the human mind (Gillies
1945, 37). From this it may be obvious that there developed a growing emphasis upon the German language as a medium capable and
worthy of expressing man's highest achievements in art, philosophy,
poetry and science in as good a fashion as the medieval Latin or the
contemporary French (Barnard 1965, 29). In a similar vein, Fichte's
stress upon the mother-tongue as being the basic factor in nationality also served as an example of 'linguistic' self-assertion (Gillies
1945, 119). Herder considered language to be not only an expression
of the individuality of each human being but also the psychological
matrix in which a person's consciousness of distinctive social heritage was aroused and deepened. This emphasis on language as the
"natural" foundation for social and political association had significant consequence in the twentieth century. It led to prodigious philo-

logical research and provided the ideological basis of nationalist agitation. The close bond between language and politics helped give rise to the belief that many of the social and political ills that afflicted empires comprising diverse language communities could be successfully cured once each of these communities acquired its own political independence (Barnard 1965, 142 f.).

Generally speaking, during the period of Enlightenment, art was considered a means to an end, with the primary purpose being to instruct. The production of art was an activity of rational decisions. Hamann and Herder were among the first to raise feeling, emotion, and empathy to unique means of perception. For them, poetry emanates from the spirit of the people. As Hamann's famous dictum reminds us: poetry is the original language of humankind ("*die Poesie ist die Muttersprache des Menschengeschlechts*"). For Romanticists, language is an expression of feeling, of spirit, of intellect; it is a creative act, and thus language and poetry are one. The communicative function of language is second to its expressive, poetic qualities. Among the consequences of the Romantic movement for poetry are the recognition of the infinite changeability of genres, their mixing, the emergence of new literary forms, the idea that the poetic unity of a work means inner conformity with itself, and the forging of a multiplicity of phenomena into a self-originated unity.

Above all, Romanticists eschewed the application of rules in favor of the shaping power of the imagination. This is evident in a path that leads from Herder to the Grimm brothers. It begins with Wackenroder's romantic conception of art that is Herderian, with the philologists influenced by Herder who awakened in Wackenroder an interest in German medieval, sixteenth century poetry. It continues in Wackenroder's intellectual executor, Tieck, whose *Songs of Courtly Love* (*Minnelieder*) attracted Jakob Grimm to Middle High German spheres (Gillies 1945, 117 f.).

The belief in the transcendence of art was key to the Romanticists' concept of aesthetics. For the Romanticists, poetry reaches into a realm beyond earthly existence into a realm that can be opened only by means of longing, and the purpose of art is to disclose this transcendent realm. To them, poetry was like religion, transporting one into another sphere; like a god, the artist creates living works of art. For Novalis, creativity, poetry, and the spiritual (*Geist*) are one. Poets create from an original union with nature and are capable of revealing nature. It is their mission to serve as cosmic rescuers of mankind. In this sense, poetry is not merely a personal confession but also serves the community and one's own people. Another function of poetry is to glorify the past, and thus literature has to be national. Hence the preference of Romanticists for folk poetry of any sort: song, legends, fairy tale. Novalis regarded the fairy tale as the canon of poetry, maintaining that every poetic manifestation has to be like a fairy tale. The world has to become romanticized. For the Romanticists, poetry tries to effect feeling, emotions, passion. It should move the heart. The task of the artist, they claimed, was to produce works analogous to creation in nature and to depict the infinite in the finite. Romanticism was opposed to the concept of mimetic art and asserted that it is not the work of art but the artist who imitates nature, and that the artist be conceived of as an independent creator of an art that is independent of nature.

Finally, Herder synthesized his lasting contributions to literature, history, and culture in the special emphasis he accorded to the folk song. By raising it to the rank of poetry, he confirmed it with canonical status. A poem of unknown origin handed down by oral tradition, the folk song is characterized by simple stanza form (four lines, with *abab* or *aabb* rhyme) and associated with a simple, easily remembered melody. Herder collected such folk songs, engaging the help of Goethe and Lessing, among others. Herder's comprehensive volumes contain verses whose origin and subject matter range across a wide spectrum: folk songs of unknown authorship mingle with translations of verses by Shakespeare. The headings of the different sections provide a glimpse of the wide scope of Herder's interest: I: Songs of the High North, Greenland, Lapland, Estonia, Latvia, Lithuania; II: Greek and Roman, Latin, Italian, Spanish; III: Songs from Romance countries and Romances; IV: Ossian, Icelandic, Danish; V: English (including the ballad of Chevy Chase, The beautiful Rosamunde, Edward, and some by Shakespeare); VI: German; and finally, VII: Tropical (Madagascar, Brazil, Peru). The totality of this work reflects Herder's innate sensitivity for the poetic creativity of different peoples, his consummate skill as translator, and his success at conveying the genuine tone and feeling of poetry of diverse origins. In sum, it is a true example of *Volksseele* (the people's soul).

Herder's collections of folk songs, as much as his *Ideas,* resonated with German poets and thinkers on several levels. First, poetry as a genre was revolutionized by Herder's elevating the folk song to paradigmatic status. Not only did some of these songs undergo ingenious revisions at the hands of poets, as for example Goethe's best known ballad, "Erlkönig," which he derives from Herder's "Erleking's Daughter" ["Erlkönigs Tochter"] in Book IV of *Volkslieder,* but also their simple form and personal content inspired a new type of lyric. Goethe began to write love lyrics in the manner of folk songs; some of these have become part of *Urfaust* (the first, prose version of *Faust*) and others are included in the *Sesenheim Songs (Sesenheimer Lieder)*.

Second, by stimulating an awareness of one's own literary past, Herder inspired generations of poets to preserve their own native folk songs. The best known and most influential collection are the three volumes of *The Youth's Magic Horn (Des Knaben Wunderhorn)* by Achim von Arnim and Clemens Brentano which became the Bible of the German Romantic movement. This collection contains about seven hundred folk songs, religious, secular, love, drinking, and war songs. Arnim's and Brentano's work came under criticism for not preserving pure texts and for selective appropriation in accordance with their own taste, though to their credit, they do cite the source of their songs. Despite these criticisms, *The Youth's Magic Horn* succeeded in widely disseminating the extraordinary wealth of German folk songs and spawned numerous imitators. Tieck produced a similar collections with his *Songs of Courtly Love (Minnelieder)*, poems from the early Middle Ages. Collections specific to certain German regions soon followed: Ludwig Uhland (1787–1862), a Swabian, edited *Ancient High and Low German Folk Songs (Alte hochund niederdeutsche Volkslieder)*, 1844/45 while August Heinrich Hoffmann von Fallersleben (1798–1874), the author of Germany's national anthem, "Deutschland, Deutschland über alles," brought out the regional collection of *Silesian Folk Songs (Schlesische Volkslieder, 1842)*.

Third, collectors broadened their search to encompass fairy tales, legends, and the earliest records of a poetic tradition. Known for their collections of fairy tales, *Kinder- und Hausmärchen,* the brothers Grimm offered German epic poems in *Deutsche Sagen*. They were first to edit *The Song of Hildebrand (Hildebrandslied)* and *The Prayer of Wessobrunn (Wessobrunner Gebet)*, the earliest monuments of German literature. "Indeed, taken all in all," Gillies has claimed, "the philological achievements of Romanticism, leading to the researches of the Grimms . . . and others, grew directly from Herder's pioneer work. His philosophy of language was taken over by Wilhelm von Humboldt, [and] his folk song collection was a standing source of inspiration to all" (Gillies 1945, 118).

CONCLUSION

Scholars generally agree that Herder exercised a major influence on the Romanticists. The scholarly view notwithstanding, the Romanticists seem to have had no awareness of Herder's influence and credit Goethe instead. (Silz 1929, 5; Gillies 1945, 116; Tymms 1955, 10). Whether or not Romanticists acknowledged their debt to Herder, or whether the extraordinary vitality and fertility of Herder's ideas make it impossible to disentangle the roots of Romanticism, there is no doubt today of Herder's impact on the German Romanticists. They built on Herder's intellectual legacy by developing and making the most of his suggestions. Romanticism's achievement in the folk song, discovery of and new attitude to the past, especially to the Middle Ages, rejection of uncompromising formalism in art, emphasis on religion, emotion, and feeling as essential in the creative process, and conception of language as the most important determinant in artistic consciousness—all have their origins in Herder's work (Clark 1955, 417). Furthermore, Romanticists learned from Herder their fine historical sense and poetic intuition, their enthusiasm for Shakespeare, their high estimation of the unique, the original, and the irrational, and their estimation of individuality and personality. In the way Herder regarded poetry as the expression of a person's profoundest creative powers and emphasized above all else those factors that produce poetry, he was responsible for the "poetization" of all life which was the ambition of the Romanticists.

Herder and the Romanticists stand at the threshold of monumental social changes; the French Revolution (1789) ushered in a new social order, and the industrial revolution, with its technical innovations originating in England, began to transform European life. To understand such forces that impact on social stability and profoundly change society, new questions demanded new answers. What are we to make of these changes in light of our growing scientific knowledge? How are we to understand the forces at work in modern society? The success of the sciences in explaining natural phenomena prompted thinkers to emulate the scientific method in the study of human activities and social phenomena. To be sure, the study of the human sciences benefits from methods of empirical investigation. It appears, however, that Herder was the first to see that we miss something essential if we try to explain specifically human phenomena in terms of the scientific method that aims to know universal truths. For Herder, human phenomena are irreducible. While science explains natural phenomena by their subsumption under universal laws, the accounting for what Herder calls individuality (i.e., a human being) requires a different method, namely, empathy (*Einfühlung*). We see the influence of Herder's claim in Dilthey's distinction between *erklären* (to explain) and *verstehen* (to understand), in the notion of interpretive social sciences, or in the role of hermeneutics. In the human sciences, as presently understood, there is hardly a branch not indebted to Herder, directly or indirectly, though few are aware of their ultimate obligation.

NOTES

1. Under Romanticism I include Weimar Classicism. The word 'romantic,' according to Behler, has two basic meanings in the literary criticism of the late eighteenth century, a chronological and a typological one. The chronological one referred to a tradition of literature originating in the Middle Ages and pervading literary writing in modern Europe, but which was held in low esteem by neoclassicists and even excluded from the literary canon (Behler 1993, 25). "The typological referred to certain exotic traits in literature, including compositional and structural ones, which were originally expressed in Romanesque literature, but which were now found everywhere. Friedrich Schlegel still used the word in these two ways" (Behler 1993, 25 f.). But for A.W. Schlegel, the word took on a new meaning. In his Berlin lectures on Romantic literature (1803–1804), Schlegel distinguishes between "classical" and "romantic," and that "romantic" refers to "genuinely modern works, not organized according to the models of antiquity and still to be considered as valid according to the highest principles" (Behler 1993, 27). In the Fragment 116 of the *Athenäum,* Friedrich Schlegel declares: "Romantic poetry is a progressive, universal poetry."

REFERENCES

Barnard, F. M. 1965. *Herder's Social and Political Thought.* Oxford: Clarendon Press.

Behler, Ernst. 1993. *German Romantic Literary Theory.* Cambridge: Cambridge University Press.

Beiser, Frederick. 1992. *Enlightenment, Revolution, and Romanticism, The Genesis of Modern German Political Thought 1790–1800.* Cambridge, MA: Harvard University Press.

Clark, Robert T., Jr. 1955. *Herder His Life and Thought.* Berkeley: University of California Press.

Ergang, Robert Reinhold. 1966. *Herder and the Foundations of German Nationalism.* New York: Octagon Books.

Gillies, Alexander. 1945. *Herder.* Oxford: Basil Blackwell.

Herder, Johann Gottfried. 1989. *Werke in zehn Bänden.* Ed. Martin Bollacher. Frankfurt a.M.: Deutscher Klassiker Verlag.

Kluckhohn, Paul. 1966. *Das Ideengut der deutschen Romantik.* Tübingen: Max Niemeyer Verlag.

Koepke, Wulf. 1987. *Johann Gottfried Herder.* Boston: Twayne.

Pascal, Roy. 1953. *The German Sturm and Drang.* Manchester: Manchester University Press.

Silz, Walter. 1929. *Early German Romanticism. Its Founders and Heinrich von Kleist.* Cambridge, MA: Harvard University Press.

Todorov, Tsvetan. 1982. *Theories of the Symbol.* trans. Catherine Porter. Ithaca, NY: Cornell University Press.

Tymms, Ralph. 1955. *German Romantic Literature.* London: Methuen.

Ziolkowski, Theodore. 1990. *German Romanticism and Its Institutions.* Princeton, NJ: Princeton University Press.

3
Hegel on History and Freedom: An Exposition and Marxist Assessment
Paul Gomberg

INTRODUCTION

The tradition of German social theory provided at least two influences on Hegel's social philosophy: one is Immanuel Kant's moral universalism and hopeful view of human history as progressing toward just relations among states; a second is Johann Gottfried von Herder's moral relativism and endorsement of the unique development of the cultures of different peoples. Kant believed that all rational beings were under the moral law and that this moral law commanded us to respect the dignity of all rational beings (Kant 1983 [1785]). Related to this view of morality was a hopeful view of human history: Kant speculated that the strife and struggle of warfare among peoples would be the school from which they would learn to construct lawful and peaceful relations among nations (Kant 1963 [1784]; 1963 [1795]; 1965 [1797], 114–129).

Herder does not share Kant's concern with justice within nations or with progress toward peace among nations. He focuses on the diversity among peoples and the ways nature suits each people, or nation, to its climate and geography. Thus, Herder thought, nature produces in each people its own incomparable genius and way in which that genius unfolds (Herder 1968 [1784]). Generally, Herder denies a common standard by which we can judge the cultures of different peoples; that is, he denies that there is precisely the sort of universal standard that Kant tried to provide.[1] The contrast between Kant's moral universalism and Herder's cultural relativism could hardly be more stark.

Hegel retains a kind of universalism, but he synthesizes it with a recognition of the individuality and particularity of the culture and of the social and political institutions of different peoples. For Hegel history culminates in a world of separate states, sometimes at war with one another. People achieve human freedom through the ethical life [*die Sittlichkeit*] of their various states, particularly those states whose social life is grounded in the freedom of capitalist markets and other liberal freedoms.

The present essay is a brief summary of some important themes in Hegel's social and political thought, particularly as this thought is developed in the *Introduction to the Philosophy of History* and *Philosophy of Right* (Hegel 1988 [1840]; 1991 [1821]). My focus is Hegel's synthesis of particular commitments and identities with a universal point of view. On the one hand, Hegel recognizes and honors the various particular attachments and passions of individuals and the particular institutions and values of each society. On the other hand, he sees these characteristics of particular people and societies in the context of an overarching historical narrative, a story of progress toward freedom.

For Hegel the end of that story of progress is in liberal capitalist society. In assessing Hegel's views of history and freedom from a Marxist point of view, I argue that there are better possibilities, ones developed in the social thought of Karl Marx.

HEGEL'S THEODICY

Hegel believes in human progress. In the *Philosophy of History* he defines philosophical history as the explanation of historical process according to an *a priori* conception (a conception one arrives at independently of empirical investigation) of history (Hegel 1988 [1840], 10–11). His particular history is a kind of theodicy, showing how Reason is manifesting itself in human history (Hegel 1988 [1840], 15–18).

The word "theodicy" derives from the philosophical study of religion. It refers to the project of showing that human suffering does not provide us with reason to abandon faith in God. Theodicy addresses a problem that arises in monotheistic religions: putting the difficulty most simply, it seems as if the suffering of the innocent provides reason to reject traditional Judeo-Christian-Islamic faith in a good and loving God. What does it mean to be good and loving? Good and loving people prevent the suffering of the innocent if they can. But if God is all-powerful, He can prevent this suffering. So the suffering of the innocent seems to show either that God is not all-powerful or that He is not a good and loving God, at least if we are to understand God's goodness and love as we understand the good-ness and love of people.

There are numerous responses to this problem. One of the harsh-est is to deny that any are innocent and to affirm that all deserve to suffer; all are born into sin as a result of the Fall of Man, and all con-stantly sin. Thus suffering is compatible with God's justice. Other re-sponses to the problem of evil see our suffering as part of a project of working our way through to a perfection that would make us worthy of being with God. Hegel's theodicy is of this latter sort, but for Hegel the culmination of this project is not in another life or another world. Hegel interprets God as Reason. He understands history as Reason's coming into the world. The agent of this process is humankind. The process of Reason's entering the world is the process of our becoming more rational; we rationally order our social lives and in doing so we become free. Salvation is a state of the world where we are free and human life accords with Reason.

Hegel's theodicy, then, is a story of human history, a story of progress toward a state where human beings live freely and ration-ally. The terrible things that have happened in the past are inter-preted as part of the process by which humanity has worked its way to a better situation.

Positive and Negative Freedom

The concept of freedom is central to Hegel's social philosophy and his philosophy of history. But the concept is one of the most contested in social and political philosophy. In Anglophone political philosophy freedom is usually understood *negatively* as freedom *from* restric-tions on what we can do. So, on the negative conception of freedom, we are free if there are no laws prohibiting us from acting in what-ever ways we may wish to act. On this view, all societies with laws restrict freedom to some extent, but freer societies restrict it less.[2] In contrast, Hegel, like Kant, proposed what is often called a positive conception of freedom; on this view, freedom is conceived not as act-ing as one wishes but as acting in accordance with reason or ration-al law.

The negative conception of freedom, while apparently clear and plausible, harbors problems. There are actions that are not pre-vented through specific legal prohibition but are prevented through a complex of laws and other social arrangements. For example, lib-eral societies do not place many direct legal restrictions on travel. In contrast, in centrally planned socialist societies (such as the former

Soviet Union) travel was often restricted through government action. So in the liberal societies people seem to be freer. Yet in those socialist societies people paid little or nothing to use public transportation. Now consider the question of freedom of travel from the point of view of someone without money. In the centrally planned socialist society that person might be freer to travel than in the liberal society without explicit restrictions on travel. For in the liberal society the public transportation system is controlled by a management that makes rules for its use and is legally entitled to do so. And among the rules for its use is the requirement to pay a certain amount to use it. So in the liberal capitalist society travel is restricted without any specific restriction prohibiting travel.

In liberal capitalist societies distribution of goods and services is generally determined by how much money one has. The laws and power of the state protect property and market exchange. As long as we accept the system of private property and commodity exchange, subjectively we experience restrictions on our behavior as due to a lack of money, not as due to the laws protecting property and exchange. In contrast, a society that eliminates the use of money to determine who gets what, has to replace the social function of money with explicit policy and decisions about allocation of resources. Does that therefore make that society less free? It is not obvious that the answer is "yes."

All human social organization creates restrictions on our behavior. Restricting behavior is essential to the possibility of social cooperation, and the extent and depth of social cooperation is much of what distinguishes humans from other primates. Considerations such as these may lead us, as Hegel was led, to develop another conception of freedom, one that goes beyond the negative view of freedom dominating Anglophone political philosophy. The other prominent conception of freedom is one emphasized in the philosophy of Immanuel Kant and developed by Hegel. The central idea is that we are free when our lives and our behavior are organized rationally or in accord with reason. But what do these phrases mean?

For Kant, to be free is to be governed by the moral law within us. To act according to the moral law we must act in such a way that the principles governing our action could be willed as a law applying universally to all rational beings (Kant 1983 [1785]). That is, roughly, we could will that anyone would act the same way as we are acting. Hegel, like Kant, had a positive conception of freedom, but he was critical of Kant's particular development of the idea of positive freedom. Much of Hegel's philosophy of history and his political philosophy is an attempt to develop a nuanced positive conception of what it means for human beings to live together rationally, a positive view of what constitutes a society where we are free.

Progress toward Freedom

Hegel believed that the goal of history is that *Geist* (mind or spirit manifest as human consciousness of freedom) becomes aware of itself as free. To achieve this goal Reason works through the particular aims and purposes that motivate individuals. This is the *cunning of Reason*. Hegel's account of the cunning of Reason involves the general theme of reconciling the particular with the universal (1988 [1840], 25–40). On one hand, Reason—like God of traditional Judaism or Christianity—has an overall plan for the course of human history. This plan represents a universal and objective reality. On the other hand, people are motivated by their particular interests (for example, to make a mark in one's profession or to succeed in business), projects (to unify a nation or to end slavery), attachments (to one's family and friends), and norms (the social rules of a particular human community). These constitute the subjective element in human life, our "passions."

For Hegel, the central problem of history is how to bring Reason and the subjective passions of particular people into an alliance so that the particular interests of people serve the objective purposes of Reason in human history. Thus the cunning of Reason refers to the way Reason uses the particular passions and interests of world-historical individuals (such as Julius Caesar and Napoleon) to achieve its own purposes (such as drawing people into larger and more rationally organized human communities). These world-historical individuals thus become agents of Reason's universal plan, but Reason works through the subjective passions of these people.

These world-historical individuals, particularly those who establish new states, may violate ordinary morality for a higher purpose. Their projects move human history toward its ultimate goal of freedom. Thus these individuals are beyond the censure of ordinary morality.

The goals of history may not be the same as the goals of world-historical individuals. Rather in striving to achieve their goals, whatever they are, these world-historical individuals bring about consequences that are no part of what they intend, but are objectively implied in what they do. Suppose, for example, Napoleon sought fame. In order to achieve this he launched wars of conquest to the East, disrupting elements of feudal social order in Central and Eastern Europe. Thus he may have hastened the dominance of capitalist social relations (free labor, market economies) over more archaic ones that bound European serfs to the land. In doing this he was, Hegel believed, bringing us closer to human freedom, even if this was not part of his intention.

Hegel criticizes those who put forward moral ideals from their sense of what is right without regard to the subjective and objective conditions necessary to realize these ideals. His main target here is Kant's *Perpetual Peace*. In that essay Kant articulates a goal of perpetual peace among nations. How will peace be achieved? For Kant, duty commands us to act morally, that is, to act in such a way that we could will that the principle guiding our conduct could serve as a universal law governing the conduct of all; duty also commands us to seek peace among nations. The solution to *how* peace is to be achieved is that everyone (including heads of state) must act morally and have faith that the two moral duties, to act morally and to seek peace, are so related that by acting morally we bring about peace (Kant 1963 [1795]; cf. Gomberg 1994, 555–56).

Hegel rejects this Kantian proposal; he believes that plausible moral ideals require that we be able to identify agents who might bring these ideals to realization. These agents must be motivated not by a recognition of an objective and universal duty to be moral, but by the sorts of subjective passions that make us recognizably human.

ETHICAL LIFE IN THE STATE

Hegel believed that the cunning of history reconciles the universal and objective purposes of Reason with the subjective passions of world-historical individuals, using the passions of these individuals to achieve Reason's purposes. In the same way, Hegel believes that ethical life in the state combines the universal will, as represented by the state and the life of the community, with the subjective will, that is, individual purposes and interests; this combination occurs as the individual freely identifies with that life and becomes aware of its norms as her own creation (1988 [1840], Chapters 3 and 4).

At an early stage in ethical development we may accept the norms of our community without reflecting on them or considering alternatives. For example, egalitarian peoples living in societies that neither centralize the means of coercion nor develop formal legal institutions nevertheless maintain social order. They discipline their conduct by shared norms. This is possible because in the process of growing up in such egalitarian communities people internalize these norms and accept them as defining what it means to be the people they understand themselves to be. Among the Kung San foragers of the Northwestern Kalahari Desert, for example, norms require modesty and sharing of food. These norms define for them what it means to be a Kung, a "real person." So there is no great difficulty in securing conformity with norms in the absence of centralized state coercion (Lee 1979; Gomberg 1997). But, Hegel reminds us, adherence to these norms is "natural" and unreflective; these traditional norms are not consciously chosen in preference to alternative norms as best representing the interests of the individual and the group. The Kung have an *unreflective* idea of virtue.

Hegel believes that at a higher stage of human development we may become aware of an abstract morality distinct from the norms that govern the conduct of any small group or individual. Yet we may conceive that abstract morality as in *conflict* with the individual will governed by natural passions and interests. This is how Hegel analyzed the moral philosophy of Kant, as representing a historical stage where Reason had not yet done its work of reconciling human passions with the universal will represented by the commands of morality.

Nevertheless, in Hegel's highest stage of freedom society consists of individuals who freely identify with the state. Here the state is an organic whole, subsisting on its own account and rationally self-conscious. For each people the state consists of its unique combination of religion, law and social norms, art, poetry, and philosophy. At this highest stage of human development individuals consciously prefer their state to alternatives.

Hegel's conception of progress is based in part on a recognition that our social arrangements can come under our conscious control, that is, can themselves become human artifacts. In classical Athens (and probably in earlier states) lawmakers made conscious decisions about the basis of social cooperation. In earlier times Athenian legal processes had been based on kinship: each person was identified with one of four tribes (each of which was in turn divided into smaller kin groups). Originally these tribes and smaller kin groups had a geographical base; settlement of disputes was simple because the tribal legal administration corresponded to the residence of the people under its jurisdiction. But as commerce developed in ancient Attica, people moved about and intermarried. The people who lived in a given locale were no longer of the kin group that was the supposed basis of legal processes. As commerce and geographic mobility made the tribal classifications unworkable, the framers of the Athenian constitutions replaced the old tribal basis of accounting citizenship with one based on residence (Engels 1972 [1884, Chapter V]). In such decisions the framers were aware of alternatives and consciously chose how to organize the shared social life of a people.

In earlier societies, whatever their virtues, norms were "natural"; acceptance of them was unreflective. The members of that society accepted these norms but did not choose them. But, at least for the framers of the Athenian constitutions, conscious choices had to be made about the best ways to organize legal administration. As we come to control our shared social life, we are more free. As more people participate in rational, informed discussion of the norms that govern our shared social life, we are more free. That is, it would seem, as we discuss questions such as unemployment, health care, and housing and choose social norms and policies to address these questions, we are more free.

According to Hegel states go through stages of development, waging wars in their youth to establish themselves and their authority. In their transition to old age the spirit of a people self-consciously criticizes the old ways from the point of view of universal rationality (as Socrates asked Athenians to justify their neglect of the moral training of youth). In this philosophical act of negating unreflective ideas of virtue, spirit defines itself as a people. A people is a community that shares a culture and political organization. Thus for Hegel the social life of a people is reconstituted based on reflective endorsement of its shared culture. This represents the highest stage of history, human freedom.

Hegel's conception of historical progress thus incorporates elements from both Kant and Herder. Like Kant, Hegel espouses a kind of universal progressive history. But he combines this universal history with a cultural relativism that recognizes that different peoples achieve human freedom in their own unique ways, an element he shares with Herder. Hegel also acknowledges that conflicts among peoples may result in wars between states; in these wars there is no objective right or wrong side.

Hegel and the British Tradition

In medieval Europe the countryside was dominated by feudal social relations of personal service to one's lord. There arose in the cities and towns a new capitalist social order centered on trade in (and later manufacture of) commodities. By the late eighteenth and early nineteenth centuries, when Hegel lived and wrote, capitalism was coming to dominate European economies and even states. A new social philosophy was needed for this new order. In England and Scotland, at roughly the same time as Hegel (a little earlier and somewhat later), Adam Smith, Jeremy Bentham, and John Stuart Mill were developing this new philosophy. Hegel was doing the same in Germany. To better understand Hegel's liberal capitalist social philosophy, particularly as developed in his *Philosophy of Right,* it will be useful to compare his views to those of these British social theorists. For both a central question was how to reconcile individual interest with the general or social good.

Bentham and Hegel had very different ways of understanding human motivation. Bentham believed that human motivation could be reduced to the pursuit of pleasure and the avoidance of pain (Bentham 1970 [1789]). The human agent is *reactive* to these incentives and active only in calculating the greatest balance of pleasure over pain. For Bentham the agent and her interests can be identified independently of the ways the agent is embedded in a community of others. The social relationships we seek are the *result* of our pursuit of pleasure. Our pleasures are *independent* of our relationships and *explain* them.

For Hegel, however, the agent does not just react to prospects of pleasure and pain, but actively constructs an identity in a community of others. The agent's interests arise from and find satisfaction in that community. For example, the development of intimate relationships is not correctly understood on Bentham's model; that is, friendship does not derive simply from pursuit of pleasure and avoidance of pain. Rather the pleasures of friendship and love arise from the relationships, and it is only through such relationships that we define who we are and what pleases us.[3] Of course, we do seek pleasure in our relationships. On Bentham's view the pleasures of friendship are independent of it and explain it. But for Hegel because the pleasures of friendship arise from it, they cannot explain the friendship. In developing friendships and the interests that arise from our being bound to others, we develop an identity, a self that has interests.

Bentham and Hegel also thought differently about the norms that discipline our conduct. On Bentham's view morality is *derived* from basic values, pleasure and pain (a disvalue): what is morally right is what leads to pleasure and minimizes pain. Pleasure and pain are basic; what is right and wrong is defined in terms of them. For Hegel the norms of conduct that govern our lives arise through our social relationships with intimates or in a community. For example, conjugal norms arise in a relationship with a spouse, parental responsibilities in our relationships with our children. And our obligations to a larger community develop in the social life of a larger group as we find our place among others; for example, our obligations to a football team or a sorority arise from the particular social life and shared understandings of those groups.

Hegel was particularly influenced by Adam Smith (as was Bentham). Hegel adopts from Smith a view of capitalist markets as systems where free action leads to mutual advantage. Suppose, for example, that I buy your watch from you for $20. I freely make the exchange because I prefer having the watch to having the $20. You freely make the exchange because you prefer having the $20 to having the watch. So free exchange occurs—and only occurs—when both parties to the exchange see themselves as benefiting from the exchange. It is easy to extrapolate from such a model of exchange to a view of capitalist markets as systems where exchange works to the advantage of all. This is how Adam Smith understood what he called the "system of natural liberty."

Moreover, Smith argued, prices work so as to promote the general good as each individual seeks his or her own good. As soon as a shortage arises for any essential commodity—for example, a particular food—prices for that commodity will rise. Then as prices for the commodity rise and hence more profit can be made from producing it, as if guided by "an invisible hand," capital will stimulate production of that commodity. As more is produced, the social need for the commodity is met, and prices will drop to their normal level. The system of natural liberty works not only for the mutual advantage of those who exchange; the system also contributes to the general or social good.

Hegel seems to agree that there is a *general tendency* for markets to work as Smith described (1991 [1821], 220–21, 227, 229–30, 233), but Hegel thinks the civil authority (what is usually meant by "the state")[4] needs to intervene in the market to protect the consumer against being cheated, to control prices, and to moderate vicissitudes to which markets give rise (Ibid., 261–63). Thus, in Hegel's view, while the markets that characterize civil society tend to create a natural harmony of interests, civil authority must intervene to extend that harmony. In this regard his views of capitalism are very much like those of the British utilitarian reformers, Bentham and particularly John Stuart Mill.

For Hegel civil authority also has a role outside the market economy to provide resources to all citizens and to alleviate poverty. For example, Hegel thought that civil authority should supervise education for all children to the extent that this education affects their ability to assume the status of citizens. Hegel condemned poverty as essentially reducing the poor to a status of noncitizens, unable to provide for themselves and assume the equal dignity of citizenship. He argued that civil authority should assume responsibility to provide for the poor, that this was preferable to making the poor dependent on private charity (Ibid., 264–67).

Hegel's Liberalism

Hegel defended several kinds of individual freedom, including the freedom to choose an occupation, a spouse, and where to live. These freedoms are thought of as essential to the flourishing of individuality within community. In choosing an occupation we become part of a corporation (Ibid., 270–74). For Hegel a corporation is something like a trade association of all those participating in a particular trade or profession, modeled on the guilds of medieval Europe. These corporations are institutions that mediate between the nuclear family and the civil society and state as a whole; they provide not only individual identity but political representation, education in the particular trade or profession, and relief from poverty for members of the corporation.

The most important function of corporations is their ethical role of making the individuals aware of their participation in a political and economic community. As we participate in the market economy, we contribute to the general good, but our awareness of this contribution is abstract and remote from our life experience. In the life of a corporation our connectedness to the good of other members of the corporation and to the civil society as a whole becomes more concrete, thus strengthening our ethical awareness and commitment to the common good.

Hegel's social philosophy thus synthesizes individualism and individual freedom (an element shared with British liberals) with a conception of individual identity as arising in community and defined through the ethical life of a community. Hegel is attempting to steer a middle course between, on the one hand, extreme individualism that ignores the ways our communities construct our personalities and define our norms of conduct and, on the other, extreme communitarianism that ignores the importance of individual freedom and self-definition within the institutions of capitalist market economies.

The key to Hegel's middle course is his idea of ethical life as uniting the subjective particularity of an individual's interests, projects, and commitments with the good of the larger community (which he sometimes calls the universal will). How are these two to be united? Part of the answer is that, on Hegel's view, the market institutions of civil society tend to unite our interests. This tendency by itself is insufficient, however, because it leaves out the ethical dimension of our lives.

Our subjective particular concerns and the larger good of our community can be united as we choose our own norms and freely identify with the ethical life of our society. I interpret Hegel's central thesis here to be the following: As we enter into specific relationships and undertake projects and commitments, we develop normative conceptions that define what these projects and commitments mean. We get married, and in doing so we define a set of obligations to a particular person. These norms not only guide our conduct; they penetrate to the core of our being. I *become* the husband of a particular person, and in becoming her husband I redefine who I am through the normative commitments I have to her: loyalty, caring, emotional sustenance, and material support. These are not externally imposed moral imperatives; these ideas of my responsibilities toward a particular other define what it means to be the person I am.

Ethical life is the central notion that enables Hegel to steer a middle course between extreme individualism and extreme communitarianism. His idea of ethical life applies not only to intimate relationships as they arise in marital and family life but also to our participation in the life of market society, in our trades or professions, and in the larger patriotic community. This larger patriotic community should be governed under a constitution by a sovereign; the laws should be made by an elected representative legislature and executed by professional civil servants. This is the state, the fullest, most developed stage of human freedom.

For Hegel, pursuit of self-interest in the market is not unbridled self-aggrandizement. As we saw earlier, Hegel followed Adam Smith in believing that all who participate in market exchanges benefit from the exchange. Hegel believed that as a result of this mutual benefit, we become aware that we are part of a system that promotes the general or universal good. Thus we develop an ethical awareness of the universal. And this awareness, he believes, limits our pursuit of individual interest (Ibid., 220–22).

This tendency to reconcile the particular and the general good is strengthened and made more concrete by our participation in the social life of a corporation. For example, one may identify deeply with being a teacher. In thinking of ourselves as teachers we develop a normative conception of what this means to us, for example, maintaining patience with students or encouraging students to develop their own ideas. We construct and embrace the identity of a teacher and define it through norms of conduct. Where these norms are shared by teachers they may constitute a social ethic with which teachers identify. An individual's conception of what it means to be a teacher becomes an ethical bridge between that person's particular concerns and the good of the larger social group.

Similarly, commitments to the state can be understood through a normative conception of citizenship. For example, during World War II, many Soviet citizens went into combat against the Nazis knowing that they were likely to lose their lives. (Roughly ten million Soviet combatants perished.) How was it possible to motivate such conduct? Young people came to maturity identifying themselves as Soviet citizens. There was a consensus that the Nazi invasion had to be defeated and that young people had to serve in the military. Virtually all agreed with these norms. So despite the price to be paid, young people freely identified with these norms as defining what it meant to be a Soviet citizen and went to war. The ethical norms of their society moved its members, and this occurred because we identified with them. Ethical norms define what it means to be a member of that society.

For Hegel the highest development of human freedom is ethical life in the state. The state, through its sovereign, legislature, and professional bureaucracy, rationally orders the social life of the patriotic community. We reflect on these institutions in comparison with alternatives and consciously affirm this ordering of our lives as representing the best and most rational life for us, a unity of our own particular interests with the general social good. For Hegel this is the highest development of freedom (Ibid., 282–88).

Hegel's conception of ethical life in the state is thus meant to bring together a number of elements and solve a number of problems. Because each person chooses her own trade or profession, individual liberty is preserved. Because we freely embrace the norms that define our intimate relationships, our professional commitments, and our patriotic duties to the state, we are free and at the same time embedded in community with others in a way that gives our lives meaning. So while Hegel embraces the individualism of market relations under capitalism and the conception of individual freedom that arises in liberal capitalist society, he embraces these in a way that emphasizes our social embeddedness in a life we share with others in a human community. Our subjective individuality becomes reconciled with our ethical involvement in a community with others.

Hegel's liberalism is another synthesis of the particular and the universal. Each individual develops a self-conception through her own particular relationships with others. Finding her identity in these relationships, she pursues life goals that have meaning for her. Her society likewise has a history. As capitalism develops, the tendency of the market to harmonize our interests is amplified by the particular cultural and social and political institutions of each state. Each citizen, in pursuing her own life projects in the context of the ethical life of her state, contributes to the general good. In the liberal capitalist state, each citizen becomes free, aware of herself as free, and affirms the state through which she realizes her freedom. In this way, history reconciles the subjective concerns of each individual with the universal good, both the good of each society and history's progress toward freedom.

ASSESSING HEGEL'S POLITICAL PHILOSOPHY

Thus far I have presented Hegel's social philosophy in the most favorable possible light, leaving aside any disagreements or criticisms. As a social philosopher who works in the Marxist tradition, I find I do not always agree with this philosopher whom Marx called "that mighty thinker." So here I assess Hegel's social philosophy: What in it must be rejected? What in it is valuable? What can we learn from it about how social philosophy must proceed?

It is difficult to defend Hegel's theodicy to an audience that is secular and skeptical of religious dogma. Hegel's contemporaries may have found it plausible to develop a conception of history *a priori,* that is, based on a religious view of the direction history *must* follow, a view developed prior to and independently of what the events of the past by themselves can justify. But Hegel presented this philosophy of history nearly two hundred years ago, when Europeans could take for granted some shared religious culture and were not nearly so skeptical of such *a priori* argument. If we are to defend a view of history as progressing toward a better human condition, we will have to do so *a posteriori* (based on evidence) without recourse to a faith in Reason in history. Hegel's "from the top down" style of argument would have to be replaced by argument "from the bottom up."

Yet parts of Hegel's view of progress are reasonable, particularly where progress is identified with growing self-awareness and rationality. Generally in human history there is an accumulation of knowledge and technology (Harris 1968). With these more of our life comes under our conscious control. We are able to control how we get food and shelter, and how we transport ourselves from one place to another. But what about our shared social life? In historical times states have become the conscious artifacts of human agents trying to organize our social life (as was argued above).

Hegel argues that with the rise of Christianity we develop more egalitarian conceptions of citizenship where each citizen is entitled to respect. Thus discussion of the basis of social cooperation is extended beyond a small elite to a larger community, which is asked to freely assent to the terms of social cooperation that constitute the state in Hegel's sense. There is much room for skepticism here, but Hegel's view that all can participate in and assent to the norms that govern our shared social life becomes for now at least a *possibility*. I doubt that such freely constructed consensus exists anywhere at the present time. One central issue for contemporary social philosophy is to determine under what conditions such agreement about the terms of social cooperation might exist.

Hegel elevated the political over the moral, arguing that people engaged in projects important to human progress may violate morality. An example may support Hegel's idea. In May of 1856, during the period of civil unrest known as "Bleeding Kansas," antislavery forces were demoralized and in retreat; the free-state capital, Lawrence, had been sacked by pro-slavery settlers and raiders from Missouri. Free-state settlers were intimidated by death threats, their livestock had been killed. Three days after the sack of Lawrence, John Brown led a small group into a pro-slavery settlement at Potawatomie Creek to retaliate for the threats and livestock killing. Brown's party went into the cabins of several settlers, dragged five men and teenage boys out of their beds and hacked off their heads. As word of the massacre at Potawatomie Creek spread across the territory, pro-slavery settlers left Kansas, and pro-slavery forces became more timid in battle. The tide in the civil war turned, Kansas eventually entering the Union as a free state; it seems that the Potawatomie Creek massacre helped to turn it, reversing the balance of terror. This act was immoral by any standards I can imagine, but because of the role it played in the struggle to end chattel slavery, it may have been justified on Hegelian grounds. This justification rides on Hegel's claim that the political takes precedence over the moral.[5]

However, some of what Hegel writes seems very doubtful, particularly as viewed from the last years of the twentieth century. (1) He

has no idea of progress beyond a system of states autonomously defending their interests and engaging in preemptive and defensive
wars. This view of the end of history seems to need justification, and
it ignores the question of what alternatives are possible for us in history, a central one for social and political philosophy. (2) Hegel recognizes that poverty may exclude some from dignity and rational
participation in a shared social life. He was aware of the tendency of
capitalism to create a "rabble," large numbers of people who were the
object of social contempt. He has no satisfactory answer to this problem, and in the time since he wrote, the problem has become much
worse: there is immense poverty in contemporary capitalist societies,
where roughly a third of the world's workforce lives in poverty, either
unemployed or earning wages that are below subsistence (Sachs
1995). (3) His conception of peoples as separate seems increasingly
inappropriate: we live in a world where huge populations migrate
and economies are increasingly interdependent. Capitalism tends to
create a world culture that crosses national boundaries.

Let me develop two other criticisms in greater detail.

My first point is methodological. Hegel offers a justification for the
authority of the norms and the cultural life of a community: these realize human freedom. But we would like to distinguish between societies and norms. We do not regard as equally good all societies that
realize the freedoms of capitalist markets. Some more than others
engage in predatory wars of conquest. Even more, we would like to
distinguish among norms, accepting some and rejecting others. Consider norms of military service. Do we not wish to distinguish between norms that required German youth to serve in Nazi armies
and norms that required Soviet youth to fight on the other side? Do
we not wish to distinguish between norms that required American
youth to serve in Europe in the Second World War from those that
required service in Vietnam? A political theory should at least provide a background for settling such questions about wars and norms
requiring service in them. It seems, however, that Hegel's justification of the state gives us no basis for distinguishing these cases.

More generally, what makes Kant, Hegel, or anyone else correct
about what we should accept in the society around us and what we
should change? We want a political and social philosophy that can
provide a guide to action. While Hegel wishes to reconcile and synthesize elements of previous philosophical traditions, he does not
give us a theory in which political philosophy is seamlessly connected with practical political decision making. His philosophy does
not help us to decide questions like the above. In Hegel's writing the

practical agent disappears because Hegel conceives himself as a philosopher, not a political agent. (Kant is better about this, addressing himself to potential revolutionaries and statesmen and telling them what practical consequences his theory has.) It would be better to overcome the separation between political philosophy and practical politics.

My methodological suggestion is this: The central question for political philosophy is to identify the alternatives that lie before us and the implications of those alternatives. This suggestion is somewhat Hegelian in spirit because it sets our practical choices in a historical context. But Hegel takes for granted that liberal capitalism is the end of history. Marx and his followers (as well as others inclined to egalitarian alternatives) have argued that something better than capitalism is possible, a society without capitalism's inequality and poverty. My methodological suggestion is that the issue of *what* is possible should be the central one for discussion. The question of what is possible is usually the question that divides us politically.

This conception of the method of political philosophy connects philosophy more closely with practical decisions such as those about norms of military service. If the best human society can offer us is the present social order with its constitutional liberties, market economies, extensive poverty, domination of the world's economies by Europe, Japan, and North America, occasional wars between nation-states, and military interventions by dominant nations in other countries, then perhaps a citizen of an economically and militarily dominant nation such as the United States owes military service when the government goes to war in Vietnam or Iraq. If, on the other hand, there are more egalitarian alternatives that enable many more people to take control of their social environment and shape it for common ends (a quasi-Hegelian conception of freedom) and if, by resisting government-imposed military service, we can help to bring these about, then we should resist military service or organize revolutionary resistance within the military. Putting questions of what is possible at the center of political philosophy, we connect that philosophy with the practical arguments that have in fact divided people about what norms of military service they should support.

This conception of political philosophy allows for many normative arguments traditionally associated with political philosophy, for example, about what freedom is and what social institutions best realize human freedom. These normative ideas are relevant to what is possible: if we define freedom negatively as explicit social restriction of conduct and if more egalitarian societies would constrict freedom so defined by replacing the social function of money with explicit law (see the discussion above), then it is impossible to establish liberating egalitarian societies. A different conception of freedom would likely yield a different conclusion about the compatibility of planned egalitarian societies with human freedom. This conception of political philosophy makes philosophy seamlessly connected with the social sciences (in making arguments about what social forms are possible and not possible) and with practical politics (as we saw above in the example of deciding what norms of military service we should support). This conception of political philosophy makes Hegel's view of the end of history the pivotal issue.

My second criticism of Hegel is substantive. Hegel endorses capitalist market institutions as part of his conception of human freedom. In owning property and in disposing of property as she sees fit, the entrepreneur is able to take a measure of control over her life. She expresses her individuality and freedom by making decisions about what business to open and where to open it, how to use her time, how to advertise, how to treat customers, and so forth. Through her property and her free control of it she is able to define herself as an individual and succeed or fail by her own actions. She seems to have some control of her daily life.

As an *individual* an entrepreneur may have a measure of control over her fate in the market order, but the international market order creates outcomes, locally and internationally, which are *outside* anyone's control. (For example, no one can control the world level of unemployment and poverty; these are the result of innumerable individual decisions of large and small capitalists fighting for market advantages and of governments and their associated banks trying to influence national unemployment and wage rates.) Most important, workers, who are the vast majority and must survive by working for others, have little or no control over the social norms governing relations at work or in the larger society.

Can rational control of our social institutions for our shared good be extended? In many of his writings Marx argued that we can extend this control only by (1) rejecting nationalism and national identities and (2) rejecting the use of markets to organize production and distribution of the means of life (Marx and Engels 1973 [1848]; Marx 1974 [1875]). From a Marxist view, nationalism and nation-states arise with capitalist society as a way of stabilizing national markets governed by capitalist norms of exchange (Tilley 1986, Chapter 2). They enable the powerful imperialist nations to dominate the economies of most of the rest of the people on earth. Nationalism and national identities, and the related idea that patriotism is a virtue, create an ideological loyalty to these capitalist forms of social organization. Marx proposed that the alternative was to organize production and distribution on an egalitarian basis, where the *abstract* freedom of the market is replaced by the *concrete* freedom of respect for people as contributors to our shared welfare. Marx articulated this as a principle of social organization: "from each according to ability, to each according to need" (Marx 1974 [1875], 347).

The Marxist alternative articulated in the previous paragraph is a political argument that something better than capitalist society is possible. To reject it the possibility of such an alternative social order must be denied or the alternative must be shown to have necessary consequences (denial of *individual* freedom and development) that we would find unacceptable. The defense of communism is the defense of a better possibility. So the substantive criticism is connected with the methodological point raised earlier.

Let me close by bringing us back to an issue in the tradition of German social theory. Kant and Hegel disagreed about the future prospects for peace among nations. For Kant the *universality* of morality, its application to and protection of all rational agents regardless of nationality, was an *a priori* that needed no justification against more parochial conceptions of the moral community. (Yet as David Felder has pointed out, this moral universalism itself was grounded in the social life of European cosmopolitans, intellectuals who communicated with one another in a shared community that took no regard of nationality [Felder 1995].) In this sense Kant was an idealist: he believed that real moral obligation, real restrictions on human conduct, could be derived from the mere *idea* of morality. Moral argument consisted in explicating moral ideas, not assessing the consequences of action. From the idea of morality Kant deduced the moral requirement for peace among states. Both Herder and, in his own way, Hegel challenge this idea of universal morality, a morality to which all are bound and one which governs conduct of all toward all merely by virtue of their rational agency. For Hegel there is no general morality which can adjudicate conflicts between states. How is this disagreement to be resolved?

This issue too is best understood as a question about history, about how it may go. If pure practical reason can lead to reconciliation among peoples, then Kant may be right. If we are at the end of history now, then there are conflicts between states which a universal morality cannot adjudicate, and Hegel is right.

Substantively there is a third possibility, that conflicts among

states are inevitable in capitalist society, but that capitalist society
is not the end of history. How then may change occur? Marxism has
proposed that the material basis of the eventual unity of humanity
is the international working class, whose conditions and problems
tend to become similar everywhere; Marxists have argued that revolutionary egalitarian change and a worldwide social order come
from this class. How would we know whether this is a possible course
of history?

In the Marxist tradition, in contrast to German idealism, such questions are best settled by looking at the world, by development of scientific argument about human society and what is possible. The mas-
terwork of the Marxist tradition, Volume I of Marx's *Capital,* is an
interdisciplinary argument incorporating history, political economy,
sociology, and philosophy (Marx 1976 [1867]). It attempts a scientific
understanding of the development of capitalist society and of a social
force, the working class, that can bring the capitalist era of history to
a close. It is simultaneously a scientific argument about the development of capitalism and a political argument about the possibility and
necessity of change. In that text, the two arguments are interwoven.
Marxism, then, departs methodologically from the more abstract,
philosophical early German social theory. Marxism is nevertheless
heavily indebted to Hegelian conceptions of history and freedom.

NOTES

1. Herder finds it hard to maintain his relativism consistently. In the *Reflections* Herder at one point affirms that each nation "bears in itself the
standard of its perfection, totally independent of all comparisons with that
of others." Then *in the following sentence* he affirms that "the more pure and
fine the maximum of which a people hit, . . . the more brilliant the figure it
made in history" (Herder 1968 [1784], 98). So in consecutive sentences he
seems to deny that there is any objective standard by which the perfection
of one nation can be compared with that of another and then implies just the
sort of comparison that he has denied can be made.

2. In his *Second Treatise of Government,* John Locke defines freedom in
just this way; as an absence of legal restrictions on action (Locke 1924
[1690], ch.II). Anglophone political philosophy generally follows Locke in
this regard.

3. In section 158 in the *Philosophy of Right* Hegel writes of the love
which characterizes family relationships that "one is present in [the family]
not as an independent person [*eine Person für sich*] but as a *member.*" And
in the addition he says that "I find myself in another person, that I gain
recognition in this person [das Ich in Ihr gelte], who in turn gains recognition in me" (1991 [1821], 199). I interpret this as implying that Hegel regards
personal identity as developing in our relationships with others.

4. Hegel uses the German word *Staat,* usually translated by its English cognate "state," with further connotations. For Hegel the *Staat* includes not just the civil authority but the entire ethical order (*Sittlichkeit*), the culture, the art, and the philosophy of a people, its entire way of living and its understanding of the way it lives.

5. Truman Nelson's *The Surveyor* (1960) contains a historically informed fictionalized depiction of the Potawatamie Creek massacre. My assessment of the effects of the massacre is based in part on what James Townsley, a reluctant eye-witness to the killings, wrote in the Lawrence *Daily Journal:* "I then thought that the transaction was terrible, and have mentioned it to but a few persons since. In after time, however, I became satisfied that it resulted in good to the Free State cause, and was especially beneficial to Free State settlers on Potawatamie Creek. *The pro-slaverymen were dreadfully terrified,* and large numbers of them soon left the Territory. It was afterwards said that one Free State man could scare a company of them" (Ruchames 1971:208–09, emphasis in original). My view here is also deeply influenced by anonymous 1979.

REFERENCES

Anonymous ("R.A."). 1979. "John Brown's Raid—Guns against Slavery." *Progressive Labor Magazine* 12:14–53.

Bentham, J. 1970 [1789]. *An Introduction to the Principles of Morals and Legislation.* London: Athalone.

Engels, F. 1972 [1884]. *The Origin of the Family, Private Property and the State.* New York: International Publishers.

Felder, D. W. 1995. "Immanuel Kant on the Cosmopolitan Ideal and the Role of Philosophers in Its Attainment." Paper presented to the National Endowment for the Humanities Seminar on Freedom and Culture in Classical German Social Theory. Chicago, IL, June.

Gomberg, P. 1994. "Universalism and Optimism." *Ethics,* 104:536–57.

———. 1997. "How Morality Works and Why it Fails: On Political Philosophy and Moral Consensus." *The Journal of Social Philosophy* 28:43–70.

Harris, M. 1968. *The Rise of Anthropological Theory.* New York: Crowell.

Hegel, G. W. F. 1991 [1821]. *Elements of the Philosophy of Right,* Ed. A.. Wood; Trans. H. B. Nisbet. Cambridge: Cambridge University Press.

———. 1988 [1840]. *Introduction to the Philosophy of History.* Trans. Leo Rauch. Indianapolis: Hackett.

Herder, J. G. von. 1968 [1784]. *Reflections on the Philosophy of the History of Mankind.* Ed. Frank E. Manuel. Chicago: University of Chicago Press.

Kant, I. 1983 [1785]. *Grounding for the Metaphysics of Morals* in *Ethical Philosophy*. Trans. James W. Ellington. Indianapolis: Hackett.

———. 1963 [1784]. *Idea for a Universal History from a Cosmopolitan Point of View* in *Kant on History*. Trans. and ed. Lewis White Beck. New York: Macmillan.

———. 1963 [1795]. *Perpetual Peace* in *Kant on History*. Trans. and ed. Lewis White Beck. New York: Macmillan, 1963.

———. 1965 [1797]. *The Metaphysical Elements of Justice*. Trans. John Ladd. New York: Macmillan, 1965.

Lee, R. 1979. *The !Kung San: Men, Women, and Work in a Foraging Society*. Cambridge: Cambridge University Press.

Locke, J. 1924 [1690]. *Two Treatises of Government*. London: Dent, 1924.

Marx, Karl. 1976 [1867]. *Capital: A Critique of Political Economy*. Trans. Ben Fowkes. Harmondsworth: Penguin.

———. 1974 [1875]. *Critique of the Gotha Program* in Marx, *The First International and After*. Harmondsworth: Penguin.

Marx, Karl, and Friedrich Engels. 1973 [1848]. *Manifesto of the Communist Party* in Marx, *The Revolutions of 1848*. Harmondsworth: Penguin.

Nelson, Truman. 1960. *The Surveyor*. New York: Doubleday.

Ruchames, Louis (ed.) 1971. *John Brown: The Making of a Revolutionary: The Story of John Brown in His Own Words and in the Words of Those Who Knew Him*. New York: Grosset and Dunlap.

Sachs, Ignacy. 1995. "Dismantling the Mechanism of Exclusion." *The Unesco Courier* 48 (March):9–13.

Tilley, Charles. 1986. *The Contentious French*. Cambridge, MA: Belnap-Harvard.

4

THE NEO-KANTIAN PREDICAMENT

Gary Backhaus

INTRODUCTION TO THE NEO-KANTIAN PROBLEMATICS

Neo-Kantianism dominated the German philosophical tradition from roughly the second half of the nineteenth century through World War I. The origins of the neo-Kantian movement could be dated perhaps as early as 1820 with Friederich Eduard Beneke's appointment as *Privatdozent* at the University of Berlin. The movement ended in 1945 with the death of its last adherent, Ernst Cassirer. The two qualifications that identify neo-Kantians are (1) a return to the critical task of philosophy espoused by Kant, and (2) the imposition of a revision to Kant's philosophy. The critical task of the neo-Kantians involved the elimination of metaphysical speculation from the interpretation of scientific research. According to Kant, metaphysical speculation consists of claims to knowledge that illegitimately transcend the parameters of human understanding.

Neo-Kantianism erupted as a result of the disillusionment with Hegel's Absolute Idealism and other transcendental systems based upon metaphysical speculation. Neo-Kantianism also posed a critical counter to the metaphysical interpretation expressed by the materialists concerning the burgeoning wealth of scientific factologies.[1] Revisions of Kant were necessary in order to properly delineate the new scientific fields, conduct rigorous scientific investigations, and interpret from the critical standpoint the plethora of scientific information. Revisions had to accommodate facets of Hegel's philosophy of history that could not be dismissed. After Hegel it was recognized by the neo-Kantians that sciences had to be created that could research history, culture, and the sociopolitical life-world, that is, the human sciences. Some revisionists sought to promote Kant's notion of the transcendental categories of the mind to the advances in the natural and positive sciences, especially in physiology and experimental psychology. Their goal was to combat the materialist interpretation of the new findings in these areas. Two internal revisions of Kant's philosophy involved the elimination of the Doctrine of the Thing-In-Itself, which was viewed by some neo-Kantians as a scepter of metaphysics, and the modification of the "excessive" formalism of Kant's deontology (the universal rules of conduct), which was viewed as necessary for the creation of a viable neo-Kantian sociopolitical philosophy. My exposition investigates the neo-Kantian polemics against both materialism and idealism and the subsequent neo-Kantian involvement with both the natural and human sciences.

I will try to show why the neo-Kantians, in their various revisions, could not successfully resolve the broadening rupture between Kant's Transcendental Idealism and his Empirical Realism. These revisions are examined systematically by displaying their problematical consequences. The philosophers selected serve as exemplars in the exposition of the main areas of revision. These nineteenth century neo-Kantian developments compromised Kant's position by interweaving incompatible philosophical orientations, or by expanding beyond the critical parameters. This thesis does not judge a priori that a revisionist synthesis is impossible; it claims that the neo-Kantians did not achieve viable (nonproblematic) syntheses. Generally, the problematics consisted of naturalizations of Kant's transcendental categories, or ontologizations of the noumenal realm, or both. The naturalization of the transcendental categories involves devastating concessions to the metaphysics of naturalism and materialism, to the epistemologies of empiricism, relativism or skepticism, and to the methodology of reductionism. It also exhibits the tendency to assume the quasi-religious eros of scientism. In order to avoid these consequences in the human sciences, some neo-Kantians returned to idealism via Plato or to Realism via Aristotle by ontologizing the noumenal realm. The naturalization of Kant's ethics was perceived to rectify the excessive formalization in Kant's ethics. This approach either led to a relativistic sociology of morals or to an eudaemonistic ethics, positions which concede too much to sociohistorical content. Both consequences are incompatible with the deontological universalism of Kant's ethics. The attempt to overcome this dilemma led to the ontologization of transcendent values, which exceeds the epistemological limits of critical philosophy.

My analysis builds upon a discussion of two fundamental terms: 'transcendental' and 'transcendent.' 'Transcendental' refers to the conditions for the possibility of knowledge. 'Transcendent' is that which is *beyond* experience or exists apart from experience. Kant's critical philosophy renders the transcendent, which he calls the noumena or the thing-in-itself, absolutely unknowable. This means that knowledge is limited to phenomena. In the modern epistemologies before Kant, phenomena were regarded as mere appearances and thus were not considered to exhibit epistemic (knowledge) status. Prior to Kant it had been thought that in the process of understanding, the mind conforms to objects. But Kant's most brilliant philosophical contribution—his "Copernican Revolution"—was the proposal that objects conform to the mind. The mind is composed of categories that organize experience. Thus, the mind supplies the transcendental *a priori* for knowledge. Phenomena are the results of the transcendental construction of objective reality. Because knowledge can be nothing but the manner in which the categories of the mind organize the phenomenal realm, it was necessary for Kant to posit the unknowable noumenal realm that is prior to the phenomenal organization. Unlike the rationalists, Kant proposed the epistemological thesis that the corresponding objects of mathematics and physics, which comprise the fundamental *scientia,* do not transcend the mind, but are products of the transcendental categories *inherent* to the mind. Kant agreed with empiricism that knowledge cannot transcend sense experience. His critical philosophy was in agreement with Hume's skepticism concerning the mind's ability for metaphysical knowledge, that is, supposed pure, rational knowledge of objects that have not entered the mind through the senses. However, through the elucidation of the *a priori* categories, Kant showed that even though knowledge begins with sense experience, it does not follow that it arises out of sense experience. The rational faculties of the mind coherently organize experience. Kant's grounding of the mind's transcendental structure legitimized the objectivity of scientific knowledge and foils Hume's skepticism.

For Hume, all synthetic judgments (judgments whereby the predicate is not contained in the subject) are *a posteriori* (based on sense impressions). Since there is no sense impression of causality, for example, causality is merely a subjective habit of psychologically associating certain juxtaposed sense impressions. Hume's radical empiricism destroys the objectivity of scientific knowledge. Kant maintained that causality is one of the *a priori* categories and thus synthetic judgments concerning causal events begin in sense experience but do no arise from sense experience. Causality, which is transcendentally ideal, legitimizes the objectivity of the empirically real observations. Kant's critical philosophy demonstrates the objectivity of scientific knowledge, for the *a priori* categories provide synthetic judgments about necessary connections between causes and their effects.

Kant explains that reason demands that its transcendental ideas be brought to completion, which means that the conditioned phenomena must be traced to an unconditioned source. For example, every effect is conditioned by a cause. Reason demands that there be a first cause that is unconditioned in order to complete the totality of the series of conditions. However, there is no unconditioned cause that is given in sense experience, that is, as a phenomenon. Such transcendental ideas are legitimately employed as regulative concepts, that is, they prescribe rules of how we ought to proceed in our empirical employment of reason. The noumenal objects that are substituted in place of the regulative principles are self/soul, world/cosmos, and God/unconditional cause. When soul, world and God are *ontologized,* which means provided with metaphysical content, then the reasoning faculty has been illegitimately employed. Nonetheless, these noumenal objects are necessary for the foundation of practical reason, the moral life of persons. Ethical principles and values are based upon a transcendental freedom that we can think but cannot know.

The terms 'transcendent' and 'transcendental' can be used to distinguish some basic philosophic orientations. These characterizations help to distinguish the various problematics associated with the neo-Kantian revisions. For the ancients, the transcendental ground is a transcendent metaphysical reality. The epistemological foundation is objective. Plato held that the Forms/Ideas (Good, Beauty, Justice) are a transcendent reality that comprise the transcendental conditions for knowledge. Aristotle held that the objects perceived through sense experience are real entities of a transcendent objectively real world. The mind has the capacity to abstract the essential nature of those individual entities that it encounters. These real existents are the manifestation of a transcendental qualitative teleological universe. The transcendental ground for the universe is the Unmoved Mover, the Pure Act. All other entities are mixed with potency and thus are in a state of becoming. These entities purposely actualize themselves in order to mimic the perfection of the Pure Act. According to the limitations imposed by Kant's critical philosophy, these metaphysical systems speculate beyond the limits of human understanding. Both Plato and Aristotle supply ontological content to ideas, such as the nature of the world as a whole, of which we can have no experience.

Modern philosophy emerged through Descartes' epistemological grounding of the transcendental in the subject as knower. Descartes' universe is a quantitative mechanistic plenum of atomic matter in motion. The nature of physical reality is deduced mathematically and cannot be known through sense experience. Descartes is the progenitor of scientific reductionism, which means that all scientific knowledge reduces to physics. Descartes is also the progenitor of physiological psychology. With the advances in physiology and experimental psychology in the nineteenth century, there was a strong materialistic tendency to reduce the human life-world to "the physics of the brain."

Speculative philosophers after Kant thought it possible to provide a metaphysical system that would replace the rationalistic dogmatic metaphysics, such as Descartes', that Kant's critical philosophy had eliminated. In fact the transcendental idealists treated Kant's critical philosophy as only the prolegomena for a transcendental metaphysics. Hegel's Absolute Idealism conflates history and ontology whereby the transcendental Absolute Spirit becomes realized gradually in concrete, historical reality through a dialectical process. The transcendental Absolute Subject loses its transcendence in its temporal concretization. The dialectical process of Spirit progressively brings the noumenal realm into the phenomenal world through its concretization in historically determined consciousness. Such idealistic systems of reality are criticized by the neo-Kantians as speculating beyond the possibilities for human knowledge. However, it was apparent to many neo-Kantians after Hegel that the methodologies of natural science were insufficient for the study of the human life-world.

The relationship of the transcendental (the conditions for the possibility of knowledge) and the transcendent (that which objectively stands against) is precisely determined by Kant' critical philosophy in a way that overcomes both skepticism and speculative metaphysics. Kant's Transcendental Idealism-Empirical Realism is a delicate synthesis of opposing philosophical orientations that characterizes the extent and the limit of human knowledge. To say that Kant's critical philosophy abjures the speculations of pure reason beyond the limits of the understanding in order to make room for practical reason and faith is not to assert that it is incomplete. Kant's achievement was to discern the natural limits of the understanding without falling into the dogmatic assumption of the metaphysics of naturalism, which posits that Being in its entirety exists in the manner of material objects. The neo-Kantians sought to discredit the materialist reduction that paralleled the development of the natural sciences. However, the consequences of some neo-Kantian revisions promoted concessions to naturalism and to reductionism. Specifically, the neo-Kantians misappropriated the transcendental in their concern to interpret the research developments of psychology, physiology, and the histology of the brain.

Psychologism is a naturalistic epistemology that emerged after Kant. This position was defined by the neo-Kantians, Jakob Friederich Fries (1783–1844) and Friedrich Eduard Beneke (1798–1854). Any natural psychology that claims epistemological status may be labeled 'psychologism'. Yet it is more appropriate to reserve 'psychologism' for a psychological foundation that replaces and naturalizes Kant's *a priori* categories to provide a methodology that unifies the burgeoning fields of science. Psychologism traces all areas of knowledge back to the real, causally produced psychological processes of human thinking. Psychology was envisioned as the foundational science for ethics, metaphysics, logic, mathematics, etc.

The neo-Kantian proponents of psychologism sought to discredit the speculative excesses of the metaphysical idealisms that retarded the growth of legitimate science. One of their means was to naturalize Kant's transcendental categories. This involved stripping the categories of their status as the *a priori* conditions for knowledge by reducing them to the status of conditioned effects in the process of perception. However, in doing so psychologism severely weakens Kant's transcendental idealism and does not strengthen Kant's empirical realism as intended. Instead, it loses the source for the objective legitimacy of the empirical content of thought. The objective content of consciousness becomes naturalized (causally formed thought products, or the epiphenomena of brain states), which consequently denies its ideal status. Kant's effort to legitimize the objective status of mathematics and physics against the Humean position is negated.

In their reaction to both the speculative expansion of Idealism and to this reduction to naturalistic psychology, other neo-Kantians, for example, Johann Friedrich Herbart (1776–1841), countered with the expansion into metaphysical realism. Herbart attempted to account for phenomena through real entities discoverable behind the empirical sense data that were viewed as epistemologically primary according to the naturalistic reduction.[2] This example shows the form of these neo-Kantian debates: a metaphysical proposal is countered with a problematic naturalistic proposal which is then countered by another illicit metaphysical proposal. The emergence of these debates had to do with managing the huge volume of new scientific information that continually called for interpretation.

Psychologism generally resulted in the reification of consciousness—the employment of ontological categories that are proper to a material object to characterize consciousness. Two particular forms of psychologism result from the naturalization of the transcendental categories. A faculty psychologism of "the mind"—the naturalistic reduction of consciousness—followed upon Kant's acceptance of Descartes' mind/body dualism. Unlike the first form, physiological psychologism, or the naturalistic reduction of the lived-body to the physical body, did not resist reducing the transcendental to physicalism. Physicalism is the view that scientific concepts are those that refer to empirically observable and testable phenomena. The transcendental, then, receives scientific legitimation only if it is linked to an observable and testable operation in the brain, on this latter view. But how can the conditions for the possibility of knowledge rest upon conditions of its location in the brain? One is motivated to inquire about the conditions for the possibility of the activity of the investigator to locate the transcendental conditions in the brain. One then must address the conscious intentions of the investigator who forms the question, who performs the procedures, and who bases her findings upon certain direct observations, which, of course, makes the reduction to "transcendental physiology" logically problematic at the least.[3]

Reductionism in Psychologism and its Consequences

Friedrich Eduard Beneke (1798–1854) produced an *Erkenntnislehre,* a new critical science of knowledge, which reformulated traditional logic in terms of a theory of perception.[4] Beneke's psychologism renounced the *a priori* categories in the naturalization of the relationship of logical forms to perceptions. The insistence upon perception in his arguments against speculative systematizations of reality seem to reassert the position of Hume. But Beneke did not hold to Hume's "theater of the mind" or to his "bundle theory of perception." Beneke promoted the transcendental of Kant by arguing that the mind creates perceptions through the externally caused impressions. Upon these perceptions the mind then forms *a posteriori* "elementary faculties" (*Urvermögen*), i.e., "a bundle of genetically formed capacities," that replace Kant's transcendental categories.[5] In this way Beneke's doctrine promoted a causal genesis of the mind's productive activities. However, these elementary faculties cannot fulfill the requirements that constitute the transcendental conditions for experience, because they are an intermediate step in the natural formation of experience. He denies that these faculties are *a priori* (nativistic), for consciousness forms new faculties in learning to accommodate new kinds of stimuli. These points foreshadow Piaget's position of genetic epistemology.[6] Beneke claimed that Kant made a mistake in attempting to uncover in a manner independent of experience the forms of intuition, the categories of the understanding, and the transcendental ground for the objectivity of knowledge. Psychologism does not recognize that the objectivity of empirical knowledge is dependent on conditions that are independent of causal mechanisms. The causally dependent, real structuring of experience results in a conflation of form (the acts of consciousness, Beneke's "active impulses") and matter (the contents of consciousness, Beneke's assimilation of external stimuli) such that there is no transcendental that guarantees the ideality of knowledge.

Following Hume's metaphor, Beneke's neo-Kantian revision characterized the mind as the "director" of the theater production. However, the script corresponds to that which transcends the experience. Beneke disagrees with Hume's skepticism and Kant's thing-in-itself with a move that could be labeled neo-Aristotelian.[7] Beneke maintained that a relation of adequacy holds between thought and being. The crucial questions concern the problematic status of this relationship, which Beneke must ground through his doctrine of causal genesis. What is modern, and not simply a return to Aristotle, is the replacement of the logico-ontological foundation (Aristotle's categories of Being) with the science of psychology, and the assumption of the modern epistemological doctrine of representation, that is, consciousness is only aware of its own states. The fundamental epistemological problem for modern philosophy shows up here: how is it possible for the "in-here" (consciousness) to know the "out-there" (transcendent reality)?

If Beneke did not smuggle in rationalistic notions, for example, substance, then how is it possible that thought is adequate to Being? Naturalisms that remain empirically pure and that assume Descartes' representational epistemology can do no more than beg the question. Unlike Herbart, Beneke was unwilling to argue the realist position, that is, to provide ontological content to the thing-in-itself. The standard nineteenth century argument in support of Beneke is that because the objects of science are natural and since human beings are natural entities, the effects of the natural world upon human beings correlate with the natural world, even though human beings can only know representations of that world "inside" them. But this argument assumes that all of reality is ontologically structured like material objects, which is a metaphysical posit. The recourse to the apparent circularity of such an argument is typically the factual enumeration of the progressive predictability (theoretical accomplishments) and the manipulability (practical accomplishments) concerning the achievements of scientific research. But this does little to strengthen knowledge claims about the nature of reality. This recourse is like Johnson's kicking a "material object" in his attempt to refute Berkeley's doctrine of phenomenalism—a doctrine which denied the existence of the material substratum.

Even though the relation of the immanent and transcendent worlds characterize the basic problematics of modern philosophy, it is erroneous to view Beneke's philosophy as an ontological construction of transcendent reality in the Cartesian manner. Yet, an analogous structure continues the Cartesian legacy as well as characterizes the dominant self-understanding of science in the nineteenth century. The only way Descartes could guarantee the existence of the transcendent world was through the establishment of the existence of God and of God's nondeceiving character. Beneke eschews the rationalistic deductive method and thus he must secure his adequation of thought and Being in another manner. "Science" replaces Descartes' benevolent God. The Double World Theory, the Doctrine of the Inner and Outer Worlds, is maintained, but in place of Descartes' purely rationalistic deductions that characterize scientific method, it is the inductive factologies of the empirical sciences founded upon a faculty psychology that guarantee an adequate relation between thought and Being. This position, which may be labeled 'scientism', promotes the independence of empirical science from "philosophy" and implicitly makes the claim that natural science is foundational. Scientism characterizes a quasi-religious reverence and faith in the progress of science. But scientism has no argument without the premise of the progress of science. In this instance, the solution to the double world problem is not demonstrated philosophically, but posited by a leap of faith in scientific progress. Scientism may be a reaction to abstract idealism, but those thinkers who fall into scientistic thinking err by abandoning philosophy and substituting the deification of scientific progress in its place. Naturalizations of the transcendental in Kant by the neo-Kantians are sublimations of the nineteenth century *eros* of scientism.

Other neo-Kantians sharply attacked Beneke and others like him who advocated the reduction to natural science. Ernst Adolf Eduard Calinich was the first (1841) to use *'Naturwissenschaften'* and *'Geisteswissenschaften'* as technical terminologies (Köhnke 1991, 54). Calinich maintained that the mind has laws of its own that cannot be discovered or handled through natural science. Calinich accepted that psychology's role is to trace science back to inner perception in order to epistemically ground the relationship between thought and Being. But, Calinich carefully avoided reductionism by promoting the distinction that would preempt the reduction of such a psychological foundational science to physiological research. This strain of argumentation eventually led to the establishment of the *Geisteswissenschaften,* which included the most fruitful flowering of the neo-Kantians in the field of sociology, for example, Max Weber and Georg Simmel.

Eduard Zeller (1814–1908) represents the position of physiological psychologism. He retreated from his Hegelian origins and thematically evoked Kant in his 1862 address at Heidelberg (Willey 1978, 73). Against a main tenet of Hegelianism, Zeller argued that logic is only a methodological propaedeutic for the study of material reality. Zeller sought to rid Kantianism of the source for unfounded speculation, the thing-in-itself (*Ding-an-sich*). To accomplish this, Zeller's psychologism promoted Kant's *a priori* forms of the mind as the analog of brain physiology. Brain activity is only in immediate relation with the states of the organism and is not in relation with the external world. What linked this physiology to the transcendental is the notion that what happens in the brain is not merely the result of atomistic mechanisms. The brain actively creates "for-itself" the organization that is essential for ordered experience. "Now the manner in which we receive the impressions of things, the quality and strength of sensation . . . is conditioned by the constitution of our sensory equipment and the laws of our sensory faculties. . . . Space, time and causality reside in the physical nature of man" (Willey 1978, 74). The thing-in-itself is eliminated, for once brain physiology is thoroughly understood, the thing-in-itself is none other than the external world organized into conscious experience by the natural entity, the brain. However, Zeller's position is problematic because brain physiology as the condition for knowledge eliminates the essential nature of the transcendental. The transcendental conditions for the possibility of experience can only be described and can never be explained, that is, examined through scientific laws. Zeller's attempt to do so sets up the absurdity of founding the unconditional upon the conditioned. The transcendental *a priori* is the very ground that allows for the possibility of explanation, including the scientific explanation of how the brain operates.

Hermann Ludwig von Helmholtz (1821–1894) argued for a critical philosophy that would establish a new collaboration between philosophy and science. The strength of his philosophical position rested upon Johannes Muller's Doctrine of Specific Nerve Energies. "The central and fundamental principle of the doctrine is that we are directly aware, not of objects, but of our nerves themselves; that is to say, the nerves are intermediates between perceived objects and the mind and thus impose their own characteristics upon the mind" (Boring 1950, 82). "That the idea in the mind is the result 'not of anything received'. . . from the external object by way of the nerves, that 'the nerves of the senses are not mere conductors of the properties of bodies to our sensorium' " (Boring 1950, 83). Since the source of the phenomenal world is the physiology of the sense organs, Helmholtz determined that the materialists could no longer argue against the reality of the phenomenal world. The qualities of our sense perceptions are the phenomenal outcomes of the nature of our physiology, which involves the entire connected cohesion or organization of the physical apparatus. Unlike Kant and Muller who espoused nativism (inborn structures rather than acquired characteristics), Helmholtz employed his physicalist foundation to argue for empirical geneticism. This he defended while at Konigsberg, the university at which Kant had taught! Thus, not only was Kant reduced to physiology but Kant's entire discussion of the synthetic *a priori* had been discarded. Helmholtz elaborated his position by arguing against the intuitionism of space and time and against the *a priori* status of geometrical axioms. Even though Helmholtz defended Kant's idea of the reality of the phenomenal realm, his research interpretations really supported materialism.

Helmholtz proved that Kant was incorrect in his belief that psychology could never be experimental. The mind/body relationship Helmholtz thought to be instantaneous. Helmholtz "brought the mind into time" by measuring the rate of nervous impulses.[8] This breakthrough brought the mind under the direct purview of the experimental sciences. It is through his monumental research in experimental psychology that Helmholtz argued against the nativist doctrine. The whole controversy, however, would not have affected the notion of the transcendental if the necessary conditions for conscious experience were distinguished from the transcendental itself. Brain activities are necessary for conscious experience but the conditions for the possibility of experience are the structural rules by which consciousness proceeds. Analogously, it is necessary to possess a ball and a bat to play baseball, but the condition for the possibility of baseball is knowledge of the rules. The rules for baseball are not found in the ball and bat. The rules for experience are not found in the brain. What is found in the brain are only necessary electrcochemical activities within a highly complex physiological organization of matter. Once certain fundamental misunderstandings occur, psychologism reduces the transcendental to arguments over whether the brain has inherent capacities that create the forms of experience (Kant reduced to nativism) or whether the brain becomes "wired" only in response to external stimulations (empirical genesis). The fact that the intervolvement of mental and physical events occurs in time does not warrant the materialistic reduction that mental events can be adequately explained on the basis of physical events.

Psychophysical parallelism is the view that the brain as a physical entity and the mind as a spiritual entity form parallel activities. The source for this conception of a preestablished non-interacting correlation is Leibniz with his monadological preestablished harmony. But Leibniz is a source for the Austrian school of act-psychology, which can be traced through Brentano, Stumpf, Husserl, Kulpe, McDougall, and the Gestaltists—Koffka and Köhler.[9] In this school, the integrity of consciousness *qua* consciousness is upheld, which means that the structures of consciousness are to be accurately described according to the manner by which they show themselves. In contrast, the particularly science-minded neo-Kantians tended toward reductionism and empiricism and their attempt to locate the transcendental in the brain fails.

If there exists a psychophysical parallelism, then must the transcendental conditions for experience have a material parallel? But then the transcendental conditions are subject to parallel material cause and effect. Damaging the brain would result in the parallel modification of the transcendental conditions for experience, which is an absurdity. In Kant's language, the schemata would be alterable through physiological damage, and thus in parallel fashion, the pure concepts of the understanding would be alterable. It is true that brain damage can alter experience in a fundamental fashion, but unless an ideal of experience is guaranteed through the transcendental, there is no objective distinction between pathology and healthy functioning. The absurd consequences of the physiological reduction of the transcendental are such that if a brain damaged person experiences no distinction between the imaged schema of a triangle and a square, then there would be no distinction between these entities as pure concepts either. This supposition does not even conform to research findings, for what a brain damaged person intellectually knows and what she can image or perceive are not necessarily the same.

Despite Helmholtz's physiological reductionism, he ironically remained an "idealist" in terms of Kant's practical philosophy. Like Kant he argued that while nature is deterministic in the sphere of empirical phenomena, the domain of freedom cannot be explained through causation. Helmholtz argued that if the judgment, 'no effect without cause', is an empirical law, then freedom of the will is impossible. Freedom of the will is an *a priori* law of thinking (transcendental) that precedes all experience. But Helmholtz's position can only be maintained as an untenable bifurcation of mental faculties. Thus, the "theoretical faculties" are reducible to the physiology of the nervous system, and the "practical faculties" (Will) are nonreducible, transcendental, *a priori* Kantian forms of conscious experience.

Arthur Schopenhauer (1788–1860) established a neo-Kantian philosophy—based on the primacy of the Will—upon the advances made in biological research. Schopenhauer's position suffers a similar weakness to that of Helmholtz in the bifurcation of the will and the understanding. Like Helmholtz, Schopenhauer held that Kant's *a priori* categories of theoretical knowledge were merely functions of the brain. But far more metaphysically stalwart than Helmholtz, he elevated the Will to the level of the thing-in-itself. But the transcendental will, even though it is *a priori,* is only known *a posteriori.* The teleology of the will correlates with ontology. The transcendental condition is the Will, which manifests as the *a posteriori* reality of the visible world. Reality is characterized pessimistically by Schopenhauer, because the teleology of the fundamental biological impulses (instincts) is blind. Thus, there can be no social progress as envisioned by Hegel.

If Schopenhauer and others eliminate theoretical reason from the transcendental and reduce the theoretical mind to physiology, then the hypertrophy of the will, practical reason, also leads to a materialist reduction. Caldwell, an early commentator, states, "man seemed to him [Schopenhauer] a creature led and dominated by his instincts, and therefore a mere puppet in the hands of nature" (Caldwell 1896, 39). Because teleology rather than mechanism characterizes the will, a materialist reduction is best handled by biology rather than by physiology.

Biologism is the position that the social order is derived from the structure of the biological organism. The physiological reduction of the Schopenhauerian position has happened only recently with the Sociobiologies of E. O. Wilson and Richard Dawkins.[10] The physiological counterpart to the consciousness of freedom is the gene through which the actions of human beings are only the outer manifestation. Thus, the consciousness of will is only an epiphenomenon to the genetic code. If DNA had been discovered in the nineteenth century, "Kantian physiologists" likely would have argued that they had found the transcendental material source for the experience of freedom, which would have been another tenuous position.

The Methods and Scope of Critical Philosophy

Another major interest of neo-Kantianism was to define the proper method and the scope of philosophy. In the year 1852, the university was restructured in a manner that delimited philosophy as a mere branch of learning alongside the others (Köhnke 1991, 79). This situation was not only externally imposed; it was a self-constraint imposed on philosophy by neo-Kantians.[11] This strain had originated with Eric von Berger who, throughout the 1820s, argued that philosophy's role is not normative when questions pertaining to the foundation of science are at issue. Philosophy analyzes the principles actually employed by the sciences themselves. Moreover, the legitimation of these principles would evolve from the sciences themselves as self-correcting endeavors (Köhnke 1991, 12). Following von Berger's espousal, Friedrich Adolf Trendelenburg (1802–1872) sought to discredit the speculative systems of Idealism and to return philosophy to a Kantian critical foundation. Grasping the structure of the new age of scientific research, Trendelenburg shared the prognosis of his skeptical generation that no single individual could master the ever-increasing quantity of scientific knowledge. He recognized that scientific progress occurs through research limited to specific problems. Against the Hegelians he asserted that only an increase in positive knowledge yields progress (Köhnke 1991, 69–70). The strength of Trendelenburg's position, like Kant's, is that it forces philosophy to critically question its speculative goal of attaining a systematically complete metaphysical exposition of reality.

However, Trendelenburg romanticizes science in his model of Organicism, which is the view that the connection of all things corresponds with the empirical experiences as comprehended scientifically.[12] Scientific Organicism holds that reality as a whole functions as the coordinating principle of the activities of scientific progress.

What this means is that each scientific fact receives its meaning in the context of the entire body of scientific knowledge. In isolation, the consequences of a scientific fact cannot be apprehended. Even though reality is not systematized as in Hegelianism, organicism still makes claims about the nature of reality in its relation to the evolution of scientific knowledge that exceed critical parameters. Specifically, Kant's second regulative rule, which concerns the concept of world, prescribes how to proceed in forming a synthesis of the many events in experience. Organicism proceeds beyond experience to posit an ontological structure to the regulative synthesis. Nevertheless, this position reduced critical philosophy to explaining the meaning of scientific progress. Influenced by scientism, Trendelenburg attempted to manage an organic synthesis of the inductive collection of individual facts by limiting the role of philosophy to the parasitic reception of content from the sciences. Trendelenburg attempted too much and too little. He limits philosophy to accepting the empirically given scientific paradigms, whereas critical activity should be expanded to include the questioning of the paradigms themselves.

The neo-Kantian critical revision of the methods and scope of philosophy also led to the expansion of philosophical concerns. These developments concerned axiology, the philosophy of culture, and the methodologies of the human sciences. Otto Liebmann (1840–1912) is a neo-Kantian critic who derides each of the Kantian epigones: the Idealism of Hegel, the Realism of Herbart, the Empiricism of Fries (the contemporary of Beneke), and the Transcendentalism of Schopenhauer (Willey 1978, 80). Liebmann argued that all of these faulty revisions of Kant can be traced to the mistaken notion of the thing-in-itself. With these diatribes, one expects a critical restriction to the analysis of scientific factologies. But, Leibmann is important for his contributions toward the formation of a philosophy of value that influenced the Baden and Marburg neo-Kantians (Willey 1978, 82). He advocated a critical philosophy of culture (judgments of will) that would avoid the extremes of absolute idealism and naturalism. Liebmann revised Kant's synthesis by posing, through a doctrine of intuition, that the transcendental is between consciousness (idealism) and the body (naturalism).

Rudolf Hermann Lotze (1817–1881) established a new metaphysics that augmented but remained consistent with the inductive methods of the empirical sciences. The role of metaphysics is to organize into an open-ended system the concepts, theories, and factual findings of the empirical sciences (Gotesky 1967, 88). Lotze did not

advocate the philosopher as a mere collator for science. The natural
mechanisms uncovered by scientific research should not be given a
materialist interpretation because mechanism is the necessary condition for the autonomy of the will. It is necessary for neo-Kantian
metaphysics to incorporate scientific knowledge into an open system
that includes value. Science can never on its own render experience
intelligible because science is incapable of incorporating the experience of feelings and values. Reality is both teleological and mechanistic and it is only by logical analysis that these aspects become separated. The neo-Kantian metaphysician integrates theoretical and
practical reason into a meaningful whole.

Lotze's eudaemonisitic value theory concretizes Kantian ethics.
Feeling and willing are much closer to reality than the concepts of
the understanding (Willey 1978, 50). Theoretical thinking can not be
exhaustive because the immediate phenomena exist for some practical purpose. Love, which is the essential nature of feeling, drives
human beings toward a truth that ought to be, that is, a reality of
transcendent significance. This impetus of love is augmented with a
moral individualism, which creates a neo-Leibnizian teleology.
Lotze's eudaemonism also implies empiricism, which demonstrates
his Kantian-like strategy to fashion a synthesis between the rational and the empirical. Values, which have transcendent (Platonic)
universal validity, nevertheless are fundamentally indexed in the individual's feelings of pleasure and pain. Lotze's view is situated in a
very difficult philosophical cul-de-sac; he maintains that free individuals strive toward the concretization of transcendent values derived from individual feelings of self-worth (Willey 1978, 51). It is
necessary for him to argue that pleasure and pain are not merely
functions of subjective inclinations. Rather, pleasure and pain are
the means by which individuals discover a transcendent objective order of values. Thus, feeling is the ultimate judge of value because
pleasure and pain lead to the universally-binding moral duties.
Lotze believed that his revision corrected the fundamental error in
Kant's formalistic ethics, which consisted in the failure to provide a
moral barometer for actual moral decisions.

For Kant, moral judgments proceed by the universalizability of a
subjectively formed maxim; that is, the judgments are founded on a
universalizable rule. Lotze argues that love prescribes the rule of how
we ought to act in our experience of feelings. Since feelings are not a
universizable rational rule, Lotze argues for transcendent values that
guarantee the legitimation of the moral prescription. However, the
ontologization of values—giving content to formerly "noumenal" en-

tities—exceeds the parameters of Kant's Critical philosophy. Lotze's neo-Kantian metaphysics proved to be influential because of the emphasis to include discussion of value. Instead of looking to metaphysics to complement scientific research with the study of value, some neo-Kantians, like those of the Baden school, sought to incorporate the study of value in the creation of the human sciences.

The Baden Neo-Kantians and
the Philosophy of History

The Baden or Southwestern School of Neo-Kantianism included Wilhelm Windelband (1848–1915), Emil Lask (1875–1915), and Heinrich Rickert (1863–1936). Windelband's dictum,' "To understand Kant is to go beyond him," led to the fruitful creation of a theory for the human sciences. Windelband claimed that because Kant's philosophical considerations were limited to the Newtonian paradigm of natural science, the Kantian doctrine did not solve the problem of the bifurcation of reality into spirit and nature. According to Windelband this philosophical dilemma would dissolve by uncovering the transcendental deduction for historical phenomena. Kant's transcendental deduction purportedly demonstrated the set of categories basic to human understanding and experience. However, Windelband contested that these categories fail to consider the nature of history.

His strategy was to identify the conditions for the possibility of historical cognition. He developed transcendental parameters by recognizing three things: an individualistic conception of value, the nomological (necessary and universally valid laws) limitations of the natural sciences, and the idiographic (the particular and contingent individual) nature of historical science.[13] Windelband argued that the addition of such a science destroys the bogus ontological categories of spirit and nature, because the same object can be a datum for both the natural and historical sciences. The two sciences are grounded on the proper epistemological distinction that does not entail an ontological bifurcation. The transcendental does not only present the conditions for the possibility of the nomothetic abstraction from concrete reality; it engenders the conditions for the comprehension of the concrete and singular features of reality.

Emil Lask refashions Kant's noumenal realm with his notion that reality cannot be conceptualized. The relation between concepts and objects is not ontological; it is purely logical. Lask's Doctrine of the *Hiatus Irrationalis* is that the sole reality, which is the concrete object of immediate experience, resists conceptualization. *Irrationalis* means that reality is fundamentally irrational. *Hiatus* means that there is a fundamental gap between knowledge and reality such that there can be no correspondence between a concept and an existent. The goal of historical knowledge is to establish a conception of value that only applies to individual entities. This value-conception must be universal so that the selection of idiographic historical events is not determined idiosyncratically or in a culturally restricted manner.

Though Windelband and Lask provide key concepts for a methodology of the human sciences, Heinrich Rickert produced the complete formulation of *Kulturwissenschaft* with his work, *The Limits of Concept Formation in Natural Science*. Rickert holds that access to the full content of reality is given only through the immediacy of life. However, this reality is an infinite, irrational, inchoate manifold. Nomological formations function to ameliorate the goals of natural science through progressive reduction of the irrational to the rational. The consequence of this function entails the progressive departure from the real as such. Natural science can not reproduce reality but it represents what holds validly through a transformation of its content in the formation of concepts.

In contrast to natural science, idiographic science is founded upon the unique, individual event. History must be capable of forming an individualizing representation of reality. Rickert distinguishes two kinds of individuals. Individuals are discrete, identifiable phenomena, but not all of them are irreplaceable. *In-dividuals* are characterized through a coherence and an indivisibility that they possess due to their uniqueness. It is because values are ascribed to certain individuals that they become irreplaceable *in-dividuals*. In order to guarantee the objectivity of the scientific description of historical-individuals, Rickert makes a distinction between valuations and value-relevancies. Valuations are either positive or negative concerning an in-dividual. Whether Luther is valuated positively or negatively, the historian does not claim that Luther the in-dividual is not value-relevant.

It is with the criteria for establishing *in-dividuals* that the *hiatus irrationalis* engenders problems. Without this doctrine the critical position would be indistinguishable from positivism or realism. Value-relevance requires a value-relation in order for there to be an objective selection according to criteria. Thus, there is the necessity of assuming objective values that exhibit unconditional validity and that are transcendent of the merely empirical normative values that

characterize a socio-historical situation. Rickert argues that unconditional validity is a formal meta-empirical assumption.

> But we must be allowed to assume that they [normative general values]
> are more or less closely related to *some* values that are unconditionally
> valid, or whose validity is independent of every *de facto* recognition. Thus
> we must be allowed to assume that human culture possesses some objec-
> tive meaning or other—perhaps still completely unknown to us—with ref-
> erence to unconditionally and general valid values. (Rickert 1986, 206)

The historian then must proceed by the rule that measures the
value-relevance of the in-dividual in its value-relation with the assumed transcendent unconditional values.

Rickert's position is untenable because this procedure is not possible without assuming unconditional-value *content*. Unless there is
content there is no possible way of measuring the value-relation. To
ascribe content to the transcendent value, that is, to give it ontological status and not merely logical status, is to circumvent the *hiatus
irrationalis* through a method of measuring the in-dividual according to ideal criteria. Rickert avoided positivism and realism but he
smuggled in Platonic idealism, which exceeds critical parameters.
Unless there is transcendent content there is no way to measure the
value-relation, because the historian would not recognize the value-
standard from which he measures the empirically given in-dividual
candidate. The critical historian assumes that there are unconditioned, transcendent values, but as regulative principles they are not
sufficient to ensure scientific objectivity. Without having positive
knowledge of the content of the transcendent values, the historian at
least tacitly must assume such candidates. Otherwise, there can be
no way of determining value-relevance according to his criteria for a
value-relation.

Rickert's "solution" presupposes the enlightenment ideal of universality and the Christian ideal of an absolute value attributed to
the individual (soul). The enlightened Christian thinkers actually
found it quite difficult to wisely evaluate the conceptions of other
ages, races and cultures. This point strongly suggests that even with
ideals of universality, the very ideal of universality can be peculiarly
culture bound. Thus, the in-dividual may indeed be culturally idio-
syncratic—unless the historian can achieve the cognition of Plato's
philosopher king. Obviously, such metaphysical cognition is impossible according to Kant's critical philosophy.

The Marburg Neo-Kantians and the
Problem of Social Ethics

The Marburg philosophers, Hermann Cohen (1842–1918), Paul Natorp (1854–1925), and Rudolf Stammler (1856–1938), were the most politically and socially conscious of the neo-Kantians. The overall history of neo-Kantianism began with the rejection of Hegelianism and then ironically ended with its reappropriation by the Marburg group. Cohen's epistemology promoted a purely formal study of conceptualization. He elaborated this position by arguing that thought produces its own reality (Hegel), that truth is in agreement with reason and is independent of experience (Plato), and that the ethical Ought of practical reason is primary over the phenomenal Is of theoretical reason (Fichte). Since rational thought produces Being, the conditions for producing an ethical culture are found in logic, especially in the logic of jurisprudence. This transcendental method, which establishes the logical coherence of formal concepts, reveals the rational law intrinsic to the Will in the production of objects, promotes the freedom underlying purposive conduct, and finds its highest expression in a form of ethical socialism. By transforming the thing-in-itself into the function of the ethical, Cohen espouses a teleological idealism. This means that through human freedom, the Will progresses towards the ideal ethical society by establishing conceptual realities. To establish this vocation of man, Cohen reformulates Kant's categorical imperative into a social imperative: "Act as though the element of humanity in one's own person, as well as in the person of every other individual, is treated at all times as a purpose, never merely as a means. The conduct of every person must have an absolute purpose, the infusion of the universal principles of humanity" (Willey 1978, 112).

Paul Natorp reintroduces a kind of Hegelian dialectic with his Doctrine of the *Aktcharakter* of Values. Practical reason can mediate between the empirical and the intellectual through a life process that takes into account transcendent values. Unlike Cohen, who sought to develop the moral state through formal laws, Natorp envisions the source for the Kingdom of Ought in the empirical character of human beings. Kant's method, which begins with the pure moral will and deduces formal principles of conduct, is inverted by Natorp in the ascension from the natural impulse to the transcendent values. His society is an integral association of self-willing individuals forming a community that transcends empirical conditions by striving toward moral ideals. In contrast with Cohen's juristic socialism, Natorp de-

veloped a socialist theory of education by which the organic community of wills morally educates the individual as a social and cultural
being.[14]

Both Cohen and Natorp had to rely upon ontological transcendence to save their philosophy from sociologism. Sociologism is the
position that holds that reality is nothing more than the manner in
which it is socially constructed. The Marburg philosophers rejected
dialectical determinism in the process of society. Through the freedom of individuals, there exists the never-ending striving toward the
transcendent values. Thus, society can overcome itself through the
free striving toward the transcendent Ought, which is not conditioned by the Is as it would be in a deterministic dialectic. However,
it is only through the metaphysical transcendence of values that sociologism is avoided. Morality rests upon societal efforts to organize
in light of the transcendent, universal values. The ontologization of
transcendent values is obvious for Natorp, as he straightforwardly
acknowledges super-experiential values. Cohen's position is more
complex, for he argued that the moral thing-in-itself, noumenal freedom, exists and resides in the Kingdom of the Ought. He claimed
that ethical realities possess Being but not phenomenal existence. It
is difficult to discern whether he transgressed critical philosophy by
ontologizing transcendent values, or whether he fell into prescriptive, dogmatic sociology by providing his Kantian formalism with the
positive content of socialism.

CONCLUSION

This essay has elaborated the philosophical problems of the neo-
Kantians that emerged as they tried to create a philosophy that
avoided speculative idealism and materialism. Their sociohistorical
situation consisted of having to interpret a wealth of new scientific
data, especially the relevant research in physiology and experimental psychology, in a way that accommodated scientific facts within
the limits of critical philosophy. They also attempted to forge a
deformalized ethics, or at least to provide an experiential addendum
to the abstract nature of deontology, in order to reinterpret the
Hegelian notion of the concrete process of historical reality. Neo-
Kantian criticism weakened Hegelian Idealism and the general tendency for speculative philosophy. It also controlled the general impulse toward naive positivism and materialism. However, their
contributions did not overcome the egregious difficulties involved in
maintaining the critical position. They either made epistemological

concessions to empiricism, for example, psychologism, that led to metaphysical naturalism and materialism, or they made ontological concessions to Hegelianism that led to the metaphysics of idealism or realism. The purest critical philosophy of the time limited philosophy's role as subservient to the empirical sciences. The greatest advance gained through the neo-Kantian movement had been toward the establishment of the human sciences and the actual research of those scientists who had been prepared for such activity through their neo-Kantian background.

NOTES

1. 'Factology' refers to the consequences of a positivistic viewpoint that eliminates philosophic concerns from scientific research. The result is to assume without question the methods of science, what counts as a fact, etc.

2. For a clear comparison of Herbart's reals and Kant's things-in-themselves, see Harold B. Dunkel, *Herbart and Herbartianism* (Chicago: University of Chicago Press, 1970), 110–111.

3. For one of the best discussions concerning this point, see Wolfgang Köhler, *Gestalt Psychology* (New York: Liveright Publishing Corporation, 1947), 26. "I do not avoid direct experience when I am working in physics; for I cannot avoid it. . . .Thus at least some observations which refer to direct experience must constitute an entirely adequate basis for science."

4. See the discussion by Klaus Christian Köhnke, *The Rise of Neo-Kantianism,* Trans. R. J. Hollingwood (London: Cambridge University Press, 1991), 93.

5. See Arnulf Zweig, "Beneke, Friedrich Eduard," in *The Encyclopedia of Philosophy* Volume I (London: Collier Macmillan, 1967), 279. The four basic psychological processes are clearly outlined.

6. See Jean Piaget, *Genetic Epistemology,* Trans. Eleanor Duckworth (New York: Columbia University Press, 1970), 77–78. After rejecting both empiricism and nativism Piaget writes, "By contrast, for the genetic epistemologist, knowledge results from continuous construction, since in each act of understanding, some degree of invention is involved; in development the passage from one stage to the next is always characterized by the formation of new structures which did not exist before, either in the external world or in the mind" 77.

7. Köhnke, 24–25. The influence of Aristotle on the neo-Kantians is elaborated throughout Köhnke's text.

8. See Edwin G. Boring, *A History of Experimental Psychology* (Englewood Cliffs: Prentice Hall, 1950), 41–45. Boring argues that Helmholtz's experiments were some of the most important in the contribution towards the materialistic viewpoint

9. See Boring, 167. A nice formulation of the position of Leibniz is given by Austin Farrer in his introduction to G.W. Leibniz. *Theodicy,* Ed. with Introd. Austin Farrer, Trans. E. M. Huggard (LaSalle: Open Court, 1985), 25: "Leibniz himself says that the very nature of representation excludes interaction. . . . The act of representing is simply the act of the mind; it represents

in view of the environment, of course, but not under the causal influence of environment. Representation is a business carried on by the mind on its own account, and in virtue of its innate power to represent." Any causal account of the mind cannot properly handle the transcendental and inevitably leads to psychologism. It is Husserl who finally founds a non-naturalistic psychology that defeats psychologism.

10. For an excellent formulation of these positions see, Robert Augros and George Stanciu, *The New Biology* (Boston: New Science Library, 1987), 9.

11. See Köhnke, 90. Köhnke states that Stahl, professor at Berlin, remarked in an 1854 address that, "Respect for philosophy is now lower than at any time in the history of civilized nations."

12. See Köhnke, 17. Köhnke argues that Romanticism paves the way for Positivism

13. Guy Oakes, "Introduction: Rickert's Theory of Historical Knowledge," in *The Limits of Concept Formation in Natural Science* by Heinrich Rickert (Cambridge: Cambridge University Press, 1986), ix. Oakes discusses both Windelband and Lask in light of their influence on Rickert

14. For further discussion of this theory of education see Willey, 118–122.

REFERENCES

Boring, E. G. (1950). *A History of Experimental Psychology.* Engelwood Cliffs, NJ: Prentice Hall.

Gotesky, R. (1967). "Lotze, Rudolf Hermann," in *The Encyclopedia of Philosophy* Volume 5. London: Collier Macmillan.

Köhnke, K. C. (1991). *The Rise of Neo-Kantianism.* Trans. R.J. Hollingale. London: Cambridge University Press.

Rickert, H. (1986). *The Limits of Concept Formation in Natural Science.* Ed. and trans. Guy Oakes. London: Cambridge University Press.

Willey, T. E. (1978). *Back to Kant.* Detroit: Wayne State University.

5

DILTHEY'S HERMENEUTICS: BETWEEN IDEALISM AND REALISM

Ronald L. Schultz

All science, all philosophy, is experiential. All experience derives its coherence and its corresponding validity from the context of human consciousness. The quarrel between idealism and realism can be resolved by
psychological analysis, which can demonstrate that the real world given
in experience is not a phenomenon in my representation; it is rather given
to me as something distinct from myself, because I am a being that does
not merely represent, but also wills and feels. (Dilthey 1989, 493–4)

INTRODUCTION

Nineteenth-century European thought involved a protracted philosophical struggle between idealists and realists. Idealists held the position that the mind is primarily responsible for the constitution of reality. Immanuel Kant had a profound impact on the formation of
idealist philosophy in Germany. His three important "critiques" (of
theoretical reason, practical reason, and aesthetic judgment), concentrated on the powers of human cognition. In addition to the critical idealism of Kant, idealism also included transcendental types, romantic variations, and the absolute idealism of Georg W. F. Hegel.
Indeed, by the early to mid-1830s, Hegel's influence was so strong, his
philosophy nearly became a national creed.

In contrast, realists claimed that the "real" external world exists beyond cognition and takes precedence over human ideas. Major developments in the natural sciences were led by empiricists, naturalists
and positivists who, as realists, advocated the discovery of natural
laws to explain all phenomena. Another strain of realism, materialism, gained momentum as a reaction to Hegelianism. Materialists,
like Karl Marx, argued that because human existence depends so

heavily on material conditions the idealist position becomes an excuse for economic exploitation. Between the heights attained by idealism in Hegel's thought and the urgency evoked by the materialism of Marx, this intellectual conflict became quite intense in Germany.

The intent of this essay is to demonstrate how Wilhelm Dilthey drew elements of idealist and realist thought into a synthesis. The key to Dilthey's attempted synthesis is his conceptualization of the human sciences which seeks to understand human consciousness as both formed by and active in the constitution of reality. In particular, we will examine how his formulation of hermeneutics attempts to draw together these fundamentally opposed aspects of the tradition of German social thought.

Dilthey's Life and Works

Dilthey's work is wide-ranging and interdisciplinary, yet is also incomplete and fragmentary. His inability to complete the second parts of multivolume works earned him the dubious title "the man of the half volume" and, sarcastically, he was said to have written not introductions but "introductions to introductions" (Ermarth 1978, 5). However, for every harsh judgment about the incompleteness of his work, there are several glowing assessments that point out his great accomplishments. For instance, Ortega y Gasset called Dilthey "the true father of intellectual history," and, concerning his importance to the development of social thought, Levine has said that "the role played by Durkheim [in France] as codifier and spokesman for a national tradition of social thought was in Germany taken by Dilthey" (1995, 194). The fact that Dilthey holds such a high reputation despite the fact that much of his work remained unfinished is one of the most interesting aspects of his legacy.

Born in 1833, in Biebrich on the Rhine, Dilthey arrived in the wake of the "great caesura"—the passing of the main figures of the classical period of German Idealism. In rapid succession, Hegel (1770–1831), Goethe (1742–1832), Schleiermacher (1768–1834), and Humboldt (1767–1835) all died. These figures had such a large impact on their era that many nineteenth-century thinkers felt they were mere epigones adrift without the leadership of the "great ones." This was not the case with Dilthey, who, in coming of age during the decline of German Idealism, sought to forge new philosophical pathways.

While Dilthey's father and grandfather had each been Calvinist ministers, Dilthey's father Maximilian (1804–67), a court chaplain and councilor to the Duke of Nassau, was more interested in politics and history than formal theology. Ermarth suggests that Dilthey was influenced early on by pietism which, like philosophical empiricism, "militates against rationalist metaphysics by stressing the necessity of direct inner experience of reality (and God) rather than deduction and abstract logical proof" (Ermarth 1978, 20). While Dilthey displayed a great interest in theology, by 1870 he proclaimed "I am not of a religious nature" for reasons of "simple historical objectivity" (Ermarth 1978, 22). His mother, Maria (1806–67) was the daughter of a renowned music director and instilled in him a love of music and a competence for performing that profoundly affected his philosophical work. Dilthey would maintain strong interests in both scientific/epistemological questions and aesthetic issues for the balance of his life.

Dilthey was known throughout his life to consistently work twelve to fourteen hour days and upon his death left thousands of pages of unpublished work. Though Dilthey published only a few books within his lifetime (along with numerous essays), his collected works in German now number over twenty sizable volumes and are expected to eventually total thirty. Of meeting him in 1867, William James said Dilthey was "overflowing with information with regard to everything knowable and unknowable. He is the first man I have ever met of a class, which must be common here, of men to whom learning has become as natural as breathing" (Ermarth 1978, 32).

Dilthey first studied theology at Heidelberg from 1852–53 with Kuno Fischer. It was during this period that Fischer criticized the then officially sanctioned combination of Hegelianism and Christian orthodoxy. (Fischer provoked furor and eventually was dismissed on charges of practicing "pantheism.") Like many German intellectuals of the time, Dilthey eventually switched from theology to philosophy. From 1854 to 1864, he was a student at the University of Berlin. Dilthey studied with F. A. Trendelenburg, a neo-Kantian, who was another adamant critic of the speculative nature of Hegel's idealism. Dilthey also absorbed the methods of the German Historical School under important thinkers like Leopold von Ranke, Theodor Mommsen, and Jakob Grimm. During this period he wrote a prize-winning essay that was a historical-critical analysis of Friedrich D. E. Schleiermacher's interpretive theory. He went on to write his dissertation on Schleiermacher's ethics.

Subsequently, Dilthey taught at universities in Basel, Kiel, and Breslau. Notably, at Basel he completed intensive studies in the various specialized human sciences, including anthropology, economics, statistics and various stripes of psychology. At the same time,

Dilthey also wrote interpretive essays on Goethe, Novalis, and Lessing. He completed the first volume of his acclaimed Schleiermacher biography in 1870 (the second volume was published, from his notes, only after his death). In 1875, Dilthey married Katharina Puttman, with whom he had three children.

The 1880s were very productive years for Dilthey. He was called to Berlin in 1882 to occupy the chair in the philosophy department previously held by Hegel. He published the first volume of the *Introduction to the Human Sciences* (a projected second volume was never completed). He also wrote important essays on aesthetics entitled "Poetic Imagination and Insanity" and "Imagination of the Poet." In 1894, Dilthey published his *Ideas Concerning a Descriptive and Analytic Psychology*. In 1900, his work took a fresh turn as his epistemological questions and aesthetic studies came together in the essay "Rise of Hermeneutics." Dilthey viewed his last works as contributing to a "Critique of Historical Reason," which he intended as an additional fourth component to Kant's three critiques. In 1910, Dilthey published his most advanced work on the epistemology of history, *The Construction of the Historical World in the Human Studies,* and he took up the task finally completing the second part of the *Introduction*. However, this project was left forever incomplete with Dilthey's death in 1911.

Attempting to Ground the Human Sciences

Dilthey is best known for his efforts to provide a philosophical foundation that would unite all of the "human sciences." The central dictum of this work—"the natural sciences seek to *explain* reality, while the human sciences attempt to *understand* consciousness"—is considered to be Dilthey's main contribution to the epistemology of the human sciences. In the *Introduction to the Human Sciences* (1989), Dilthey lays out an assessment of the problem of providing a foundation for the human sciences, failures in approaching their study, and his proposed solution.

In the *Introduction* Dilthey sets as his objective to "attain as much certainty as possible about the philosophic foundations of the human sciences" (Dilthey 1989, 47). What exactly does Dilthey mean in his use of the term "human sciences?" The German word that he uses—*Geisteswissenschaften*—has stimulated debates about his meaning. *Wissenschaft* is fairly straightforward and may be defined as 'science' or 'systematic study.' *Geist* might be translated in a number of ways, for example, as 'mind,' 'spirit,' or even 'ghost,' but, given the broad scope of his studies, 'human' seems the most appropriate term. Indeed, Dilthey's concept of "the human" indicates his belief that the qualities of the human mind (as interpretive, intentional, and value-positing) are central aspects of being human.

Although possible English translations of the phrase *Geisteswissenschaften* include human sciences, moral studies, studies of the mind, and even cultural studies, one common preference has been "human studies." The choice of the term "studies" over "sciences" is based, in part, on Dilthey's own attacks on the application of the methods of "natural science" to the human sphere. On the other hand, recent scholars argue convincingly that "human sciences" is really closer to his intentions. For example, Makkreel and Rodi suggest that "current conceptions about the role of interpretation in all science have made it possible to refer to the *Geisteswissenschaften* as either human sciences or human studies" (1989, 56). Indeed, "science" best fits Dilthey's intentions when we consider that he places heavy emphasis on an empirical basis and a systematic methodology for the human sciences. Given Dilthey's interest in the life of the mind and its highest achievements—aesthetic creations—he certainly considers all of the humanities to be potential sciences.[1]

In the *Introduction*, Dilthey's main objective is to completely separate the human sciences from speculation, mysticism, and superstition. In this respect, he recognizes that an "emancipation" of the sciences in general began with the end of the Middle Ages. Unfortunately, according to Dilthey, "the sciences of society and of history retained their old subservient relation to metaphysics for a long time—well into the eighteenth century" (1989, 52). He gives special credit to the French social scientists, Auguste Comte in particular, for extending Enlightenment thought to the human sciences. Dilthey states with confidence, "any metaphysical grounding of the human sciences is a thing of the past" (1989, 52). He argues that the human sciences must be empirical and scientifically grounded.

Although Dilthey calls for greater scientificity and rigor in the human sciences, he also suggests they face a threat from the natural sciences which have "subjugated them in a new manner, and no less oppressively" than previous metaphysical systems (1989, 47). From his perspective, the fact that the natural sciences developed faster led to their dominance over the human sciences. While praising Comte's vision of a "positive philosophy" that would unite all of the sciences, Dilthey suggests that he "merely created a naturalistic metaphysics of history" (1989, 154). This criticism is based on his view that Comte's recommendations for the structure of the social sciences are primarily inherited from the natural sciences. Even though Dilthey argues for a positivist human sciences, he rejects the idea of modeling them directly from the natural sciences.

In contrast, Dilthey distinguishes the epistemology of the human sciences from that of the natural sciences. Of the human sciences he writes: "The practice of regarding these disciplines as a unity distinct from the natural sciences is rooted in the depth and totality of human self-consciousness" (1989, 58). Dilthey's interest in consciousness is an indication of the influence of German idealism upon his thought. He praises members of the German Historical School[2] for viewing mental life as historical (a legacy of Hegel) but also claims they fail to take proper account of the inner experience of human life. Dilthey notes that the Historical School played a part in emancipating the historical sciences and historical consciousness from metaphysics, but he criticizes these thinkers for not making links to "facts of consciousness." Even as consciousness has been taken into account in the human sciences, he notes an overemphasis on rational thought. Dilthey writes "no real blood flows in the veins of the knowing subject constructed by Locke, Hume, and Kant; but rather the diluted extract of reason as a mere activity of thought" (1989, 50). In contrast, Dilthey posits human consciousness as containing not only aspects of thought but also willing and feeling. Interestingly, this viewpoint is shared by Marx and the materialists who tend toward a more anthropological view of human consciousness.

Of both French social science and German historical studies, Dilthey writes: "Not only can the task which these disciplines set themselves not be carried out, but their methods, while useful for dazzling us with generalizations, do not bring about a lasting extension of knowledge" (1989, 153). His conception of the human sciences, in contrast, would involve a special "kind of experience, which requires the immersion of all our mental powers in its object [and] has individuals and their deeds as its elements" (1989, 158). Dilthey criticizes Kant's philosophy as substituting aprioristic experience in place of the real concrete experiences of the individual and of the human collectivity. Dilthey's aim is to place the basis of the human sciences on the analysis of the "lived experiences" of human life.

The German Historical School, in Dilthey's estimation, while critical of Hegel, remains under his influence because they concur with Hegel's assertion that there is an absolute 'telos' or goal to history. Dilthey, as a relativist, rejects this position, "history no more has such an ultimate and simple message which would express its true sense than does nature" (1989, 141). The proper goal of the human sciences is to free history of metaphysical assumptions in the same way that natural forces have been "freed" by the natural sciences. Similarly, Dilthey sees Comte's positive philosophy as having an inherent *telos* of inevitable progress. This criticism is related to Comte's conceptualization of world history as being comprised of progressive stages.

Occasionally, Dilthey appears to say that the natural and human sciences are totally incommensurate because of their distinctive objects of study; however, this is an overly simplistic view of his position. He suggests to the contrary, that "knowledge of the natural sciences overlaps with that of the human sciences," recommending a relative delimitation of the sciences rather than one that is absolute (1989, 70). Dilthey also points out that "to a great extent, however, the human sciences do encompass natural facts and are based on knowledge of nature" (1989, 66). Indeed, he contends that humans are biological organisms and acknowledges that their experiences are shaped, in part, by this natural fact.

Although he objects to Comte's conceptualization of the human sciences, Dilthey agrees that "the theories of Comte and Herbert Spencer are justified in locating these [human] sciences in their hierarchy of all the sciences" (1989, 68). For Dilthey, quite simply, mental facts are also natural facts. Comte envisioned sociology as the "queen" of the sciences because it would reign, hierarchically, over all of the other sciences. Dilthey is largely in agreement with this conceptualization:

> Because the realm of persons, including human society and history, is the highest phenomenon of the empirical world, knowledge of it must at countless points be based on the system of presuppositions which accounts for its development within the whole of nature. Man, because of his position in the causal system of nature, is conditioned by it in a twofold respect. (1989, 69)

Human beings are, in Dilthey's terms, "psychophysical life-units" who receive natural stimuli via a nervous system. At the same time, humans also purposefully act upon nature. This makes human life unique in the natural order. Dilthey acknowledges that nature, as a causal system, conditions socio-historical reality. He also suggests that humans, as reflexive volitional beings, act on and alter natural reality.

For Dilthey, a major problem for the human sciences is that there
are two conflicting approaches to the analysis of human consciousness: an idealist "transcendental standpoint" which posits nature as
dependent on the conditions of consciousness, and an "objectivistic
empirical standpoint" which conversely views the development of
human consciousness as subject to the conditions of nature. The task
of the human sciences is to solve this problem conclusively, Dilthey
suggests:

> The conditions for such a solution would be a demonstration of the objec-
> tive reality of inner experience and a proof of the existence of an external
> world from which we can then conclude that this external world contains
> human facts and spiritual meaning by means of a process of transferring
> our inner life into this world. (1989, 72)

This is no mere philosophical pondering; for Dilthey it is *the* problem of knowledge itself. Is the natural world really "real" or a representation given in human consciousness? On this question, he is
content to accept that "natural phenomena can always be interpreted and used as signs of reality, that uniformities of coexistence
and succession can be interpreted and used as a sign of such uniformities in reality" (1989, 72). In contrast, from Dilthey's perspective, the problematic of the human sciences is that "only in the facts
of consciousness given in inner experience do we possess reality as
it is" (1989, 50).

What, then, ought be the basis for this human science?

Dilthey's Descriptive Psychology

Because the question of consciousness tends to focus on the operation of individual minds, Dilthey concentrates on psychology. From
his perspective, humanity does not exist prior to history and society.
A proper human science examines the individual human being as a
component of society. The task of psychology, for Dilthey, is to "attain
analytic knowledge of the universal characteristics of man" (1989,
83). Along these lines, he situates individual existence in relation to
social collectivities and recommends that psychology aim "to develop
general propositions, the subject of which is the individual life-unit
and the predicates of which are all the assertions about it that can
be productive for the understanding of society and history" (1989,
84). One may conceive Dilthey's objections to the German Historical
School here in another light, namely, in his assertion that its practitioners do not adequately acknowledge the concrete lived experience

of individuals. The bases of the human sciences, Dilthey asserts, lie in the individual human mind, and the problem becomes one of determining to what extent these individualized phenomena are generalizable. "The starting point for an understanding of the concept of systems of social life" Dilthey asserts, "is the richness of the life of the particular individual himself, who, as part of society, is the object of the first group of human sciences" (1989, 99–100).

This descriptive psychology is intended to have a deep affinity with social psychology. Although social psychology acknowledges the importance of individual consciousness and the biological basis of the brain, it insists on the importance of social context for shaping the mind. Dilthey writes, "a particular individual is the point of intersection of a plurality of such systems, which become ever more finely specialized in the course of cultural progress" (1989, 101). Indeed, the fact that individuals have consciousness is the basis of historical consciousness. But historical consciousness is only possible through a larger shared social consciousness.

Dilthey never completed the second volume of the *Introduction,* in part because he "gave up" on the idea of creating a descriptive psychology to ground the human sciences, but also because of other setbacks. First, his *Ideas Concerning a Descriptive and Analytic Psychology,* published in 1894, was subjected to scathing criticism by Hermann Ebbinghaus (Dilthey's former friend and colleague at Berlin). At the time, German psychology was dominated by more experimentally inclined explanatory psychologists who viewed descriptive psychology as a threat to their dominant position. Ebbinghaus's main objections centered on Dilthey's use of literature and personal anecdotes as evidence, and on his overly hypothetical generalizations (Ermarth 1978, 184). These criticisms were taken to heart by Dilthey, who as a result, ceased giving lectures on psychology, withdrew his subsequent essay, "On Comparative Psychology," from publication, and virtually suspended his work in epistemology. Second, Dilthey began historical studies of G. W. Leibniz, Frederick the Great, the German Enlightenment, and the (at the time) largely unexplored youthful writings of Hegel. These broad historical works essentially led him further away from psychological epistemology. Third, and perhaps the most important reason Dilthey discontinued his descriptive psychology, is that he read and admired Edmund Husserl's *Logical Investigations* thereby developing a greater interest in phenomenological issues. In fact, Husserl welcomed the support of the elder Dilthey, since his work was facing resistance at the time.

Dilthey's Turn Toward Hermeneutics

By the turn of the century, Dilthey gained fresh insight into epistemological questions through his explorations of hermeneutics. Hermeneutics is a systematic method for analyzing the interpretive practices that govern and constitute the process of understanding. In his essay, "The Rise of Hermeneutics" (1990 [1900]), Dilthey outlines the development of the method of hermeneutics and offers suggestions on how this method can be applied to the human sciences. The essay demonstrates how he attempted to reconcile the conflict between realist and idealist epistemological stances.

Dilthey begins by discussing the concept of "understanding." He argues that, through the perspective of the human sciences, historical consciousness enables human beings "to hold the entire past of humanity present within himself: across the limits of his own time he peers into vanished cultures, appropriating their energies and taking pleasure in their charm, with a consequent increase in his own happiness" (1990, 101). The capacity of the human sciences to derive general historical laws lies in the fact that the operations of understanding and interpretation are its basis. A full seventeen years after his original statement on the topic in his *Introduction,* Dilthey reconfirms that a systematic conception of understanding and interpretation form the basis of the human sciences which are, in turn, the bedrock of historical consciousness.

The crux of Dilthey's problematic is that thoughts and feelings (the realm of intentional, meaningful consciousness) cannot be accessed in the way that fluctuations in time, space, temperature or chemical reactions can. This leads him to take up the question of how individual consciousness is possible. For Dilthey, consciousness of one's own individuality is experienced "only through a comparison of myself with other people; at that point alone I become aware of what distinguishes me from others" (1990, 102). In this sense, other people are only known to us through the operation of our senses. And it is through a process of "reconstruction" that sense perception is converted into meaningful knowledge.

Reconstruction appears, however, to involve a contradiction. If each person attains, in Dilthey's terms, an "individually structured consciousness" that is derived from a reconstruction of signs given from the individuality of an other, how, then, are disparate individual minds bridged? It is this problem of "intersubjectivity" that necessitates Dilthey's move toward hermeneutics. To resolve this issue, he focuses on the process of understanding. Understanding, or *Ver-*

stehen, is a "process by which we intuit, behind the sign given to our senses, that psychic reality of which it is the expression" (1990, 102). According to Dilthey, one does not merely perceive a given external reality (the commonsense take on understanding); rather, one reconstructs, understands, intuits, and interprets given physical signs through an internal mental process. This explains why a particular collection of signs can carry different meanings to different people, or how meanings shift over time for the same person.

The general process of human understanding becomes the basis for grasping socio-historical reality and Dilthey's goal, then, is to analyze the essential features of this process. He suggests that the process of *verstehen* has universal applicability: it "ranges from the comprehension of the babblings of children to *Hamlet* or the *Critique of Pure Reason*" (1990, 102). Shakespeare and Kant differ as to their subject matter and each differs from the communicative practices expected of children, nevertheless, the process of understanding or *verstehen,* in each case, is quite similar.

The only concrete difference between the interpretation we practice in our everyday activities and the hermeneutic method, is the degree to which a level of systematic objectivity may be reached. Though all kinds of understanding are systematic (even interpreting a child's communication/babblings is a systematic process), it is a matter of degree that distinguishes them. Since everyday understanding is similar to the systematic procedures of hermeneutics, Dilthey's strategy is twofold: on one hand, an exploration of the process of general understanding and how human consciousness functions; on the other hand, the refinement of hermeneutics as a methodological procedure such that it might become the epistemology for all of the human sciences.

The decision to develop a doctrine of *verstehen* for the human sciences resulted from Dilthey's intensive investigation of the development of hermeneutics. In the ancient world, hermeneutics developed in scholarly libraries (the "Alexandrian school of philology"), and in debates over the qualities and authenticity of literary and philosophical works (1990, 105). In early Christianity, hermeneutics was further refined and marshaled in the service of various theologies in their interpretations of the Old and New Testaments. During the Protestant Reformation, Protestants used hermeneutics to authorize doctrines that undermined the interpretations supported by Roman Catholics and the Papacy.

By the nineteenth century, a number of separate specialized hermeneutics had emerged in the fields of philosophy, theology, anthropology, and jurisprudence. However, it was Schleiermacher who, according to Dilthey, brought to hermeneutics "the characteristic approach of German transcendental philosophy, which sought, behind the contents of consciousness, for some creative power that, working unconsciously but in unified fashion, brought the entire form of the world into being within us" (1990, 110). Schleiermacher (1768–1834), a German Protestant theologian, was a professor at Halle and Berlin and Dilthey's massive biography of him is still recognized as a masterpiece. Prior to Schleiermacher, hermeneutical thinking had, at most, a common system of rules, but Schleiermacher's work exceeded that of his contemporaries as he sought, in Dilthey's estimation, nothing less than "an analysis of the understanding that lay behind these rules, or in other words for a formulation of the goal of the activity as a whole, and from such a formulation he derived the possibility of valid interpretation in general" (1990, 110). Schleiermacher's great contribution was that due to his hermeneutic insights "the German spirit had turned its attention from literary production to a comprehension of the historical world" (1990, 111), thus warranting Dilthey to do the same for the human sciences.

Though interpretation is inescapable, it also possesses inherent limitations. One important limitation pertains to the inexhaustibility of interpretation, in which understanding remains partial and can never be terminated (1990, 113). Therefore, one's embrace of the text must not and truly cannot end. This, in and of itself, was Dilthey's problem in finishing his Schleiermacher biography. Since there is virtually no end to interpretation, the biography of one person, for example, Dilthey's lengthy (over 2,000 printed pages) but unfinished biography of Schleiermacher, could go on to endlessly demonstrate various connections to history and one's environment.

In a famous statement, Dilthey suggests, "the ultimate goal of the hermeneutic process is to understand an author better than he understood himself. This is an idea which is the necessary consequence of the doctrine of unconscious creation" (1990, 113). Of course, the implication is that if the hermeneutic process can be applied to the human sciences, we can understand the actions of historical subjects better than they understood themselves. Knowing that the method of *verstehen* is vulnerable to criticism on the basis that it is too subjective, Dilthey argues that the purpose of *verstehen* must be "to preserve the general validity of interpretation against the inroads of romantic caprice and skeptical subjectivity, and to give a theoretical justification for such validity, upon which all the certainty of historical knowledge is founded" (1990, 114). Indeed, Dilthey desires the epistemology of the human sciences to truly be empirical and scientific.

Although this epistemology is based on the study of literary forms, Dilthey wants to extend it to the study of history and society. In his subsequent writings the operation of hermeneutical practice takes the place of descriptive psychology as his model for the primary method of the human sciences. In this regard, Dilthey asserts that a "theory of interpretation becomes the essential connecting link between philosophy and the historical disciplines, an essential component in the foundation of the human studies themselves" (1990, 114). This is the connecting link missing in the *Introduction* and his descriptive psychology. Dilthey's standpoint, now complete, is that human beings not only experience reality, they also interpret it.

The Construction of the Historical World

In his last published work, *The Construction of the Historical World in the Human Studies* (1976), Dilthey picks up where he left off in the *Introduction,* conceptualizing the fundamental differences between the natural sciences and the human sciences. Human existence is, of course, natural *and* sociohistorical. Whereas physiology may abstract from specific historical and sociocultural facts and still remain a science, the human sciences must concretely analyze intentional meaning, understanding, and interpretation if they are to truly understand sociohistorical reality. Likewise, humans may be viewed as mere physical beings, but according to Dilthey, *humanity* "only becomes the subject matter of the human studies when we experience human states, give expressions to them and understand these expressions" (1976, 175). In this sense, the goal of the human sciences is to reach behind mere external events and grasp the inner meaning of history. In the twenty-seven years following the publication of the *Introduction,* Dilthey's objective remained virtually unchanged. Now, however, his epistemology embraces three main concepts: understanding, experience, and expression. Their interrelation demonstrates how profoundly hermeneutics has affected his thought. The historical construction of the world demands that students of humanity interpret, experience, and give expression to historical reality. We have already seen how Dilthey explored the conditions of interpretation, and must now consider the other two demands of a hermeneutic method: experience and expression.

Dilthey's concept of experience, or *Erlebnis,* may also be translated as "lived experience;" indeed, for him the terms "life" and "experi-

ence" are nearly interchangeable. While ordinarily one thinks of experience in the past tense, for Dilthey, experience has immediacy. Of
course he concedes that "experience includes elementary acts of
thought" (1976, 211), but experience is not merely the contemplation
of acts; rather "experience is followed by judgments about what has
been experienced in which this becomes objectified" (1976, 212). Any
type of judgment (the rational processing of the contents of an experience) is a step beyond experience itself. In this sense, experience is
the *immediate* encounter with thoughts, objects, and/or other people.

Dilthey recognizes that while "experience presents us with the
reality of life in its many ramifications we, only, seem to know one
particular thing, namely our own life" (1976, 186). While personal
experience of life (and the knowledge it engenders) is not "scientifically" valid, he suggests it is the model for understanding historical
experience. The particular biases of an individual's knowledge of life,
in Dilthey's view, are enlarged and corrected within the context of
"common knowledge." Common knowledge includes shared beliefs,
customs, traditions, and public opinion which emerge socially and
"influence individuals and their experience; because the community
has the weight of numbers behind it and outlasts the individual, this
power usually proves superior" to the individual's will (1976, 179).

Dilthey contends that common knowledge, as opposed to that of individuals, is generalizable because extreme individual points of view
tend to cancel each other out, providing a more valid representation
of the average human experience. Common knowledge, which exists
as a whole beyond individuals yet, at the same time, is created by
those individuals, is Dilthey's conception of culture. Although individual knowledge is subjective, common knowledge is intersubjective and constitutes, as Dilthey puts it, "objectifications of mind."

In some respects, Dilthey can be read as a forerunner of sociological interactionism. He suggests that the lives of individuals are en-
riched through their relationships to their environment, to other
people and to things. Dilthey views the individual as a "point where
webs of relationships intersect." For individuals, these relationships
are said to "reach beyond their life and possess an independent existence and development of their own through the content, value and
purpose which they realize" (1976, 181). These relationships carry
meaning because they exist in the context of a mind-constructed
world.

At the same time, Dilthey says it is a mistake to limit history to
the cooperation of human beings in common purpose. He suggests
that the individual has an independent existence within an histori-

cal context. And at the same time, the life of the individual is determined by his or her position in time and space and in the interaction of cultural systems and communities. The role of the human sciences is to grasp the "whole" of the life experiences of the individual as revealed in a particular time and place. The character of society and history, for Dilthey, stems from "the whole web of relationships which stretches from individuals furthering their own existence to the cultural systems and communities and, finally, to the whole of mankind" (1976, 181). It is in this respect that he places the individual as a "logical subject of history." Interestingly, this is the point of Dilthey's biography of Schleiermacher—that individual biography is part of a much larger whole but is also indicative of that whole.

The third component of Dilthey's hermeneutic epistemology, that of expression or *Ausdruck*, could also be interpreted as "objectification" because of his intent to focus on concrete manifestations of experience, rather than feelings. Dilthey suggests "we cannot understand ourselves and others except by projecting what we have actually experienced into every expression of our own and others' lives" (1976, 176), and it is only through the manifestations of expressions that the internal world of others may be apprehended.

In summary, for Dilthey the human sciences must be founded on a full recognition of the relationship between experience, expression and understanding in the construction of the historical world. Dilthey sees this interrelationship as the "starting-point not only for the human studies but also for philosophy; we must try to get behind its scientific elaboration and grasp life in its raw state" (1976, 178). He contends that lived experience and the expressions it engenders must be understood in the context of objective mind. Indeed, this point brings together both Dilthey's treatment of hermeneutics and his effort to reformulate the human sciences.

Objective Mind and Dilthey's Hermeneutic

Though experience is the foundation of individual knowledge and therefore plays a key role in understanding, Dilthey asserts that it is only "through the idea of the objectification of life [that] we gain insight into the nature of the historical" (1976, 192). Although the concept of "objective mind" is central to the philosophy of Hegel, what precisely is the meaning of Dilthey's conception of "objectification"?

In Hegel's system, there is a progression in the development of the mind from a subjective stage, to objective mind and finally a culmination in absolute mind. The attainment of objective mind is the historical precondition for all human civilization—it is the background for the social, cultural, historical conditions that make the experience, meaning, and interpretation of all cultural pursuits possible. While accepting much of Hegel's system, Dilthey, nevertheless, objects to Hegel's overly idealistic conception of objective mind. Hegel "constructed communities from the universal, rational will," but Dilthey desires to start from the "reality of life" or "lived experience" (1976, 194). His purpose here is to free his epistemology of the concept of the "absolute" that is so central to Hegel's thought. In Dilthey's view, "once the objective mind is divorced from its one-sided foundation on a universal reason (which expresses the nature of the world-spirit) and from any ideal construction, a new conception of it becomes possible" (1976, 194). In this break with Hegel's absolute idealism, Dilthey conceives of history as being relative to historical conditions, not preconditioned by the prerogatives of an absolute world-spirit on a dialectically predetermined path, as it is in Hegel's thought. This move helps Dilthey to escape Kantian "universalism" as well.

At the same time, Dilthey maintains (along with Hegel and Kant) the importance of the human mind as constitutive of sociohistorical reality. However, he adds the caveat that objective mind is not to be conceived of as rationalistically imposed upon individuals from without, but is rather the result of lived experience in a historical context.

CONCLUSION

We have seen in the development of Dilthey's thought a continuing desire to create an epistemology to better ground and unite the various human sciences. In the course of his life's work, Dilthey moves from a "psychological" toward a more "sociological" understanding of human life. Likewise the goal of the human sciences, for Dilthey, requires that one move from understanding the individual to analyzing human consciousness as a function of lived experience or *Erlebnis*. In turn, lived experience is best understood in its relation to human expressions conceptualized as the objective mind. In part, Dilthey's descriptive psychology always held sociohistorical phenomena as its object, and perhaps the most important transformation in his work was a shift in his terminology. However, it is in his hermeneutics that Dilthey explicitly realizes that an understanding of individual and social experiences emerges in processes of interpretation.

Dilthey promotes a position that is rigorously empirical but not empiricist, and for him ideas should be understood as objectively real phenomena, but ought not be studied under the model of the natural sciences. It is not that the "objects" studied by the natural and human sciences are completely incommensurate. Rather the key is that human consciousness is formed, through intersubjectivity, on the basis of a relationship between subject and object. In this sense, human subjectivity, for Dilthey, has a very objective basis.

It is in the realm of sociological phenomena, or "common knowledge," that Dilthey seeks to resolve the debate between idealism and realism. He concludes that although we live in a mind-constructed world, it is a world, nonetheless, with an objective reality. The challenge of the human sciences, then, is to *understand* human life as existing amid mind-dependent interpretations and concrete lived-experiences of sociohistorical conditions.

NOTES

1. While I favor the use of "sciences" over "studies" many of the quotations in this paper use "human studies" as per their specific translation.

2. Dilthey's discussion of the "Historical School" refers to a specific group of nineteenth-century German historians (including Leopold von Ranke, Friedrich von Savigny, and Barthold Niebuhr) whose work focused on a realist interpretation of historical events.

REFERENCES

Dilthey, Wilhelm. 1989. *Introduction to the Human Sciences.* Edited by Rudolf A. Makkreel and Frithjof Rodi. Princeton, NJ: Princeton University Press.

———. 1976. "The Construction of the Historical World in the Human Studies," in *Wilhelm Dilthey: Selected Writings.* Translated and edited by H. P. Rickman. Cambridge University Press.

———. 1990. "The Rise of Hermeneutics," in *The Hermeneutic Tradition.* Edited by Gayle L. Ormiston and Alan D. Schrift. Albany: State University of New York Press.

Ermarth, Michael. 1978. *Wilhelm Dilthey: The Critique of Historical Reason.* Chicago: University of Chicago Press.

Levine, Donald N. 1995. *Visions of the Sociological Tradition.* Chicago: University of Chicago Press.

6

SOCIAL SCIENCE AND THE *VERSTEHEN* THESIS[1]

David L. McNaron

INTRODUCTION

How do I know what the motorist's vulgar gesture means? How does a field anthropologist comprehend the rituals of an exotic people? What explains the rise of capitalism in Protestant countries? How does a good biographer reveal his or her subject? Why did Socrates remain in prison?

I model the motorist's behavior on my own: I know what my *own* gesture would mean if I were to raise my finger in that way while driving. The anthropologist assimilates into the alien culture, thereby adopting an "internal perspective" on its practices. Perhaps Calvinist religious beliefs motivated Protestants to succeed materially to demonstrate their membership in God's elect. Skilled biographers write from the perspective of their biographical subject. Plato tells us that Socrates remained in prison because he reasoned that escaping would unjustly violate an implied contract he held with the state. The common ground in these examples is *verstehen:* the method of explaining behavior by sympathetically understanding others. Persons who use this method imaginatively identify with their subjects, projecting themselves into their position, vernacular variations on which include "getting inside someone's head" and "walking a mile in someone's shoes." The underlying model views understanding as achieving psychological parity with the other, a condition to which one cannot attain with atoms, rainbows, magma, or other purely physical phenomena. Hence, the social sciences' use of the method of *verstehen* demarcates them from the natural sciences, or so *verstehen* theorists would have it.

---

[1] I am grateful to Professors Stephen Levitt and Steven Alford and also to Gordon Patterson of Krieger for making helpful comments on this paper. Most of their suggestions have found their way into the essay.

This paper is an argumentative tour of versions of the *verstehen* thesis. One main formulation of the thesis holds that the social and natural sciences have fundamentally different goals and methods, the former requiring the method of *verstehen* or understanding. A more radical version maintains that both the social and natural sciences rest on *verstehen*. We shall evaluate arguments for and against the *verstehen* thesis from classic German social theorists and contemporary philosophers.

VERSTEHENDE SOCIAL SCIENCE VERSUS NATURALISM

The classical German tradition of social thought, rooted in Kant, is committed to a controversial view of the philosophical status of the social sciences. According to this view, the *Geisteswissenschaften* or human studies and the *Naturwissenschaften* or natural sciences rest on different foundations. While the experimental methods of the natural sciences have proven enormously successful in the explanation, prediction, and control of physical phenomena, they are inappropriate for the study of meaningful human phenomena. The natural sciences seek causal explanations via universal laws of nature, while the goal of the social sciences is to understand human actions, to render them intelligible in light of agents' own meanings.

Kant's view that human phenomena are essentially different from nonhuman natural phenomena is axiomatic for the German tradition and underpins its commitment to *verstehen*. For followers of Kant, *verstehen* is the appropriate social scientific method because human subjects are free and capable of acting from reason. Kant evoked two standpoints from which we may regard humans: the standpoint of nature and the standpoint of freedom. The natural sciences explain physical phenomena by discovering universal causal laws of which particular events are instances. The social sciences as well may adopt this "standpoint of nature" and attempt to explain human behavior empirically. But Kant insisted that while adopting the natural standpoint is valid for the purposes of scientific explanation, the transcendent human subject must not be viewed from the standpoint of nature alone. Because we are rational moral agents who deliberate and choose, we must also be viewed from the practical standpoint of freedom.

Plato anticipated *verstehen* theory in his dialogue *Phaedo* wherein he urged a teleological mode of explanation for human action. Teleological explanations are purposive; they explain by appealing to the agent's reasons, beliefs, desires, goals. A mechanistic physical explanation for Socrates' presence in his cell in terms of the positions of his muscles, bones, joints and the like fails to explain *why* Socrates remained in prison—*mutatis mutandis* for the other examples in my introduction. The right sorts of explanations of behavior invoke the agent's meaningful intentional states. *Verstehen* is the means for grasping those meanings.

On the *verstehen* view, social science is interpretive. As Charles Taylor (1985, 15–17) points out, the subject matter for an interpretive study must be a text or text-analogue, that is, something that has meaning. Human thought and expression may be said to have meaning in several senses, including semantic meaning and experiential meaning. What is philosophically interesting for our treatment of meaning is the "aboutness" or "intentionality" of mental states exhibiting semantic meaning and the "what-it-is-like-ness" of experiential meaning.

The following briefly explains the role of semantic meaning in psychological phenomena. Intentional mental states, such as beliefs and desires, have been called (following Bertrand Russell) propositional attitudes because statements expressing those states contain 'that' clauses. For example, a fictive Jones believes that the Yankees will win the World Series. The proposition following the 'that' ('The Yankees will win the World Series') carries the meaning or content of the psychological state or attitude. These meanings in turn may refer to material objects. The metaphysically peculiar aspect of semantic meaning is its "aboutness," its directedness beyond itself. In virtue of its content, Jones's belief is about the Yankees. Oddly, thoughts can be about nonexistent objects, such as Santa Claus. This "intentionality of the mental" is often held to pose problems for a physicalistic view of humans because natural phenomena lack this feature of meaningfulness or aboutness. The cognitive stance that we take toward meanings is to interpret and understand them. *Verstehen* is that operation needed to put us in touch with an agent's meanings.

Experiential meaning is the felt quality of experiences, what it is like to have an experience of, say, love, anger, or perceiving a sunset. It is *like* something to be a sentient creature but presumably not like something to be a neutrino, planet, gust of wind, or pebble. Some argue that *verstehen* is needed to understand what another's experiences are like; sympathetically experiencing another's mental state is a necessary condition for correctly ascribing that state to others. Both kinds of meaning imply similarity between others and oneself. Critics argue that this condition of psychological similarity places undue limits on our ability to comprehend and explain human conduct since social scientists who rely on *verstehen* are limited by their own psychological sets. For example, if sociologists and psychologists were committed to *verstehen* they could not explain the behavior of exotic subjects whose experiences and beliefs were radically dissimilar to their own.

The global philosophy of social science that opposes *verstehen* is naturalism. Naturalism claims that the predictive, explanatory methods of the physical sciences are the only legitimate means for acquiring empirical knowledge, and that the social sciences should be incorporated into the natural science framework. The logical canons are the same for each. Advocates of this position argue that the social sciences will progress only when they emulate the methods of the physical sciences.

B. F. Skinner advanced a radical naturalistic program. In *Beyond Freedom and Dignity* (1971) he argued against the Kantian tradition, which has fostered the "myth of autonomous man." By promoting the view that humans are "free," that tradition has frustrated the search for the causes of human behavior. The social sciences should mimic the physical sciences and eliminate appeals to unobservable, spiritual causes; they should also abandon subjective, mentalistic, purposive explanations of behavior, and introspective methods. Physics, chemistry, and biology failed to progress until they abandoned teleological and spiritualistic explanations in terms of *entelechies* and vital spirits. By analogy, if "the sciences of man" are to progress, they should do the same. Psychology should become a science of behavior, explaining all human behavior only through lawfully linked observable events.

Radical behaviorism is rarely held today in its pure form, but philosophers and scientists have sought a materialistic replacement for behaviorism or at least a naturalistic understanding of mental phenomena. The cognitive science revolution against behaviorism promised to reconcile intentionality and causality, social and natural science, in ways that would "save" belief by finding a place for intentionality in natural science. This revolution would unite the humanistic and scientific cultures and restore the lost moral order longed for by Romantic poets. But there is danger for *verstehende* social science from the cognitive science quarter.

Some naturalistic philosophers think that explanations in terms of the agent's intentions can be pressed into service by cognitive science, but only if mental states are understood functionally or computationally. This strategy involves defining mental states in terms of their causal properties, thus sacrificing the primacy of the meaning or content of mental states. Many philosophers have come to think in the following way. Those who accept intentional explanations think of reasons as causes. If events only under physical descriptions are causes and do the explanatory work, then reasons must be identified with or reduced to physical causes. Although continuing to talk in terms of the intentional vocabulary may be useful to us, the view of the explanation of behavior based on those concepts is a false theory, dubbed "folk psychology." Intentional states are reduced or eliminated in favor of physical or functional states; intentional explanations at best have a heuristic value. But if one does *not* think reasons are causes, the relation that intentionality bears to behavior becomes utterly mysterious. If forced to choose between reasons and causes, then we must favor causes and eliminate intentionality from any ultimate explanatory account of human behavior. This is so because our understanding of matter is superior to our understanding of mind—*contra* Descartes.

The problems of intentionality, reasons and causes, understanding and explanation will resurface in our discussion of the *verstehen* theses of Wilhelm Dilthey and Max Weber, key figures in the German tradition of social thought. Dilthey and Weber agree that the social and natural sciences are distinct by virtue of subject matter and method. Let us now turn to an examination of their positions.

The Dualistic *Verstehen* Thesis

Verstehen has been variously described as empathic projection, empathy, imaginative identification, reliving and reexperiencing. The goal of *verstehen* is to identify with agents' "subjective meanings" and thereby understand actions in agents' own terms, from the inside, so to speak. The resulting intentional explanations are uniquely appropriate for the social sciences. The *verstehen* thesis in its dualistic formulations methodologically demarcates the social and natural sciences. Consequently, those advocates of the dualistic *verstehen* thesis oppose attempts to "naturalize" the social sciences.

Dilthey's and Weber's work exemplifies the orthodox, dualistic formulations of the *verstehen* thesis. Their theories offer distinctive visions of what social scientific practice ought to be. Whatever the methods of the natural sciences, the social sciences must practice a unique method of interpretive, empathic understanding since the latter deal with meaning-intending human agents. Different subject matters require different methods. Hence, Dilthey and Weber defend a thesis of the duality of scientific method. The dualistic *verstehen* thesis, especially Dilthey's version, is an exclusion thesis: The natural and social sciences rest on different logical canons.

As Donald Levine (1985) has argued, Dilthey and Weber are part of the hermeneutic and historical tradition of German social thought, a tradition whose central notions are:

> . . . that human phenomena are constituted by the expression of intentions, such that to describe and explain them adequately requires an act of empathic understanding (*Verstehen*) of the subjective orientation of actors, and that historical phenomena are not reducible to the exemplification of general laws, but involve a unique constellation of elements embodied in concrete cases, the interest in which depends on some particular angle of relevance to the values of inquiring subjects. (127)

Yet within this tradition Dilthey's and Weber's versions of the dualistic *verstehen* thesis contain important differences. Dilthey stresses the reading or interpretation of the expressions or objectifications of *Geist* (mind or human spirit) to unravel and understand an artist's, agent's or culture's meanings. Understanding these meanings is an end in itself, the goal of the human studies. Weber stresses subjecting empathically arrived at hypotheses to empirical constraints and tests, and producing causal explanations of social actions. Accordingly, Weber's position seems closer to current forms of naturalism.

Dilthey's Hermeneutic *Verstehen* Thesis

Dilthey's vision of the social sciences places them closer to the humanities than to the natural sciences. The social sciences, so conceived, offer explanations that are quite different from empirical causal explanations. The social sciences are about interpreting and understanding the meaning of human action rather than causally explaining it: "We explain nature, we understand mind."[1] (As we shall see, some contemporary hermeneutic theorists of social science go very far in Dilthey's direction and advance a thesis of *reasons-versus-causes*.)

Dilthey was influenced by German hermeneutics and historicism. Hermeneutics is based on interpretation of texts, whose meanings we explicate. By extension, understanding is the proper cognitive goal for grasping human expression.

Understanding *[Verstehen]* is what we call this process by which an inside is conferred on a complex of external sensory signs. . . . We must . . . call Understanding that process by which we intuit, behind the sign given to our senses that psychic reality of which it is the expression.[2]

Psychological exegesis begins by a projection into the creative inner process, and proceeds onward to the outer and inner forms of the work, and beyond that to an intuition of its unity with the other works in the spiritual stance of its creator.[3]

Dilthey's appeal to intuition raises eyebrows among toughminded critics. How can appeals to intuition count as more than mere conjecture? How can one tell if one is using intuition correctly? What makes intuition reliable? What if people's intuitions differ? There must be nonintuitive "checks and balances" on such claims, not merely further appeals to intuition. If there were no constraints on intuitive appeals, there would be no way to choose rationally among rival interpretations. We are reminded of Wittgenstein's (1953, 153) point about subjective phenomena, that an "'inner process' stands in need of outward criteria." One should demand constraints on imaginative reconstructions of others' psychic processes.

Dilthey suggests that knowledge of human nature grounds or constrains *verstehen:* "In Understanding, the individuality of the exegete and that of the author are not opposed to each other like two incomparable facts. Rather, both have been formed upon the substratum of a general human nature. . . ."[4] Our knowledge of a common human nature or psychological makeup provides a background from which to frame interpretations. This view is worth considering as a possible solution to the problem of how to constrain intuitive interpretations.

The appeal to human nature to constrain *verstehen* leads to several problems. First, what counts as human nature is very controversial. Second, any understanding of human nature will be either too general to adjudicate rival interpretations, or too specific to serve as a neutral test. If this is not the case, how is one to know which propositions about human nature are of the appropriate scope? This dilemma would not damage the Diltheyan account provided that one could supply an adequate criterion for selecting appeals to human nature.

However, there is a more serious problem. Even if we knew such propositions about human nature, how did we come by this understanding? While Dilthey has offered a constraint on *verstehen,* he goes on to suggest that *verstehen* is a perfectly general method for understanding humans:

Such understanding ranges from the comprehension of the babblings of children to *Hamlet* to the *Critique of Pure Reason*. From stones and marble, musical notes, gestures, words and letters, from actions, economic decrees and constitutions, the same human spirit addresses us and demands interpretation. Indeed, the process of understanding, insofar as it is determined by common conditions and epistemological instruments, must everywhere present the same characteristics.[5]

This passage presents us with another dilemma: Either (a) *verstehen* is not a perfectly general method for understanding humans, or (b) appealing to human nature does not constrain *verstehen,* since our conception of human nature would itself be arrived at by means of that method. The original problem reappears at the level of understanding human nature rather than at the level of specific actions: What constrains our intuitive understanding of human nature? The appeal to human nature, therefore, does not adequately constrain *verstehen.* The failure of the appeal to human nature to constrain *verstehen* should not surprise us: What counts as human nature is ultimately what is at stake in social science. Reasoning from a conception of human nature to justify our hypotheses that in turn inform our understanding of human nature is circular. One has failed to justify a demand for a constraint on a practice when that constraint itself presupposes the practice.

Without adequate constraints, *verstehen* explanations that rely exclusively on interpretations of meaning are "underdetermined by the evidence." The upshot is that there is no evidential, nonquestion-begging way to choose from among rival interpretations that are internally consistent and fit the evidence equally well. Habermas (1988 [1967/1970]) makes this point:

No choice between competing interpretations can be achieved through *Verstehen* itself. The interpretations remain arbitrary until they are subjected to a test in the usual manner. Weber points this out unequivocally: "The disclosure of the meaning of an action in a given situation . . . is merely a hypothesis taken on for the purpose of interpretation, which in principle always requires empirical verification, however certain it may seem in thousands of cases." (59)

Weber and Empirically Constrained *Verstehen*

The above objections should motivate us to move to a version of the *verstehen* thesis that provides empirical constraints on interpretive understanding. Within the classical German tradition, Weber's account fits the bill. Armed with these constraints Weber avoids the difficulties attending Dilthey's position.

Weber builds causal explanation and the interpretation of meaning into the very definition of "sociology," seemingly combining in a single vision the usual competitors for the soul of the social sciences: "'Sociology' . . . means the science whose object is to interpret the meaning of social action and thereby give a causal explanation of the way in which the action proceeds and the effects which it produces" (1978a [1922], 7). Marianne Weber (1975 [1926]) reiterates Weber's commitment to these goals:

> Weber teaches the truth content of the empirical sciences whose point of departure is extrascientific, is created by subjecting the connections that were at first grasped "understandingly" or "intuitively" to the rules of rigorous thinking—above all, to the rules of "causal attribution." There must be a logically adequate explanation of the causal connection between the processes: "Only what is causally explained is scientifically treated." (313)

Nothing counts as sociology that does not fulfill two conditions: It must treat the meaning of and give causal explanations for social actions. While Weberian *verstehen* remains an interpretive approach that stresses the uniqueness of human studies, it is hemmed in conceptually: Empirically constrained, idealized, pragmatized, and thoroughly tamed, metaphysically, it is a lean, trim, desert-landscape *verstehen*.

Weber softens his accounts of meaning and causal explanation. As it turns out, his notion of causal explanation is a species of teleological explanation. More surprising, Weber does not require that the meaning postulated by social scientists to explain behavior be the agent's own. We are left wondering whether Weber merely pays lip service to those two cornerstones of *verstehende* and naturalist social science, meaning and causal explanation, to effect a compromise. Be that as it may, we can learn much from following Weber's argument: He strikingly anticipates crucial problems and theories in the contemporary philosophical debate.

Weber distinguishes a clear interpretation from the point of view of meaning from a causally valid interpretation, the former oftentimes remaining "a peculiarly plausible hypothesis." The agent's motives may remain hidden even to himself, or he may suffer from conflicting motivations whose relative strengths may be unknown. In such cases we cannot be certain of our interpretation: "Only the actual outcome of the conflict gives a solid basis of judgment. More concretely, verification of subjective interpretation by comparison with the concrete course of events is, as in the case of all hypotheses, indispensable" (1978b [1922], 9). Weber thinks that controlled psychological experimentation is required to verify hypotheses. Lacking that, we may resort to comparative sociology for partial confirmation of hypotheses. Here we find an example of the needed empirical constraint on *verstehen* that eluded Dilthey's theory: Interpretations are testable by their observable consequences.

Causally valid interpretations require subjective adequacy, which is achieved when one has correctly posited the agent's meaning and fit that motive into a complex of meanings (*Ibid.,* 12–13). Weber has recognized what has been called the "holism of the mental." We explain people's actions with *sets* of beliefs, desires, and other mental states. One desires a newspaper, believes there is a newsstand on the corner, and therefore goes to the corner newsstand. The holism of the mental is usually considered an essential ingredient in the intentional (belief-desire) type of explanation, and is widely regarded as a fact that defeated behavioristic translations of "mentalistic" sentences. Subjective adequacy, then, is finding the right set of mental states to explain the behavior.

For Weber, actions are explained causally by fitting motives into a set of purposes: "To 'explain' . . . for a science concerned with the meanings of actions, is to grasp the complex of meanings into which a directly intelligible action fits in by virtue of its subjectively intended meaning" (1978a [1922], 12). Actions that are less than fully rational are explained as deviations from an idealized assumption of perfect rationality. *For Weber, the goal of causal explanation of action is to render the action rationally intelligible.*

Does causal explanation so understood capture the agent's own meaning? To answer this, consider Weber's disjunctive definition of meaning: The meaning of a social action can be the meaning actually intended by the agent, a meaning calculated as an "average" of a group, or a meaning attributed to an abstract, pure, ideal type. After sketching the three types of meaning-of-social-action, Weber continues: ". . . in neither case is the meaning to be thought of as somehow objectively 'correct' or 'true' by some metaphysical criterion" (1978a [1922], 7).

The above passage reveals the main tension, if not inconsistency, in Weber's philosophy of *verstehen:* the commitments (a) to capture the agent's psychological reality (the main point of *verstehen*), and (b) to employ a scheme that aims at explanatory adequacy rather than truth as correspondence with fact. The attribution of meaning turns out to be a methodological device used to render the action intelligi-

ble. Can Weber have it both ways? Requiring that explanations capture the agent's own subjective meaning *does* seem to commit Weber's account to objective truth or correspondence in some metaphysical sense, despite his disavowal, and hence to a realism of inner
psychological states.

A strategy that aims at explanatory adequacy rather than realist
truth is instrumentalism. Instrumentalists in the philosophy of science regard scientific theories as tools used to predict our experiences. Theories are not "ontologically committed" to the existence of
referents of their theoretical terms. In Weber's theory, beliefs could
remain "virtual"—that is, explanatory fictions.

Weber's position resembles in important respects some naturalistic views currently held by Anglo-American analytic philosophers.
Intentional explanation and its alleged assumption of rationality is
one of the main topics in contemporary philosophy of mind. Some
philosophers (notably, Donald Davidson and Daniel Dennett) agree
with Weber that intentional explanations of action necessarily "rationalize" behavior (Davidson's term); that is, they make it reasonable in light of the agent's own goals.[6] These explanations assume
the rationality of the agent. The form of explanation is teleological
rather than mechanistic. Further, while these explanations may
treat reasons as causes, they do not flow from *laws* linking subjective states to behavior. (Weber also saw this.)

Opinion is divided over the legitimacy of intentional explanations.
Davidson argues that as long as we describe behavior as action we
are committed to the intentionalistic vocabulary and rationalistic
type of explanation—but it can never be made scientific. Dennett attempts to reduce intentional explanation to the adoption of a *stance,*
the intentional stance, that is instrumentally useful for its predictive
utility but ultimately a retrograde form of explanation. To use an example from Dennett (1978, 4–9), we can adopt the intentional stance
and treat a chess-playing computer as a rational opponent. This is
probably the best way to try to beat the computer. But such a strategy does not commit us to the existence of intentional states in the
computer, nor any final appeal to "ghostly" subjective mental states
to explain the workings of the computer.

Dennett argues that psychology should have no final commitment
to the intrinsic rationality of a system because psychology should *explain* rationality in nonintentional, mechanistic terms. Intentional
explanations, which assume rationality, are not scientifically adequate because science should not presuppose what it should explain.
Artificial intelligence shows us how to remove the ghost in the ma-

chine (or "discharge the homunculi," as Dennett puts it) and explain intelligence, intentionality and rationality in purely physical, mechanistic terms. Cognitive science can tolerate "folk psychological" attributions of mental states as long as those appeals are seen as merely pragmatic.

The empirical-logical tone of Weber's writing makes it tempting to think that his position is born of a certain skepticism toward the slippery category of meaning. Yet, as Weber sees it, sociology requires explanation in terms of meaning, and this form of explanation is very useful. Conceivably, however, physical sciences could capture territory formerly held by sociology. Weber has taken a position that anticipates current problems and some naturalistic responses to them. Weber's pragmatic, instrumentalist attitude toward meaning opens the door to positions such as those of Dennett or Davidson. While those positions to some extent balance meaning and cause, understanding and explanation, they are materialistic in their view of humans.

In his classic critical discussion of *verstehen,* Ernest Nagel seems to reduce Weber's *verstehen* thesis to absurdity (1961, 481–485). Is it really necessary to empathically experience another's mental state in order to explain it? Must one have experienced the terror of someone fleeing a mob or the mob's anger to explain the situation? Must the historian who tries to account for the careers of people such as Hitler have felt or relived Hitler's violent hatreds? Must a psychiatrist be mentally ill to study mental illness? Nagel does not object to positing unobservable psychological states to explain behavior. But such imputations must be based on and tested by observable evidence. Reconstructions of others' psychic states are not self-certifying.

Nagel further argued that *verstehen* is not necessary for explaining action. Although it is a useful heuristic device for generating hypotheses about behavior, *verstehen* plays no role in the validation of hypotheses. Nagel's point implicitly invokes the distinction in the philosophy of science between the "context of discovery" and the "context of justification." There are no rules to govern the context of discovery, the origins of scientists' ideas. In that context, anything goes. But anything does not go in the context of justification: Scientific hypotheses must be subjected to controlled tests. For Nagel, *verstehen* explanations unsupported by independent evidence count as conjecture, not knowledge.

But as we saw, Weber required empirical constraints on the use of *verstehen.* His theory does not entail that imputations of inner states are self-certifying. As we saw, Weber called such ideas "merely plausible hypotheses" until their truth is born out by evidence and argument. In fact, Nagel credits Weber for emphasizing that very point "with vigor and illumination" (1961, 483). Still, Nagel's arguments attack the heart of the *verstehen* thesis, as we have so far formulated it, by challenging the claim that an act of *verstehen* is a necessary condition for understanding another's actions.

There are several replies open to a defender of Weberian *verstehen*. First, one could argue that a social scientist who has not experienced violent hatred or mental illness nonetheless could and must imaginatively entertain the having of such states, say by conjuring up exaggerations of states, such as anger or confusion, that he or she *has* experienced. This move still would limit social scientific explanation to the researcher's psychology.

Second, even if one lacks the imaginative powers or experiences from which to extrapolate, one could appeal to intentional states correlated with behavior. One then *infers* such states from observing others' behavior: a logical rather than empathic procedure. One need not have experienced a state to invoke it in an explanation of behavior. This reply is not open to Nagel's objections since he does not object in principle to psychological explanations.

A third response (a) weakens the necessary condition claim to the requirement to take account of others' subjectivity rather than vicariously experiencing it, and (b) shifts the *verstehen* thesis from a claim about method to a claim about goal. The strategy is to accept Nagel's attack on the necessary condition claim and abandon *verstehen* as a necessary, empathic *method* of capturing the agent's own meaning. We take account of the other's point of view but reformulate the main point of *verstehen* as the *goal* of rendering actions rationally intelligible. The latter need not require such psychological feats by social scientists.

Taylor's Reconstruction of *Verstehen*

Charles Taylor takes the last approach (1985, 116–133). He reformulates the aims of *verstehende* social science and thereby avoids some traditional objections. What is true in the *verstehen* thesis is that the social sciences should be committed to giving meaning-explanations that render actions rationally intelligible, rather than causal explanations in the mode of the natural sciences.

Taylor argues that *verstehende* social science's commitments to empathy and capturing the agent's own meaning lead to unsolvable difficulties. Those commitments are mistaken. *Verstehende* social science should be construed differently from the classical social theorists' conception.

Taylor argues that the usual supporters of *verstehen* assent to two mistaken assumptions: (1) that understanding consists in empathy alone, and (2) that understanding the agent consists in adopting his or her point of view. Number (1) is incorrect because empathy, unlike science, is not a form of discourse, and discourse sets out the significance of actions. If we accept (2), social science would be unilluminating and in some circumstances impossible—unilluminating because the agent's point of view may be confused, his or her goals may be contradictory, etc. That is, the agent's point of view may not make sense. We must distinguish making sense of what someone does from what someone does making sense: "Simply recovering their self-description may cast no light at all on what was going on."[7] Social science would be impossible in cases of a primitive society that left no record of its view of itself or "discourse of reflective theory," as Taylor calls it (177–78). We treat others as agents by identifying their point of view—their beliefs, goals, etc.—however confused it may be. But we must go beyond their "self-ascriptions" and *make them more intelligible*.

Taylor believes his account avoids a serious problem that befalls traditional accounts of *verstehen*. If our interpretations have to be either in the agent's own terms or in ours then we have the following dilemma: Either the agent's point of view is incorrigible or we are arrogantly ethnocentric (we foist our own meanings or values onto others). We escape this dilemma through rendering the agent's behavior comprehensible—making it more understandable—by developing a language that is neither simply the others' nor our own, what Taylor calls a "language of perspicuous contrast" (125). This language involves questioning both points of view. We avoid the possible dead-end of the other's point of view and the biased imposition of our own. Taylor argues that attempts to take the others' perspectives as sacrosanct, "to adopt their point of view," are themselves ethnocentric, since such attempts foist distinctions onto cultures that the cultures would not recognize. He provides a very subtle discussion of explanations of traditional cultures' magical practices to support these points. For Taylor, understanding and criticism are not at cross purposes. They are necessary parts of a dialectic involving both points of view.

Taylor retains a remnant of the traditional thesis when he argues throughout against naturalism on the grounds that it fails to treat people as agents and ignores their self-ascriptions. Again, we should go beyond these, but we must also account for them if we are to understand their actions. Hence, Taylor retains a weakened form of the necessary condition claim that Nagel attacked and remains true to the Kantian dictate to treat people as responsible agents. Social science should render actions intelligible rather than explaining actions following the canons of predictive natural science. (It is difficult to see how one could explain phenomena such as magical practices without entering into the sort of debate that Taylor conducts over anthropological interpretations that account for the significance of those practices.)

Taylor develops the following objection to functionalist theories of religious and magical practices (122–23). All naturalistic theories (such as functionalist theories) that bypass agents' self-ascriptions (beliefs) have insufficient scope, since those theories leave unexplained particulars that cannot be accounted for by their general causal function. A functionalist theory of religion explains religious practices through their general function(s), such as making the society cohesive. This revelation, of course, would come as a surprise to the local inhabitants. They are quite unaware that their practices serve this function. The problem is this: There may be other religious practices that could fill the functional role and serve to integrate the society equally well. Why, then, are the particular practices adopted? According to Taylor's argument, the functionalist theory could not explain why. Appealing to general functions bypasses agents' beliefs; but self-ascriptions are required to explain particular intentional phenomena. Hence, functionalist theories cannot explain particular intentional phenomena. Without engaging in serious interpretation of the significance of the practices, functionalist theories fail to explain the *detail* of the *explanandum;* there will always be excess data left unexplained.

In philosophy, versions of the "Argument from Excess Data" have been leveled across the board against functionalist theories of mental phenomena and are widely regarded as posing a serious challenge to them. Common to these objections is the idea that functional definitions are defeated by counterexamples, misclassify or fail to explain mental phenomena. In the philosophy of mind functionalist theories define types of mental states in terms of their functional roles—that is, their typical causes and effects, inputs and outputs—rather than by their meaningful (intentional or experiential) contents. Recalling our earlier discussion, functionalist definitional strategy allows naturalists to argue that mental states will likely turn out to be physical states of the brain and central nervous system or computational states. Critics allege that such functional analyses are subject to counterexamples. Causally identical states could conceivably differ in mental content and thus should be classified as different types of states. For example, a blind person may learn to discriminate the color of objects by correlating others' color terms with various shades of grey. Red fire engines and ripe tomatoes would occasion the blind person's use of 'red,' yet his or her perceptual states are not the same as those of someone with normal vision.

Taylor assumes that interpreting the significance of intentional practices, which he regards as necessary for explaining them, is not a species of causal explanation. We will examine this assumption in the following section.

Acausal Hermeneutics: Reasons Versus Causes

Taylor is joined by some Continental thinkers who have argued recently that no causal explanations of behavior—including intentional ones—are correct. Some have offered a novel interpretation of Freud's theory of psychoanalysis. They argue that Freud was wrong in regarding psychoanalysis as a natural science that offered causal explanations of behavior. Instead, we should regard psychoanalysis as "hermeneutical" in that its explanations of behavior are interpretations of the meaning of patients' psychic states. Pschoanalysis, so conceived, is a prototype of interpretive social science. Like Taylor, these "hermeneuticists" oppose meaning-explanations to causal explanations. Let us call their position a "hermeneutical acausal approach." This recent version of the dualistic *verstehen* thesis raises the issue of reasons versus causes.

Contemporary advocates of an acausal hermeneutical approach to social science combine a reasons-versus-causes thesis with the claim that an interpretive, historical method alone is appropriate for understanding human activity. Only such a method can capture essential features of human phenomena. Specifically, only the interpretive or hermeneutic method squares with the historical and context embeddedness of human action. There is good reason to challenge this claim, as Adolph Grunbaum has done in his work on Freud. In a lengthy opening chapter, Grunbaum (1984, 2–93) rebuts hermeneutical acausal interpretations of Freud (by Habermas, Ricoeur, Gadamer and others) which claim that Freud was guilty of a "scientistic self-misunderstanding" of psychoanalysis as a natural science offering causal explanations and lawlike generalizations. Some points from Grunbaum's discussion throw light on our concerns.

Grunbaum argues that the hermeneutical readings distort Freud's theory and social science generally. As an interpretation of Freud, the hermeneutic readings fail to square with Freud's own view of his theory as a natural science founded on obviously causal hypotheses such as the theory of repression. This reply is ineffective since Habermas accused Freud of *self*-misunderstanding. More damaging is Grunbaum's charge that a hermeneutic acausal reading seriously distorts psychoanalysis *and the social sciences generally.* One simply cannot make sense of the psychoanalytic theory of the mind, etiology of neurotic symptoms, analytic-clinical procedures, or the explanation of action generally, from the perspective of acausal hermeneutics.

Grunbaum (69–83) argues that a fundamental mistake underlying the acausal arguments against Freud is the thesis of reasons-versus-causes. On the acausal view, reasons—whether conscious or unconscious—have content, the interpretation of which yields the meaning of the agent's action. But the reason did not *cause* the person to act because there were other reasons available from which the person could have chosen to act. Grunbaum argues that this line of thought confuses motivating reasons with deliberative and justifying reasons. While one is deliberating over reasons and possible courses of action, none of the reasons are (yet) causes. When one justifies an action with a supporting reason the reason performs a logical rather than a causal function. Justifying an action is not the same as causing it. However, when a person does act, he or she acts *from some reason.* And that reason is the motivating reason, the one that "lead to," "brought about," "moved," that is, *caused* the agent to perform his or her action.

Grunbaum offers a counterexample to Habermas's claim that context dependence distinguishes human action from all natural phenomena and makes hermeneutic acausal interpretations, but not causal explanations, appropriate for understanding action. In a lengthy scientific discussion that is difficult to summarize, Grunbaum (17–20) argues that some explanations in microphysics are radically context dependent and historical and hence that the hermeneutic critique of naturalistic social science rests on an egregious misunderstanding of physical science.

If the reasons-versus-causes thesis falls, the acausal *verstehen* thesis loses a major supporting argument. Moreover, if reasons were causes, the line dividing social and natural science would weaken. If a "compatibilism" between reasons and causes were defensible, social science could legitimately explore the causal consequences of mental states identified by their meaningful contents.

There is much more to be said on reasons-versus-causes and interpretations of Freud. But it is legitimate to wonder in what sense
we have understood or explained the agents' actions if their intentions played no causal role in bringing about the behavior. This
points to a major liability of interpretative explanation as the sole
method of social science. The reasons-versus-causes thesis and a
view of human studies that stresses the role of subjectivity on the
course of history would seem strange bedfellows.

The Universalist Version

Having discussed versions of the dualistic *verstehen* thesis, let us
explore a strikingly different, nondualistic version: what I will call
the universalist *verstehen* thesis. We have treated the *verstehen* thesis as a dualistic view that separates the social from the natural sciences: *verstehen* as the empathic understanding of meaningful phenomena. But some theorists have defended *verstehen* not as a
deliberate operation for apprehending the contents of other minds,
but as a basic epistemology that asserts the irreducibility of our
"meaningful" grasp of the world. This view is an inclusion thesis: The
social *and* natural sciences are unified under a general or universal
interpretive or hermeneutic epistemology.

Thinkers who hold the universalist thesis may find support from
remarks such as Weber's (1949 [1904], 76): "We cannot discover . . .
what is meaningful to us by means of a 'presuppositionless' investigation of empirical data. Rather perception of its meaningfulness to
us is the presupposition of its becoming an *object* of investigation."
Alfred Schutz advanced this universalist line of thought:

> *Verstehen* is . . . primarily not a method used by the social scientist, but
> the particular experiential form in which common-sense thinking takes
> cognizance of the social cultural world. It has nothing to do with intro-
> spection; it is a result of the processes of learning or acculturation in the
> same way as the common-sense experience of the so-called natural world.
> *Verstehen* is, moreover, by no means a private affair of the observer which
> cannot be controlled by the experiences of other observers.[8]

Schutz claims that Nagel's objections are off target because he has
misunderstood what *verstehen* is. *Verstehen* is not an operation of
empathic identification; rather, it is our way of grasping both the social *and* the natural worlds.

Schutz argues that *verstehen* is a two-tiered phenomenon, comprising a common-sense, socially molded experience of the social

world and an added layer of social scientific constructs.[9] An unstated assumption in Schutz's argument is that the latter should refer to the former. That is, while natural science can use its "objective" methods, ultimate accounts or reconstructions of science likewise should refer to the acquisition of social meanings and hence to *verstehen*.

Andrew Sayer (1992, 37) makes a similar point in his objection to the criticism of *verstehen* as a dispensable source of hypotheses for explaining actions. Sayer argues that identifying agents and meaningful social phenomena (such as marriage) presupposes *verstehen* as the understanding of constitutive meanings. Without *verstehen,* a critic such as Abel could not identify matrimonial practices; indeed, he would not count as a social actor himself according to Sayer. Putative counterexamples to the need for *verstehen* in social science are thus self-defeating, since they presuppose *verstehen* in the identification of social actors and their practices.

Sayer (1992) goes on to say:

> [T]his implies that verstehen is universal: it is not a special technique or procedure but is common to all knowledge, both of nature (where it is restricted to a single hermeneutic . . .) and of society (where it is situated in a double hermeneutic . . .). However, this is not to deny that it is used differently according to context. (37)

The universalist thesis, which holds that *verstehen* underlies natural science, seems to be based on an anti-empiricist epistemology. The claim is that the "naturalistic" attitude of physical science is an abstraction from our prior meaningful grasp or constitution of the world (often called the *Lebenswelt* or lifeworld, following Husserl). There is no "foundation of knowledge" in the sense of an isolable core of meaning-neutral sense data from which knowledge can be deduced.

The universalist theorist would say of *verstehen* what Taylor (1985, 25) said of interpretation, that it is an "inescapable part of our epistemological predicament," however one may try to eliminate it. *Verstehen,* then, "goes all the way down" epistemologically, even when it is not a special method deliberately employed by a scientist. The universalist does not recognize an ultimate cleavage between natural and social sciences because *both* rest on an interpretive or hermeneutic foundation. Now, the universalist view cannot charitably be interpreted as ascribing intentions to nature that the scientist seeks empathically to understand. Rather, the natural sciences involve a "single hermeneutic," while the social sciences involve a "double hermeneutic."

As a response to critics such as Nagel, these arguments merely change the subject and redefine *verstehen*. However, we could interpret the arguments as employing two senses of *verstehen*, arguing from the necessity of the one to the propriety of the other. The two notions are a strong (universal) sense and a weak (dualistic or local) sense of *verstehen*. We necessarily employ *verstehen* in the strong sense in understanding the world. That is to say, if advocates of the universalist *verstehen* thesis are correct, we could not fail to employ *verstehen* because it is basic to human nature and knowledge. However, the point of arguing for the dualistic thesis is to *get us* to adopt the *verstehen* approach to social science. The weak, dualistic *verstehen* thesis is normative: We *should* employ *verstehen* to frame meaningful explanations in the social sciences.

As we have seen, *verstehen* theorists of the universalist variety hold that *verstehen* in the strong sense is part of our way of knowing the world. However, even if this were so one could avoid using *verstehen* in the weak sense, as a specific operation. But in doing so, the universalist could argue, one would fail to be true to a method presupposed at a deeper level by one's discipline. Behaviorists, for example, who exclude the subjective orientation of humans in their descriptions and explanations of behavior, have distorted our view of human behavior.

An analogy with a debate over value judgments in science will make the universalist's view clearer. Many philosophers have traditionally viewed science as purely factual; scientists *as* scientists make no value judgments. A more radical view, often defended by thinkers in the Continental tradition, questions the distinction between factual and evaluative judgments and argues that so-called factual judgments are really value-laden or at least presuppose value judgments. Science, which relies on veiled value judgments (of "relevance" or "importance"), is shot through and through with them. On this view, scientists and philosophers of science, lamentably, fail to recognize the value-ladenness of science and promote a distorted view of scientific rationality, objectivity and neutrality. *Verstehen,* like value judgments, is claimed to have the same sort of status: It occurs in or is presupposed by science in ways that scientists may overlook. Even though scientists may avoid making specific value judgments, their activity presupposes value judgments. For universalists, the same is true of *verstehen*.

Evaluating the truth of the universalist *verstehen* thesis is beyond the scope of this paper. However, the *inference* from that thesis to the requirement to use the *verstehen* method in social science is questionable. Even if the universalist view were true, one would still have to advance reasons to justify the deliberate use of *verstehen* in the social sciences. Even if our knowledge of the world were founded on an understanding arrived at through a "single hermeneutic," one may nonetheless find alternative approaches to *verstehen* in the social sciences more fruitful. A behaviorist, for example, would refuse to employ meaningful categories altogether, describing behavior only as habitual movements in objective space rather than as "intentional practices." That is, one could choose a non*verstehen* vocabulary and method in sociology or psychology. Since one *could* consistently accept the strong, universalist thesis and reject the weak dualistic thesis, the first thesis does not logically entail the second. Hence, establishing *verstehen* in the universalist sense is insufficient to justify *verstehen* as the correct social scientific method. The argument that we must employ a method of empathic understanding to grasp meaningful phenomena because we meaningfully grasp all phenomena is invalid. 'Subject *S* meaningfully grasps *x*' does not imply 'Subject *S* grasps *x* as meaningful.' Natural phenomena are not themselves meaningful in the sense in which human actions are meaningful—that is, as expressing intentions. Hence, the attempt to justify the dualistic thesis by appealing to the universalist thesis fails. We would have to look elsewhere for arguments that show *verstehen* is the correct method of social science.

CONCLUSION

We have seen that the *verstehen* thesis has been philosophical battleground for a number of difficult issues. The concept of *verstehen* forces one to reflect on the relation between reasons and causes, explanation and understanding, meaning and fact. We have examined the confrontation between naturalism and *verstehende* social science on these problems, explored the strengths and weaknesses in the classic positions of Dilthey and Weber, and showed the relevance of their arguments to contemporary philosophical debate.

Our discussion has yielded two main themes. On the one hand, we should accept the demands for significance and intelligibility advanced by defenders of the dualistic *verstehen* thesis. On the other hand, we must demand evidentially warranted explanations. The social sciences are committed to meaning, but appeals to meaning must be constrained. Working out a defensible position that reconciles meaning and explanation is one of the main problems of contemporary philosophy and social science. The complexity of the debate over the *verstehen* thesis is a testament to the enduring power of the problem posed by Kant's formulation of the standpoints of nature and freedom.

NOTES

1. Dilthey, quoted in Levine (1995, 198).
2. Dilthey, quoted in Ormiston and Schrift, eds. (1990 [1900], 102).
3. Ibid., 113.
4. Dilthey, in Ormiston and Schrift, eds. (1990 [1900], 112).
5. Ibid., 102.
6. See especially Dennett (1978) and Davidson (1980).
7. Taylor (1985, 117).
8. Alfred Schutz, in Maurice Natanson, ed. (1963, 239).
9. Ibid., 245.

REFERENCES

Davidson, D. 1980. *Essays on Action and Events.* Oxford: Clarendon Press.

Dennett, D. 1978. *Brainstorms: Philosophical Essays on Mind and Psychology.* Montgomery, VT: Bradford Books.

Kant, I. 1959 [1785]. *Foundations of the Metaphysics of Morals.* Trans. L.W. Beck. Indianapolis: Bobbs-Merrill.

Levine, D. N. 1985. *The Flight from Ambiguity.* Chicago: Chicago University Press.

———. 1995. *Visions of the Sociological Tradition.* Chicago: University of Chicago Press.

Dilthey, W. 1990 [1900]. "The Rise of Hermeneutics." In G. Ormiston and A. Schrift (eds.) *The Hermeneutic Tradition.* Albany: SUNY Press.

Grunbaum, A. 1984. *The Foundations of Psychoanalysis.* Berkeley: University of California Press.

Habermas, J. 1988 [1967/1970]. *On the Logic of the Social Sciences.* Trans. S.W. Nicholsen and J. Stack. Cambridge: Cambridge University Press.

Nagel, E. 1961. *The Structure of Science: Problems in the Logic of Scientific Explanation.* New York: Harcourt, Brace, & World.

Sayer, A. 1992. *Method in Social Science: A Realist Approach.* London and New York: Routledge.

Schutz, A. 1963. "Concept and Theory Formation in the Social Sciences." In M. Natanson (ed.) *Philosophy of the Social Sciences: A Reader.* New York: Random House.

Skinner, B. F. 1971. *Beyond Freedom and Dignity.* New York: Random House.

Taylor, C. 1985. *Philosophy of the Human Sciences.* Cambridge: Cambridge University Press.

Weber, Marianne. 1975 [1926]. *Max Weber: A Biography.* Trans. and ed. H. Zohn. New York: Wiley.

Weber, Max. 1949 [1904]. "'Objectivity' in Social Science and Social Policy." In M. Weber, *The Methodology of the Social Sciences.* Trans. and ed. E. Shils and H. Finch. New York: Macmillan.

————. 1978a [1922]. "Excerpts from *Economy and Society,*" as cited in W. G. Runciman (ed.) *Selections in Translation.* Trans. E. Mathews. Cambridge: Cambridge University Press.

————. 1978b [1922]. *Economy and Society,* vol. 1. Eds. G. Roth and C. Wittich. Trans. E. Fischoff, H. Gerth, A. M. Henderson, F. Kolegar. C. W. Mills, T. Parsons, M. Rheinstein, G. Roth, E. Schils, C. Wittich. Berkeley: University of California Press.

Wittgenstein, L. 1953. *Philosophical Investigations.* Eds. G. E. M. Anscombe, R. Rhees, and G. H. von Wright; trans. G. E. M. Anscombe. Oxford: Oxford University Press.

7

SIMMEL'S THEORY OF CONFLICT

David W. Felder

INTRODUCTION

Georg Simmel predicted that a crisis in modern culture would occur when individuals in conflict with their culture no longer try to create new social forms but instead reject the very principle of form. For predicting the rejection of all form Simmel has been called the first postmodern philosopher.[1] In this chapter I examine his claim that modern culture has reached a crisis. I begin by examining his views on the function of conflict in society, the rise of individuality, and his claim that conflict between individuals and society increases with modernity. Then I examine Simmel's solution to the problem of increasing conflict. Simmel differs from other thinkers, including Hobbes and Marx, in that he thought the problem was not to repress or even reduce conflict but rather to find creative ways to handle conflict.

The Function of Conflict in Society

Our views on the nature of conflict determine our views on how to handle conflict. We might view conflict as an aberration from a norm of harmony, or we might view conflict as an important feature of human's living in society. Georg Simmel believed that just as cooperation has a social function, conflict also has social functions. As Lewis Coser summarizes Simmel's view, "Far from being necessarily dysfunctional, a certain degree of conflict is an essential element in group formation and the persistence of group life" (Coser 1956, 31).

In his essay "Conflict" (*Der Streit,* 1955 [1908]), Simmel sees conflict as part of our social life. He claims that "If every interaction among men is a sociation, conflict—after all one of the most vivid interactions, which, furthermore, cannot be carried on by one individual alone—must certainly be considered as sociation" (Simmel 1955

[1908], 13). Simmel is aware that viewing conflict as a sociation went against the traditional notions. He notes that sociology was once thought to include either the study of individuals or of society, a unit that included many individuals. As Simmel recognizes,

> In this conception, conflict itself—irrespective of its contributions to these immediate social units—found no place for study. It was a phenomenon of its own, and its subsumption under the concept of unity would have been arbitrary as well as useless, since conflict meant the negation of unity. (14)

The tradition was to classify relations that helped unity as distinct from those that counteracted unity. The fault with this tradition, Simmel points out, is that

> [B]oth [types of] relations can usually be found in every historically real situation. The individual does not attain the unity of his personality exclusively by an exhaustive harmonization, according to logical, objective, religious, or ethical norms, of the contents of his personality. On the contrary, contradiction and conflict not only precede this unity but are operative in it at every moment of its existence. Just so, there probably exists no social unit in which convergent and divergent currents among its members are not inseparably interwoven. (15)

The opposite of association is not conflict, as the traditional view would have it, but indifference. "Unity" Simmel writes, "in the empirical sense of the word is nothing but the interaction of elements. An organic body is a unity because its organs maintain a more intimate exchange of their energies with each other than with any other organism; a state is a unity because its citizens show similar mutual effects" (Simmel 1971, 23). Conflict is one exchange of energy and thus a part of any unity or association.

Form and Content

Simmel's analyses in sociology, as in other areas, depend on the form/content distinction. The content is the interests of each person, which is the energy that drives them. The forms are social structures in which people attempt to satisfy their interests. Simmel writes:

> In any given social phenomenon, content and societal form constitute one reality. A social form severed from all content can no more attain existence than a spatial form can exist without a material whose form it is. Any social phenomenon or process is composed of two elements which in reality are inseparable: on the one hand, an interest, a purpose, or a motive; on

the other, a form or mode of interaction among individuals through which, or in the shape of which, the content attains social reality. (24)

From Simmel's point of view, our conflicting interests are the content of our association. To try to get at the root causes of conflict to eradicate conflict is folly. Conflict will always exist. Simmel discusses at length the foolish things that people fight over, from quarrels over the color of a cow to the side on which people should button their clothes. He says that "[t]here is nothing to suggest that the soul does not have an inborn need for *hating* and *fighting*" (Simmel 1955 [1908], 31).

For Simmel conflict is a permanent feature of human life. Our interests cannot all be expressed within our benign social forms, so conflicts result. The "problem" of conflict is not to do away with interests but rather to have new social forms that allow more interests to be expressed.

Simmel is not interested in getting at the cause of conflict as if we can remove conflict. He takes our interests, and the resulting conflicts as a given. For him association "is the form (realized in innumerably different ways) in which individuals grow together into a unity and within which their interests are realized" (Ibid., 24).

The energy that drives people—one of the basic units for sociology—is people's interests. Sociology explores the social forms in which those interests interact. But Simmel did not believe that sociology has to "psychologize" about individual interests. He insists that "the scientific treatment of psychic data is not thereby automatically psychological" (Simmel 1971, 32). Further, "even where the explanation of every single fact is possible only psychologically (as it is in sociology), the sense and intent of our activities do not have to be psychological. They do not have to aim, that is, at an understanding of the laws of the psychic process itself . . . but can aim rather at its content and configurations" (Ibid.).

Conflict and Group Cohesion

Conflict can help a group preserve its unity and, indeed, its security in cases when threatened by other groups. In discussing intra-group conflict Simmel comments on social hatred:

This hatred is directed against a member of the group . . . because [the member] represents a danger to the preservation of the group. In so far as intra-group conflict involves such a danger, the two conflicting parties hate each other not only on the concrete ground which produced the conflict but also on the sociological ground of hatred for the enemy of the group itself. Since this hatred is mutual and each accuses the other of responsibility for the threat to the whole, the antagonism sharpens precisely because both parties to it belong to the same social unit. (Simmel 1955 [1908], 48–49)

Intra-group conflict can aid association because members of the group perceive the non-conformist to be a threat to the group and direct their energy at forcing conformity. A group will use internal conflict to force group cohesion.

Simmel also argues that group unity can be furthered by intergroup conflict.

[T]he group in a state of peace can permit antagonistic members within it to live with one another in an undecided situation because each of them can go his own way and can avoid collisions. A state of conflict, however, pulls the members so tightly together and subjects them to such a uniform impulse that they either must completely get along with, or completely repel, one another. This is the reason why war with the outside is sometimes the last chance for a state ridden with inner antagonisms to overcome these antagonisms, or else to break up definitely. (1955, 92–93)

Intergroup conflict can also aid association because a threat from outside forces a group to increase its internal cohesion to meet the threat. Simmel observes that "war needs a centralistic intensification of the group form . . ." (88). Far from impeding association, conflict is part of every association and in many instances increases association.

Conflict Between Individuals and Culture

Simmel thought that there is always a separation of individual life and social life. In *"Der Streit"* he comes to the view that "[t]he *a priori* of empirical social life consists of the fact that life is not entirely social. The reservation of a part of our personalities so as to prevent a part from entering into interaction has an effect upon our interactions . . ." (14).

Individuals never blend completely into societies, just as their interests are never completely satisfied within existing social forms. For Simmel, a society " . . . is a structure which consists of beings who stand inside and outside of it at the same time. This fact forms the basis of one of the most important sociological phenomena, namely, that between a society and its component individuals a relationship may exist as if between two parties" (14–15).

The separation of individual and society allows for the possibility of relations between individual and society. Just as we can speak of a conflict between two individuals, we may speak of a conflict between individual and society, between the freedom of individuals and the demands of culture. We can trace historical changes in the relationship of individual to culture and map these historical trends onto the future. The same features that have increased individuality have also intensified conflict. We can know, then, that as the objective measurement of value increases under capitalism, the need for individuals to secure their feelings of self by differentiating themselves from others increases.

Simmel traces the beginnings of individualism to the Italian Renaissance and traces the forms that its development took. First, individuals expressed their individuality in their manner of clothing: "[t]he individual wanted to be *conspicuous;* he wanted to present himself more propitiously and more remarkably than was possible by means of the established forms" (217). In the eighteenth century the move is from individual expression in fashion to freedom, "the universal demand which the individual uses to cover his manifold grievances and self-assertions against society" (218). Simmel continues,

> After the individual had been liberated in principle from the rusty chains of guild, hereditary status, and church, the quest for independence continued to the point where individuals who had been rendered independent in this way wanted also to distinguish themselves *from one another.* What mattered now was no longer that one was a free individual as such, but that one was a particular and irreplaceable individual. (222)

Simmel believes that individuals have a need to maintain their individual identity. For him, maintaining our individuality is a moral duty.

> Certainly, each individual is a synthesis of the forces that constitute the universe. Yet out of this material that is common to all, each one creates an entirely unique configuration. It is the realization of this incomparability, the feeling of a space held in reserve for him alone, that is the moral duty of each individual. Each person is called to realize his own, his very own prototype. (224)

As the use of technological means of production increases, resulting in the increased standardization of both production and products, it becomes harder and harder for individuals to differentiate

themselves. As cities get larger and life more standardized people try
to set themselves apart. Often this takes the form of fashion statements. In Simmel's day, this form was exhibited especially by women
who were relatively powerless and thus more in need of avenues of
individual expression. All individuals need to carve out a space for
themselves and this gets more and more difficult.

The Crisis of Modern Culture

There has always been a conflict between individuals *as* individuals and society. No social form can realize the interests of all of the
individuals who comprise society. But as the aforementioned technological society moves forward, the nature of the conflict between
individual and society changes. According to Simmel it becomes
harder and harder for the individual to maintain individuality. Simmel emphasizes that "[t]he *deepest problems* of modern life flow from
the attempt of the individual to maintain the independence and individuality of his existence against the sovereign powers of society,
against the weight of the historical heritage and the external culture
and technique of life" (1955, 324).

In the past the conflict between individual and society resulted in
individuals forcing social change. The expression of life, of people's
interests, clashed with existing social forms. There has always been
a process of people creating, destroying, and creating new forms.

"Life as such is formless, yet incessantly generates forms for itself.
As soon as each form appears, however, it demands a validity which
transcends the moment and is emancipated from the pulse of life.
For this reason, life is always in a latent opposition to the form"
(376–7).

We create social forms, institutions, customs, works of arts and so
on. These forms then become entrenched as if they were independent
of us and our interests. But eventually the new forms are viewed as
a hindrance to our interests, the flow of life, and then we replace
those forms with new forms that better serve our needs. This pattern
of replacing old forms with new forms is, according to Simmel, starting to change. "At present, we are experiencing a new phase of the
old struggle—no longer a struggle of a contemporary form, filled with
life, against an old lifeless one, but a struggle against the form *as
such* against the *principle* of form" (377).

This worries Simmel because he believes that "[l]ife ... can manifest itself only in particular forms; yet owing to its eternal restless-
ness, life constantly struggles against its own products, which have

become fixed and do not move along with it" (376). The pace is too fast. Change in society cannot keep up, and individuals no longer want to try to create new forms. They attack the idea of having any forms. Simmel sees this as the tragedy of modern life because "[l]ife wishes . . . to obtain something it cannot reach. It desires to transcend all forms and to appear with its naked immediacy. Yet the processes of thinking, wishing and forming can only substitute one form for another" (393).

Simmel believed that the challenge to culture is to have the maximum expression of interests. Interests are a measure of life itself. He viewed conflict as a permanent feature of society that we might handle in productive ways. The solution to the problem is to find ways to allow more interests to be expressed.

Simmel Contrasted with Thomas Hobbes

Simmel's view of conflict contrasts with that of Hobbes, who sought to *suppress* conflict. Hobbes thought that we need to have one sovereign who uses coercion to repress conflicting interests. Hobbes' attitude toward conflict is that conflict must be suppressed because it is too dangerous to let people express and act out their conflicts. His goal is to have a univocal system, a system that allows only one decision maker. The model is that of two or more parties in conflict giving all right to speak and act to a third party who will speak and act for them. Since that third party has one voice, there can be no ambiguity in act or expression. The many voices that existed before are forced into silence, so that the conflict is suppressed.

Hobbes makes a distinction between factual questions, which reason can settle, and nonfactual questions, which reason cannot settle. He believed that questions of ethical right and wrong, religion, and possession cannot be settled by individuals reasoning together. Since peace depends on settling questions that cannot be settled by reason, some other method is needed. One does not have to agree on the necessity of settling *all non-factual* questions for Hobbes's argument; all the argument requires is that we grant that there are *some* disputes that reason cannot settle. Hobbes argues for the acceptance of a nonrational method of settling the disputes that reason cannot settle (Felder 1978, passim). That method is authority.

What is authority? Above all else authority is a method of conflict resolution. Other words for 'authority' in this context are 'arbiter,' 'representative,' and 'sovereign.' Hobbes explains how this method of conflict resolution works:

A multitude of men are made *one* person, when they are by one man, or one person, represented; so that it be done with the consent of every one of that multitude in particular. For it is the *unity* of the represener, not the *unity* of the represented, that maketh the person *one*. And it is the representer that beareth the person, and but one person: and *unity*, cannot be otherwise understood in multitude. (Hobbes 1987 [1651], 220)

The institution of authority replaces the reason of many with the reason of one. The result is that "the commonwealth being in their representative one person, there cannot easily arise any contradiction in the laws" (317).

Here then is a method for removing contradictions of interests and viewpoints by having the conflicting parties accept the judgment of a third party. The representative they accept represents both; yet, because the arbiter is one person, the arbiter speaks with one voice. The arbiter represents them in that he or she acts for them, and they give up the right to act. This method resolves conflicts by creating a situation in which the formerly disputing parties are no longer allowed to press their conflicting views.

Hobbes believed that civil society required a clear hierarchy of authority and coercion. There must be one ruler who must have the power to make decisions and to force others to obey those decisions. On Hobbes's view, since conflict is a permanent feature of society, it must constantly be suppressed.

Georg Simmel took individuals' interests as a given, and was interested in examining the social forms that allowed the expression of those interests. Unlike Hobbes, Simmel did not want to suppress interests. He sought the development of social forms that would allow the maximum expression of interests and was always mindful that there is a permanent conflict between individual and culture. For Hobbes, on the other hand, the solution to the conflict between individual and culture was to repress individual interests.

Simmel Contrasted with Karl Marx and Friedrich Engels

The solution to the problem of individual and culture for Karl Marx and Friedrich Engels was to reduce or remove conflict. Like Hobbes, they were interested in examining the causes of conflicts. Whereas Hobbes saw the cause of conflict in individuals' interests Marx and Engels viewed interests in terms of economic classes and not isolated individuals. As they wrote in *The Communist Manifesto*, "[t]he history of all hitherto existing society is the history of class struggles" (Marx and Engels, 1972 [1848], 81).

Marx and Engels looked forward to the day when there might be a classless society with a concomitant reduction and even removal of conflict. The proletarian revolution would be different from previous revolutions in that it would usher in a classless society.

> All the preceding classes that got the upper hand, sought to fortify their already acquired status by subjecting society at large to their conditions of appropriation. The proletariat cannot become masters of the productive forces of society, except by abolishing their own previous mode of appropriation, and thereby also every other previous mode of appropriation. (89)

The result, according to Marx and Engels, will be the removal of class conflict: "[i]n place of the old bourgeois society, with its classes and class antagonisms, we shall have an association, in which the free development of each is the condition for the free development of all . . ." (97). In the communist society, where individuals give according to their abilities and receive according to their needs, there would be no more class conflict. Conflict for Marx is an undesirable feature which has a historical function. The goal is to remove conflict by creating a classless society.

Within the communist society there would no longer be a hierarchy of power and authority, and true equality in power and authority might exist. Since one group would no longer be oppressing another group, coercion and the instrument of coercion—the capitalist state—would no longer exist.

Simmel discussed many of the same issues that Karl Marx discussed—coercion, hierarchies, oppression—and came to very different conclusions. In writing about super-ordination and sub-ordination, the higher and lower positions that people may hold in hierarchical structures, he examines the reasons people may connect oppression to being in the subordinate position.

Simmel states that "[t]he motivation of the endeavor (to abolish super-subordination) lies exclusively in the feeling-states of individuals, in the consciousness of degradations and oppression . . ." (Simmel 1971, 340). The problem with inequalities is that it fosters these feelings. The solution is not necessarily to do away with inequality because "[i]f some kind of social organization could avoid these psychological consequences of social inequality, social inequality could continue to exist without difficulties . . ." (Ibid.).

Socialism is proposed as one way to eliminate the feeling of being oppressed. Simmel points out that it is at best one way and not the only way to eliminate the feeling. He writes that "As a mere *means,* however, socialism succumbs to the fate of every means, namely of never being, in principle, the *only* one. Since different causes may have the same effect, it is never impossible that the same purpose may be reached by a different means" (Ibid., 340).

One possible alternative means of removing the feeling of oppression while preserving hierarchical society with inequalities is "Super-Subordination without Degradation." Simmel notes that "[i]f it were possible to dissolve the association between super-subordination and the feeling of personal devaluation and oppression, there is no logical reason why the all decisive feeling of dignity and a life which is its own master should stand and fall only with socialism" (Simmel 1971, 341). Simmel's solution is to have super-ordination that is reciprocal, so that the same people are not always in the *dominant* position. If this reciprocity can be achieved, he thinks that "[w]e would then have an ideal organization, in which A is superordinate to B in one respect or at one time, but in which, in another respect or at another time, B is super ordinate to A. This arrangement would preserve the organizational value of super-subordination, while removing its oppressiveness, one-sidedness, and injustice" (342).

Simmel believes that in modern society specialization is needed, and therefore so are hierarchies of authority, since no one can know everything. He opens the possibility of a society in which different individuals are each the authority in their own area of expertise.

Simmel observes that coercion is not necessarily a bad thing. He notes that people occasionally feel that "being under coercion, . . . being subject to a superordinate authority, is revolting or oppressive . . ." (344). But he also claims that "for the majority of men, coercion probably is an irreplaceable support and cohesion of the inner and outer life" (Ibid.). He explains how this can be.

> In the inevitably symbolic language of all psychology: our soul seems to live in two layers, one of which is deeper, hard or impossible to move, carrying the real sense or substance of our life, while the other is composed of momentary impulses and isolated irritabilities. . . . [T]he second layer would give the first no opportunity to come to surface, if the feeling of a coercion interfering from somewhere did not dam its torrent. . . . (Ibid.)

We thus need some coercion in society, not because of class conflict but because of conflicts between disparate parts of our own personalities. To the extent that Simmel offers a solution, his method is to ascertain when people have the feeling of being oppressed, and to examine how changes might be made, such as to hierarchies, to lessen these feelings. He has none of Marx's notion of a false consciousness. Coercion is not always oppressive because most of us welcome some coercion in society.

Georg Simmel's views on conflict, and his views on hierarchies, coercion, and the future of conflict, contrast sharply with the views of Karl Marx. In contrast to Marx who thinks that all hierarchy and coercion were oppressive, Simmel thinks that there are ways to have hierarchy and coercion that are not oppressive. While Marx wants to reduce or remove conflict, Simmel wants to find ways to handle conflict so conflict could be used to create new social forms.

CONCLUSION

Simmel offers a partial solution to the clash of freedom and culture. By the use of creative methods of conflict resolution we can strive to create social forms that allow the maximum expression of interests. This approach contrasts sharply with the view of Thomas Hobbes who wanted a strong hierarchy that suppressed the expression of conflicting interests. In contrast to Marx, Simmel saw conflicts between individuals in society and individuals and society as a permanent feature of social life. The problem for Simmel was to improve our methods for handling conflict. Simmel's approach is consistent with the approach of modern social scientists such as Robert Axelrod (1984) who conducts empirical studies to determine what strategies a person can use to increase or decrease aggressive and cooperative behavior. The overriding goal here is to study conflict to find creative ways to handle it.

NOTE

1. See for instance, Deena Weinstein and M. A. Weinstein, *Postmodern(ized) Simmel*. London: Routledge, 1993.

REFERENCES

Axelrod, Robert. 1984. *The Evolution of Cooperation*. New York: Basic Books.
Coser, Lewis A. 1956. *The Functions of Social Conflict*. New York: Free Press.

Felder, David W. 1978. *The Relationship of Fact, Value, and Obligation in Hobbes's Leviathan.* Unpublished diss.

Hobbes, Thomas. 1987 [1651]. *Leviathan,* ed. C. B. Macpherson. London: Penguin Books.

Levine, Donald N. 1994. "Social Conflict, Aggression, and the body in Euro-American and Asian Social Thought," *International Journal of Group Tensions.* Vol. 24, #3, pp. 205–217.

Marx, Karl, and Friedrich Engels. 1972 [1848]. *The Communist Manifesto,* Part I "Bourgeois and Proletarians," reprinted in Carl Cohen (ed.) *Communism, Fascism and Democracy.* New York: Random House.

Simmel, Georg. 1950 [1917]. "Fundamental Questions of Sociology" [*Grundfragen der Soziologie*], trans. by Kurt H. Wolff in *The Sociology of Georg Simmel.* New York: Free Press.

———. 1955 [1908] "Conflict" [*Der Streit*], translated by Kurt H. Wolff in *Conflict and the Web of Group-Affiliation.* New York: Free Press.

———. 1971. *On Individuality and Social Forms,* ed. Donald N. Levine. Chicago: University of Chicago Press.

8

FROM SIMMEL'S CONCEPTION OF SOCIETY TO THE FUNCTION AND FORM OF LEGAL CONFLICT

Nathan W. Harter

INTRODUCTION

Conflict, according to Georg Simmel, may be analyzed in terms of "formal" or "pure" sociology, whereby human interaction can be seen to assume relatively stable forms.[1] As a function of methodology, Simmel characteristically distinguishes between the contents of a social relationship and its form, in order to proceed toward an analysis of the form itself. In this fashion, Simmel adopted the objective point of view, from which "it is not our task either to accuse or to pardon, but only to understand."[2] Conflict is a form of elementary social behavior through which individuals influence, suffer, and modify one another for the sake of various drives and purposes,[3] including but not limited to, egoism, altruism, hostility, and a class of neutral motives, such as the desire to see a project through to completion.[4] A thorough study of conflict would, by Simmel's own standards, therefore, attempt to discern its characteristics, its order into hierarchy, its causes, and its historical trajectory as a form.[5]

The following chapter develops one aspect of a more comprehensive theory: applying his sociology to the practice of institutionalized conflict resolution. More specifically, it concentrates on certain formal methods of resolving conflict: third-party interventions known as mediation, arbitration, and adjudication. My emphasis will be on adjudication as a form of legal conflict.

A CONCEPTION OF SOCIETY

In order to describe a particular social form, Simmel relies on a certain understanding of its context in society or groups. He conceptualizes the architecture of society and groups as a "formal matrix of tensions" and elsewhere as an "intersection of social circles." People are psychologically as well as physically oriented toward each other in a kind of constellation; in each relationship we may hypothesize that persons have approached an equilibrium of social distance, reaching proximity to one another and at the same time keeping each other at a distance.[6] Relationships can be depicted in terms of the social distance that two persons reach by mutual orientation. Significantly, no relationship, regardless how intimate, would lead to a complete unification of the participants (Simmel 1971 [1908], 72). A unification would be understood as an obliteration of individuality by the resulting social unit, which is impossible. As Simmel put it elsewhere, "the 'I' can *not* seize the 'not-I'."[7] One cannot get behind appearances sufficiently to unify with another; complete penetration of another's core individuality does not happen. One reason for this limitation is the manifold that is "me": one can access many parts of me, but aspects of me remain detached. One cannot access *all* of me.[8] Nor does anyone necessarily want others to access all of them and probe that which has been relegated to spheres of secrecy. We attract each other by degrees, and in some instances—for example, in marriage—we approach a true unification. We also maintain distance, even from the closest relation. Moreover, according to Simmel, the same forces that keep persons apart can also effectively terminate the relationship altogether. Thus, at one extreme there is no relationship at all; at the other is the intimate struggle toward unification. By definition, relationships fall somewhere in between. Without any convergence, there would be no relationship, and therefore no occasion for conflict; without any divergence, there would be no difference to serve as a basis for conflict. There must be both.

Simmel suggests that we think of a relationship as the ratio of these forces (Ibid., 72). They are two aspects of a single impulse, a disposition for a specific distance (Ibid., 78) which we might refer to as an impulse to establish distances conducive to our interests. Both persons are responding to this impulse separately; the form emerges from the tension established by their separate searches for appropriate distance. One's search for appropriate distance might not, and probably will not, arrive at the same place as another's search. The appropriate distance remains to be worked out according to reciprocal behaviors, like a dance. To put it another way, the phenomenon is bipolar, comprehending the participants.

SOCIAL CONFLICT

Simmel's treatment of social conflict begins from two premises: (a) that conflict is inexorable and (b) that conflict is also essential to well-being.[9] Conflict results from the human condition; conflict is a manifestation of ourselves as social beings. Conflict evidences a social relationship. Interpersonal conflict actually constitutes a social unit (Ibid., 70). Simmel refers to an "association," that is, an occasion of variable duration in which persons interact and thereby constitute a unity. Conflict is one way people associate. Simmel says that society produces opportunities for conflict and that in turn conflict produces society, giving it shape.[10] When subsequent theorists such as Kenneth Thomas posits that conflict originates with the perceived threat by the other to some interest of mine,[11] Simmel's influence can be readily seen.

Not every conflict episode is a fight to the death; society is not a condition in which everyone walks around frightened of each other in some Hobbesian state of nature. Conflict is rarely so intense. Instead, Simmel describes a continuum, measuring the degree of antagonism associated with conflict behaviors. At one extreme, in an attempt at a complete unification, is the antagonism reflected in the willingness to annihilate the other, thereby hoping to destroy the source of the divergence (Ibid., 80). Obviously, at this pole of the continuum, conflict risks destroying the association. On this point, Lewis Coser is right to make explicit a distinction Simmel raises with regard to intimate relationships (Ibid., 92–95), namely, that relationships tend to withstand conflicts about peripheral matters, but not conflicts that go to the fundament, the ground of the relationship itself.[12] When the parties share superordinate goals, as when they share a commitment to the relationship, they aren't as likely to feel threatened by minor disputes, and this in turn makes conflict itself less threatening to them.

Therefore, one of the limits of conflict, without which conflict becomes a war of extermination, is the existence of commonality.[13] So long as there is a shared, superpersonal objective, there is a limitation on antagonism (Ibid., 81). Another related limit arises whenever the conflict is grounded in desire for an object such that once the object is obtained, or acquired by other means, or an antagonist loses interest in the object (or substitutes something else in its place), then the conflict ceases (Ibid., 82–83). In the meantime, however, conflict has no reason to escalate beyond this pursuit of the object.

The trick would seem to be identifying the object and discovering alternative means of acquiring it. This is easier said than done, because parties are not always sure what they want. Their behavior could be merely expressive of frustration, rather than instrumental. The behavior could be displaced, targeting either the wrong person or a substitute object. Generally, people displacing their frustrations tend to implicate innocent parties and also prevent the clarity of purpose needed to resolve conflict. By the same token, those "nonrealistic" conflicts, as they are called, can serve as a kind of safety-valve, diverting hostility into healthy channels.[14]

TRIADIC STRUCTURES

A social form such as legal conflict can seem too rigid and artificial for some disputes. To avoid this rigidity, parties have sought alternative methods for resolving their conflicts. Rogers and McEwen, for example, explain the emergence of mediation in just this way: "[Many lawyers and scholars] critiquing the legal system focused on how disputes are transformed when lawyers and judges translate the conflict into legal terms for litigation [and] the exaggeration of conflict created by the litigation process. . . . [*citations omitted*]"[15] Because alternatives exist and seem to be growing in popularity, they might be construed as a repudiation of the legal system, when in fact their use evinces the resilience of the overall system. Adjudication is one form, one method for resolving disputes, and before examining it in any detail we ought to place it in the context of a range of choices. In other words, adjudication is only one of a variety of third-party interventions. Third-party interventions in any conflict, whether voluntarily sought or externally imposed, include extralegal forms such as arbitration and mediation. In each instance of third-party intervention, the geometry is that of the triangle. Simmel wrote specifically about these arrangements in his classic discussion of triads, since the triad is the form that third-party intervention assumes.

As in the legal system, so also in triads generally, a third party has two functions: to unite, and to separate.[16] With regard to unification, Simmel says that "[d]iscords between two parties which they themselves cannot remedy, are accommodated by the third or by absorption in a comprehensive whole."[17] For instance, a third party can occupy (and urge) the intermediate point between extremes held by antagonists.[18] This middle ground enables the third party to reveal to antagonists that their impasse is really only an illusion created by their insistence on a bipolar, zero-sum model: either X wins or Y wins. It is the role of the third party to identify alternatives to the entrenched positions of a zero-sum logic. In arbitration, the third party can simply declare an outcome. But this role presupposes that the issue in dispute is clear. If not clear, a third party can also distill out the factual elements of an antagonism from those rooted in subjective passions, thereby improving the odds for reconciliation based on factual grounds.[19] In this way, resolution is facilitated through a strategy of depersonalization.[20] Even before sifting the objective wheat from the subjective chaff, a third party can serve as the excuse or occasion for two persons to convene.[21] They might never have made a point of meeting were it not for the intervention. Third parties also create an opportunity for the antagonists to unite against intervention, as for example, brawling spouses turning their ire against the local police dispatched to the home.[22]

A triad may also function to separate or disunite parties. A triad disturbs "pure and immediate reciprocity,"[23] since the members risk participating in "party formation" of two against one in all permutations.[24] A and B might gang up on C, who in turn seeks alliance with A or B, and so forth. Other similar separations occur because of the presence of a third person, and it would be an incomplete representation of Simmel's account to leave them out.[25] Third parties have to beware the implications of their involvement. Properly conducted, however, third-party interventions offer alternatives to the dyad.

In any third-party intervention, the parties give up, assign, or lose control over some aspect of the conflict to the third party. An intervention in which the third party controls the *process* might be mediation: the mediator is like a football referee seeing that teams comply with the rules. A mediator must not favor one side over another. An intervention in which the third party controls the *outcome* might be arbitration, in which the arbiter, like a judge in a diving competition, simply declares the outcome. Adjudication is characterized by the third party's control over *both* process and outcome; the system makes the rules, shapes the behavior into prescribed rituals, and decides in favor of one side.[26] According to this way of schematizing third-party interventions, adjudication represents maximal control by the third party.

LEGAL CONFLICT

The Form of Legal Conflict

The practice of law largely requires an attorney to take some unique human predicament and give it a form recognized by the judicial system in order to satisfy the client's interests. It is a process of pigeonholing and conflict resolution, converting frustration into satisfaction. This particular system operates according to rules of all kinds. For example, there are rules of procedure, rules of evidence, rules of interpretation, and rules of professional conduct. And then every courtroom has its unspoken norms of etiquette. "May I approach the bench?" "I have no more questions at this time, your honor." "May it please the Court . . ." In this highly ritualized process,[27] both client and jury (as well as reporters, witnesses, and members of a curious public) feel as strangers and risk coming away with one of two impressions: (a) that the whole thing is an artificial device meant to keep lawyers employed or (b) that something mysterious is happening at the altar of Justice, where bench and bar (attorneys all) are its priests. Eric Voegelin, a philosopher whose dissertation had been about Simmel, observes in his later legal writings that for the litigant the system "sounds like an elaborate game of make-believe."[28] What then is this "game"? Here we can take up Simmel's account.[29]

Like all forms of social conflict, the legal system does have an object, which in and of itself places limits on the conflict and serves as a check on antagonism. Nonetheless, from the client's standpoint, other interests could outweigh the value of that object. For example, lawyers rapidly become too expensive and relationships become too nasty. It is sometimes tempting for parties to decide that it's simply not worth the fight. This is why alternative methods such as mediation exist. Once conflict finds its way to litigation, however, the system works toward resolution according to its own set of rules.

Simmel makes a relevant contrast when he notices that a legal process meant to resolve conflict also *intensifies* conflict, since parties obviously have a stake in the outcome and, by this time, the conflict is overt, public, and designed to reach a definite outcome. Once lawyers enter the fray as advocates, they feel pressure to win as much as possible for their clients, within the limits of the system, and so they in turn contribute to the intensification (Ibid., 86–90). Within the limits of the system, why should they hold back now? Like a river channeled into a narrow gorge, the conflict increases in intensity.

The process is meant to be objective and purposeful, admitting all that pertains to the decision and excluding all that does not, with the singular purpose of reaching that decision.[30] Thus, in the course of pigeonholing a human predicament for preexisting categories, treating it in terms unfamiliar to the people involved, clients may well wonder where they fit in. Clients just want to tell their side of a story. But then their own lawyer coaches them how to tell it, and the opposing lawyer interrupts with objections and generally tries to twist the story beyond recognition, such that even telling one's story becomes distorted. The client's narrative shall have become hedged in by rules and stratagems, for the sake of the form. In this way, a form created to serve people now appears to rob them of their individuality, their uniqueness, in order to slot them according to esoteric roles.[31] In *The Philosophy of Money,* Simmel describes this phenomenon as follows: "law [is] characterized by [its] complete indifference to individual qualities, [extracting] from the concrete totality of the streams of life one abstract, general factor which develops according to its own independent norms and which intervenes in the totality of existential interests and imposes itself upon them. . . . [It has] the power to lay down forms and directions for contents to which [it is] indifferent. . . ."[32] The participant is simply a "respondent" in another wrongful death tort action, for example, supposedly just like the respondent in a case decided two years ago in the state of Georgia, and so forth. The unique person shall have been abstracted out of the equation; the case must be made empty of individuality. For the sake of the process, the participant has to be depersonalized, establishing distance from the process and vice versa. The parties lose control of both the process and the outcome, so it is no wonder clients feel alienated. *The system was designed that way.*

This alienation would be intolerable were it not for the system's claims to legitimacy, grounded in part in its claims to objectivity. The system has to *seem* to be the application of pure reason. And it does in fact aspire to legitimacy on these grounds, even if one could save time and money and reach a comparable distribution of outcomes by flipping a coin or by some other mechanism of sheer randomness. A system that forswears being grounded in luck or an arbitrary will might attain legitimacy. But legitimacy is a product of the perceptions of the parties. The perception of fairness is a powerful aid for resolving conflicts. People often accept manifestly unfair outcomes if they accept the essential fairness of the process producing that outcome (as for example in lotteries). Contrarily, the legitimacy of the fairest distribution suffers if the people conclude it was attained by unfair means. Thus, legal systems have a stake in how the public perceives the process by which they arrive at an outcome.[33]

The broad term for this stake is "procedural justice." Implicated in procedural justice is the question: on what grounds shall authority be vested in decision makers? Parties yield to intervention only if they submit themselves to authority—whether they create that authority by means of contract (where signatories often specify how the agreement is to be enforced) or find it ready-made in the social structure they share (for instance, case law). Authority is not necessarily grounded in anyone's capacity to be fair, although authority that is not perceived to be fair is at risk.[34] The point is that litigants accept a judge's decision, not so much because of any personal qualities of the judge, but rather because the judge represents society.[35] The judge too must be depersonalized. Thus, the parties engage in an exchange of their individuality for a process they perceive to be legitimate, and it is legitimate only if everyone else gives up their individuality as well. To defy a judge, reserving to oneself the right to ignore rulings, casts an individual as anti-social and accordingly as an enemy of legitimate authority.

The legal process has an object. That object is not justice.[36] Neither is it bare reason. So Professor Rapoport, in an essay on the professionalization of conflict: "The adversary system of law [is] supposed to serve justice.... But, if success ... can be achieved in other ways, say, by adroit use of forensic skills or demagogy, professional competence and commitment will be directed toward acquisition of the appropriate skills."[37] The object of the legal system is Law. *Lex Rex:* the law is king. This the parties share or else they become outside the law, or outlaws. Litigation is not meant to challenge the legitimacy of law itself, but rather applies the law.[38] Within the form of legal conflict, one is supposed to serve the law. Thus, the role of the attorney, who stands between a unique human predicament on the one hand (the content of the struggle, as it were) and a legal form on the other, is to serve *both* the flesh-and-blood customer and the legal system itself, at one and the same time.[39]

The Vitality of The Law

Even though the object of legal conflict is the law, and the whole system is measured against that object, use of the image of "the Law" as given, an external fact, a transcendent, brooding omnipresence, misses its dynamic qualities as a human product.[40] Simmel was not unaware of the "law-creating aspects of conflict."[41] Law might settle conflict, whereas over time conflict creates law. Law and its conflicts shape each other with the passage of time. This temporal dimension of law recalls Simmel's model of unrelenting re-formation, captured in the words of the esteemed jurist Benjamin Cardozo.

According to Cardozo, "[i]n the life of the mind as in life elsewhere, there is a tendency toward the reproduction of kind. Every judgment has a generative power. It begets its own image."[42] Thus, in a legal system devoted to case law, we find ourselves confronted by the authority of precedent, and well we might, as a basis for legitimacy. "Adherence to precedent must . . . be the rule rather than the exception if litigants are to have faith in the even-handed administration of justice in the courts."[43] Speaking broadly, in terms reminiscent of Simmel, Cardozo says, "Life casts the moulds of conduct, which will some day become fixed as law. Law preserves the moulds, which have taken form and shape from life."[44] On the other hand, however, "[f]or every tendency, one seems to see a counter-tendency; for every rule its antinomy. Nothing is stable. Nothing absolute."[45] Thus, "[t]he rules and principles of case law have never been treated as final truths, but as working hypotheses, continually retested. . . ."[46]

Professor Levine identifies this aspect of the law with one of Simmel's four basic presuppositions for analyzing society, which is the presupposition of reciprocity. *"No thing or event has a fixed, intrinsic meaning; its meaning only emerges through interaction with other things or events [emphasis supplied]."* He then cites Simmel with regard to the law that "[n]o legal precept is valid in itself, but only in relation to other legal precepts."[47] In this way, the system of case law avoids what Cardozo called "the demon of formalism" so that, over time, by a process of conflict, "[t]he old forms remain, but they are filled with a new content."[48] In light of which it has been said by Professor Edward Levi that the law is *both,* at one and the same time, (a) certain and constant, as well as (b) uncertain, mutable, and case specific.[49] It is in other words an open system. Cardozo hoped this continual adaptation of the law would develop (imperceptibly) along some combination of four lines of inquiry: logical consistency, historical change, social custom, and the welfare of the community.[50] Levi simplifies this list to changes in circumstance, and changes in what people want.[51] What these two legal philosophers imply is that the law dare not change according to some individual's whim, or for light and transient reasons. The very persons entrusted with the process, lawyers and judges, as well as the litigants, must detach themselves and surrender aspects of their personality to the social form.

The form of legal conflict provides the artificiality necessary to reflect the playing of roles. As the Honorable Sarah Evans Barker has expressed it:

> The reality is that in the judicial system, judges and lawyers deal with and manage significant amounts of power ... and unless the exercise of that power is cloaked in forms and processes and rituals which are calculated to provide constant reminders to everybody involved that that's what we're doing ... the process will degenerate quickly into nothing more than arbitrary power. The forms we use and the rituals we employ prevent that degeneration into pure arbitrariness.[52]

By way of contrast, Professor Rapoport takes a dimmer view.

> [P]rofessionalism involves symbolic skills. And the nature of symbolic manipulation is such that it confers the more power the more abstract the symbols become. . . . Consequently, as there is more power to be wielded, the professions tend to be further removed in the minds of the practitioners from the concrete situations affected by their activities.[53]

In these quotations the judge and the professor are addressing themselves to the content of conflict, and yet they both speak to the same formal aspect of our legal system, that is, the distance of the professionals from the case. Without this professional distance, the participants involve too much of themselves, their feelings and their agendas, to permit a perception of legitimacy.

CONCLUSION

Conflict is a social form that, with the intervention of a third party, becomes transformed according to the dynamics of Simmel's classic triad. The resulting forms emerge as a function of life and then come to regulate the vitality of the very life from which they spring. In every such form there is the originating tension arising from the substantive conflict, and eventually, there arises a procedural tension between the participants and the institutional form designed to process their conflict. The legal system exemplifies this tension in every concrete case, and it uses these unique predicaments to amend itself as a suprapersonal system, but only at a cost—a cost an increasing number of disputants prefer not to pay, as they go casting about for alternative forms such as mediation and arbitration. These alternative forms are in their turn becoming increasingly formal, regulated, and complex, as our society generates, enjoys, and suffers a diversity of forms to express our diversity as individuals. It was

Simmel, more than any other theorist, who predicted this refraction of the single form, conflict, into the dazzling array of techniques, devices, tricks, and methods presently being differentiated in the legal literature, in legislation, and in everyday practice.

NOTES

1. Wolff (1950, "Introduction," xvii-lxiv, at xxxiv). By saying these forms are "relatively stable," I intend to incorporate Levine's depiction that forms "are not fixed and immutable, but emerge, develop, and perhaps disappear over time." See, Levine (1971, xv).
2. Simmel (1950 [1908], 424).
3. Simmel (1950 [1917], 10*ff*); *see generally* Georg Simmel, *Soziologie, Untersuchungen über die Formen der Vergesellschaftung,* 3rd ed. (Leipzig: Verlag von Duncker & Humblot, 1923). Chapter 4, translated by Kurt H. Wolff and abridged in Levine (1971). Levine's volume is the basis for in-text, parenthetical citation.
4. Simmel (1950 [1908], 60). Simmel adds the possibility of a form persisting for its own sake, as for example when boxing becomes a sport rather than combat. See, Ibid., 42*ff*.
5. Ibid., 23.
6. Levine (1971, xxv) allows as how "[i]n general .. sociology may be regarded as the geometry of social forms."
7. Simmel (1908, 128, 202). Simmel does acknowledge instances when one person treats another as a mere means, and he explicitly removes these instances from his analysis of conflict (Ibid., 182).
8. Loiskandl, Weinstein, and Weinstein (1986, xlvi); see also, Simmel (1950 [1908], 58*ff*).
9. See, Levine (1994, 208).
10. Simmel (1950 [1908], 18).
11. Thomas (1976, 895).
12. See, Coser (1956, 74).
13. Thus, the creation or maintenance of such commonality, even the institution of slavery, preserves society against the inevitable shocks of antagonism. Again, it might be depicted as a ratio, such that severe animosity can nonetheless be counterbalanced by the greater necessity at some level to get along. Interestingly, conflict often establishes, or reveals the basis for, a commonality that previously did not exist. See, Coser (1956, 121*ff*).
14. In this paragraph I am indebted to Coser (1956, 48–55, 156).
15. Rogers and McEwen (1989, § 4.2). For a description and critique of this "transformative role" for the lawyer, see, Menkel-Meadow (1985, 30) in which the author identifies "defining, channelling, and labeling a dispute," "rephrasing" the dispute into a public discourse, and serving generally as "the only source of contact with the legal system for many disputants." She makes a typically Simmelian move by alleging throughout that by these means lawyers both expand and narrow conflict.
16. Simmel (1950 [1908], 135).
17. Ibid., 87–424; See for example, Rogers and McEwen (1989, § 3.3).
18. Simmel (1950 [1908], 144).

19. Ibid., 147.
20. Ibid., 148.
21. Ibid., 146.
22. Ibid., 135*ff.*
23. Ibid., 139; also, 136.
24. Ibid., 141.
25. See for example, Ibid., 154–169.
26. The foregoing taxonomy appears in Thibaut and Walker (1978).
27. Barker (1995, 11*ff.*) writes: "Our legal processes and, in particular, our court processes virtually run on ritual. . . . The ritual transcends and gives deeper meaning and significance and value to the day-to-day work of the courts—we know that—but the question still persists: Have we become too sophisticated to keep it?" She answers in the negative. On the increasing ritualization of mediation as well, see Rogers and McEwen (1989, 1.3, 12.1–12.5); see also, Shephard (1995, § 2.4).
28. Voegelin (1991, 46).
29. In his writings on social conflict, Georg Simmel devoted scant attention explicitly to *legal* conflict.
30. A student of Simmel, José Ortega y Gasset (1946, 29) quotes Livy for the proposition that "the law is deaf and inexorable, unrelenting and remorseless even toward venial offenses."
31. See Simmel (1950 [1917], 58): "The really practical problem of society is the relation between its forces and forms and the individual's own life."
32. Simmel (1990 [1900/1907], 442).
33. Greenberg (1987).
34. See, Simmel (1950 [1908], 183*ff*).
35. Voegelin, (1993, 59).
36. Cf. Simmel (1950 [1908], 259; also 100, n.3).
37. Rapoport (1974, 214).
38. Coser (1956, 123).
39. Walter (n.d., 158): "The forms are not judged by how they serve or deny the needs of individuals, but merely by the criteria of logic and coherence."
40. Voegelin (1993, 14).
41. Coser (1956, 124–126).
42. Cardozo (1921, 21).
43. Ibid., 34.
44. Ibid., 64.
45. Ibid., 28.
46. Ibid., 23. For a similar treatment of constitutional provisions, see Levi (1948, 41).
47. Levine (1971, xxxiii) citing Simmel's German-language second edition of the *Philosophy of Money* at (1907, 66).
48. Cardozo (1921, 101).
49. Levi (1948, 3, 4): Litigants participate in law making. "They are bound by something they helped to make."
50. Cardozo (1921, 30). These changes "have their roots in the constant striving of the mind for a larger and more inclusive unity, in which differences will be reconciled, and abnormalities will vanish" (Ibid., 50).
51. Levi (1948, 3).

52. Barker (1995, 15).
53. Rapoport (1974, 220).

REFERENCES

Barker, Hon. S. E. 1995. "Ritual & Civility." *res gestae* (July) xxxix:1:11–15.

Cardozo, B. 1921. *The Nature of the Judicial Process.* New Haven, CT: Yale University Press.

Coser, L. A. 1956. *The Functions of Social Conflict.* New York: Free Press.

Greenberg, J. 1987. "A Taxonomy of Organizational Justice Theories." *Academy of Management Review* 12:1:9–22.

Levi, E. H. 1948. *An Introduction to Legal Reasoning.* Chicago: University of Chicago Press.

Levine, D. N. (ed.) 1971. "Introduction." Levine, D. (ed.) *On Individuality and Social Forms.* Chicago: University of Chicago Press.

———. 1994. "Social Conflict, Aggression, and the Body in Euro-American and Asian Social Thought." *International Journal of Group Tensions* 24:3:205–217.

Loiskandl, H., D. Weinstein, and M. Weinstein. 1986. "Introduction." In G. Simmel, *Schopenhauer and Nietzsche.* Urbana, IL: University of Illinois Press.

Menkel-Meadow, C. 1985. "The Transformation of Disputes by Lawyers: What the Dispute Paradigm Does and Does Not Tell Us." *Journal of Dispute Resolution* 25–44.

Ortega y Gasset, José. 1946. *Del Imperio Romano.* Trans. H. Weyl in *Concord and Liberty.* New York: W.W. Norton.

Rapoport, Anatol. 1974. *Conflict in Man-made Environment.* Baltimore: Penguin.

Rogers, N. H., and C. A. McEwen. 1989. *Mediation: Law, Policy, Practice.* Deerfield, IL: Clark Boardman Callaghan.

Shephard, Hon. R. T. 1995. "Judicial Perspective on Indiana ADR." In M.E. Draper and J.N. Stimson (eds.) *Indiana Practitioner Series: Alternative Dispute Resolution.* Rochester, NY: Lawyers Cooperative Publishing.

Simmel, G. 1990 [1900/1907]. *The Philosophy of Money.* Second Enlarged Edition. Trans. T. Bottomore, D. Frisby, and K. Mengelberg. New York: Routledge.

———. 1950 [1908]. *Sociology.* [*Soziologie*]. Trans. K. Wolff. In Wolff, K. (ed.) *The Sociology of Georg Simmel.* New York: Free Press.

———. 1950 [1917]. *Fundamental Questions of Sociology.* [*Grund-*

fragen der Soziologie (Individuum und Gesellschaft)] Trans. K. Wolff. In Wolff, K. *The Sociology of Georg Simmel.* New York: Free Press.

Thibaut, J. and L. Walker. 1978. "A Theory of Procedure." *California Law Review* 66:541–566.

Thomas, K. 1976. "Conflict and Conflict Management." In M. D. Dunnette (ed.) *Handbook of Industrial and Organizational Psychology.* Chicago: Rand McNally.

Voegelin, E. 1991. "The Nature of the Law." In R. A. Pascal, J. L. Babin, and J. W. Corrington (eds.) *The Collected Works, Volume 27.* Baton Rouge: Louisiana State University Press.

Walter, E. V. (n.d.) "Simmel's Sociology of Power: The Architecture of Politics." in K. Wolff (ed.) *Essays on Sociology, Philosophy and Aesthetics.* New York: Harper & Row.

Wolff, K. 1950. "Introduction." Wolff, K. (ed.) *The Sociology of Georg Simmel.* New York: Free Press.

9

CENTRAL THEMES IN SIMMEL'S *THE PHILOSOPHY OF MONEY*

Paul Kamolnick

INTRODUCTION

Georg Simmel's sociological contributions are frequently neglected in sociological theory courses, or if taught, often trivialized. For example, Simmel is often considered in an exclusively micro-sociological context through a brief discussion of dyadic and triadic relations, social distance, and possibly a discussion of his famous essay "The Metropolis and Mental Life." This Simmel-Lite approach transpires in the span of a lecture or two, and is likely the last time most students will encounter Simmel's ideas.

In the past forty years or so, several scholars have sought to remedy this situation, in the process contributing a formidable body of commentary and secondary literature on Simmel.[1] As a result, sociological theorists, cultural theorists, and modern intellectual historians now generally regard Simmel to be one of the most creative thinkers of the great generation of sociological writers in turn of the century Germany.[2] Moreover, several of Simmel's key works have finally been translated into English, and several special conferences assessing Simmel's sociological contributions have been held.[3] It is likely that future generations of interested students will have at their disposal a wider array of Simmel scholarship, and this ought instill an even deeper regard for Simmel's significance.

Owing to this ongoing reappraisal of Simmel's legacy, his most important work, *The Philosophy of Money*,[4] was finally translated into English in 1978, and republished in a second edition in 1990. This work, like Marx's *Capital*, Durkheim's *Division of Labor*, and Weber's *Protestant Ethic and the Spirit of Capitalism*, was Simmel's genuine masterpiece, most fully expressing his ideas, and the one book he never disavowed. Indeed, Simmel's *The Philosophy of Money* is a testament to his struggle to comprehend the elemental foundations of life; it is also a book of social theory. Unfortunately, like Marx's *Capital,* it is a difficult book, and without guidance regarding its central structure, themes, and goals, it can be somewhat intimidating. *The Philosophy of Money* is a densely argued, carefully structured, five-hundred page masterpiece written in 1900 at the height of Simmel's career and revised in 1907 just eleven years prior to his death in 1918.

This chapter provides an overview of key themes in Simmel's *The Philosophy of Money.* I believe it will be of use to introductory students of Simmel and also to anyone who has not yet had the opportunity to analyze the book's structure. Obviously an overview can be only accomplished by omitting many details and digressions constituting the book's genuine beauty. To accomplish this, I organize the chapter under seven subsections, corresponding to the Preface of *The Philosophy of Money,* and the six chapters of that text: (1) Methodology, (2) The Relations of Value, Exchange, and Money, (3) Money as Universal Social-Psychological Institution, (4) Money and Human Agency, (5) Money as Positive Force for Human Freedom, (6) Money as Negative Force for Human Freedom, and (7) Money and Culture.

METHODOLOGY

Simmel's approach to the phenomenon of money is best understood in relation to the view it was intended to replace or at least supplement: Marxism. According to historical materialism, the driving force of human history resides in a given society's economic foundations. This base consists of productive forces such as machinery, science, technology, and the division of labor. Such forces are essential, given that for human history to be possible, one must first produce one's means of physical subsistence through the process of laboring on nature with the use of these productive forces. According to Marx, these productive forces, in tandem with existing natural resources, determine other aspects of organized social life, such as social relations among persons, ownership relations, and prevalent political, religious, and intellectual ideas. For example, a hunter-gatherer society has a meager level of productive forces, does not generate a social surplus, and is socially regulated by relatively egalitarian forms of familial authority. However, the great agrarian empires of classical civilizations, for example, Chinese, East Indian, Egyptian, Aztec, Incan, and Mesopotamian, were possible because of greater productive powers, since slave-labor, metallurgy, animal domestication, and plant cultivation greatly enhanced the level of energy expended, the size of the population that could be sustained, and so forth. Because of these material achievements and the key role that productive forces play, Marx and those who embrace historical materialist explanations grant a deterministic role to a society's economic foundations.[5]

Simmel believes, however, that Marx's theory is incapable of grasping the actual foundations of human history, and that historical materialism has failed to unearth an even *deeper* layer of reality, one that precedes even the economic foundations of a given society.

> Methodologically, [my] basic intention can be expressed in the following manner. [An] attempt is made to construct a new story beneath historical materialism such that the explanatory value of the incorporation of economic life into the causes of intellectual culture is preserved, while these economic forms themselves are recognized as the result of more profound valuations and currents of psychological or even metaphysical preconditions. (1990, 56)

Though economic structures clearly matter, and money is certainly an economic phenomenon, life itself has metaphysical and psychological dimensions that to Simmel are even more basic. One's struggle to make the world meaningful, to develop a sense of value and to translate one's desires, passions, and visions into concrete real forms, shapes the nature of economic life. In sum, money must be understood first and foremost as a reflection of deeper *noneconomic* determinants, and the most important of these is a human being's quest for self-realization and self-valuation.

VALUE, EXCHANGE, AND MONEY

Simmel first discusses the nature of, and relations among, three basic concepts—*value, exchange,* and *money.* Each of these concepts expresses a basic Simmelian thesis, namely, that human life is dualistic. It may be viewed on one hand from the point of view of subjective individuality and particularity, or on the other, with a view to its sociality, objectivity, and universality. Every social phenomenon reveals this inherent dichotomy. *Value* for Simmel is defined as the basic sacrificial price a person is willing to pay or endure to attain a psychologically rewarding existence. This view is similar to the utilitarian and neoclassical economic view that value arises when something is considered a utility or is considered useful and desirable by us. It also has affinities with earlier classical political-economic and

Marxian doctrines that claimed that the use-value of a thing is based on the useful properties and qualities we seek or perceive in an object. For example, an automobile has a use-value, since it provides transportation; a pen likewise has value, since it is a means of expression and communication.

But Simmel's conception of value is also distinct from these views. Value for Simmel has a profoundly and inalterably psychological significance, since value originates for him in the metaphysical quest of each individual's ego to render the world meaningful. Moreover, it is only through an individual differentiating herself from the object she seeks, by separating the desiring act from the object desired, that the peculiar structure of value is revealed.

> [V]alue does not originate from the unbroken unity of the moment of enjoyment, but from the separation between the subject and the content of enjoyment as an object that stands opposed to the subject as something desired and only to be attained by the conquest of distance, obstacles and difficulties. (1990, 66)

Like neoclassical, classical, and Marxian economists before him, Simmel identifies value as a humanly created phenomenon. But unique to Simmel is the deeply metaphysical, psychological, and aesthetic twist he provides; value most profoundly expresses our basic desires, and central to the achievement of value in the world is the constant satiation and renewal of desire in the process of continual sacrifice centered around newly demanded desires.

Exchange performs the essential function for Simmel of organizing subjectively unique, psychologically based valuations into an elementary structure of social interaction. Just as Durkheim insisted that a suprapersonal "society" exists *sui generis,* Simmel insists that ". . . [E]xchange is a sociological phenomenon *sui generis,* an original form and function of social life" (1990, 100). One tends to think of exchange as an exclusively economic phenomenon involving the exchange of money for goods, or vice versa. But just as economic value is merely a more developed form of value as such, Simmel claims that

> Every interaction has to be regarded as an exchange: every conversation, every affection (even if it is rejected), every game, every glance at another person. The difference that seems to exist, that in interaction a person offers what he does not possess whereas in exchange he offers only what he does possess, cannot be sustained. For in the first place, it is always personal energy, the surrender of personal substance, that is involved in in-

teraction; and conversely, exchange is not conducted for the sake of the object that the other person possesses, but to gratify one's personal feelings
which he does not possess. It is the object of the exchange to increase the
sum of value; each party offers to the other more than he possessed before. (1990, 82)

Exchange is the form that enables relativity of all values and the
incomparably individual nature of desire to be organized in a social
relation of reciprocal interaction. The basis of exchange is the desire
to gain something of greater value than one now possesses, whether
that be love, honor, recognition, erotic fulfillment, or material wealth.
The genius of exchange and the true secret to its *sui generis* character is this: exchange simultaneously preserves individuality yet does
so in and through social interaction. Exchange overcomes the purely
subjective as a formal structure of reciprocity, and simultaneously, it
enables fulfillment of subjective desire by providing a social arena for
the positing and realization of value.

> The profound relationship between relativity and socialization, which is
> a direct demonstration of relativity for which mankind presents the
> material, is illustrated here: society is a structure that transcends the in-
> dividual, but that is not abstract. . . . From this arises the unique signifi-
> cance that exchange, as the economic-historical realization of the relativ-
> ity of things, has for society. (1990, 101)

Simmel next introduces his concept of *money*. Normally when one
thinks of money one views it as an instrument for paying bills, or
purchasing products one needs and wants. Often one thinks of the
freedom that money allows: the freedom to engage in leisure, to pursue desires, to do something other than waged-labor. But for Simmel,
in addition to any instrumental role money may have, it also has a
profound philosophical and psychological significance. Money represents, Simmel says, "pure interaction in its purest form . . . money
is the adequate expression of the relationship of man to the world"
(1990, 129). And: "[M]oney as abstract value expresses nothing but
the relativity of things that constitute value; and, at the same time,
that money, as the stable pole, contrasts with the eternal movements, fluctuations and equations of objects" (1990, 121). In short,
money for Simmel symbolizes the highest, most abstract, and therefore complete expression of the fundamental relativity of all things,
values, and subjective human dispositions. Because of its abstractness and symbolic nature, money provides for an indefinite expansion of exchange, of reciprocity underlying exchange, and the ex-

pression of subjective valuation. It is critical to keep in mind that Simmel does not mean here that with time money as a means of payment has simply become a more important feature of life. His argument is more basic than that. Money is to society what blood is to the human body; it is the currency that renders possible the expression of an infinite quantity and quality of values, and it is in principle a permanent feature of modern modes of organized human existence.

Money as Social-Psychological Institution

Simmel develops the varied implications of money for the social-psychological experience of life. Simmel begins this discussion by tracing both the history of money and contradictions arising from that history, as well as concluding with a discussion of the institutional reality of money. Preceding the introduction of money was a system of barter, when specific goods are exchanged for other goods, each being incomparable and therefore traded on the basis of an assessment relative to each transaction. Barter involves the intrinsic, substantive qualities of each product. Replacing barter is the particular equivalent form of money, one that takes the form of one specific commodity established through convention by which all others will be measured, as for example cowrie shells, cattle, salt, or some other valued good. But to perfect money, one must attain the level of a complete abstraction from the qualities of specific properties of goods, and achieve a purely universal and *symbolic* level of representation. This ideal level of symbolic representation, represented in the gold standard, and the American and European currencies of Simmel's time, was viewed by Simmel as an extraordinary achievement of the human mind.

> Money, as a product of this fundamental power or form of our mind, is not only its most extreme example, but is, as it were, its pure embodiment . . . . The significance of money is only to express the value relations between other objects. It succeeds in this with the aid of man's developed intelligence, which is able to equate the relations between things even though the things themselves are not identical or similar. (1990, 147)

Fully developed money expressed as pure symbol is of profound philosophical and sociological significance. Philosophically, pure symbolic money allows the mind to conceive psychological and social infinity. In principle, any conceivable value can be exchanged for money. The entire universe of valued goods, and therefore human valuing itself, has come under a completely universalizable notion. It perfects in philosophical form the basic structure of our psychological life as well. Since for Simmel money is merely an expression of the metaphysical quest confronting each individual in a relativistic world that must be rendered meaningful, money provides an ideal form for the facilitation of this process.

Though a tension must exist between the intrinsic psychological values money is designed to express, and the purely symbolic and universalizable abstractness of money, money nevertheless establishes itself as an elemental sociocultural institution. Simmel unequivocally views money as a sociological institution, through and through.

> A certain comprehensiveness and intensity of social relations is required for money to become effective—otherwise it does not differ at all from other goods that are exchanged—and a further intensification of social relations is needed in order to intellectualize its effects. These conspicuous phenomena illustrate clearly that the inner nature of money is only loosely tied to its material basis, since *money is entirely a sociological phenomenon, a form of human interaction,* its character stands out all the more clearly the more concentrated, dependable and agreeable social relations are. (1990, 172; my emphasis)

This "further intensification of social relations" draws heavily upon Simmel's notions of association, choice, and interaction that make up a "society" and also relies on social differentiation theory. Simmel views the modern, complex social division of labor as a key causal agent giving rise to money, and his interactionist conception of society further allows one to understand precisely what he meant by his terms "sociological phenomenon."

> Society is not an absolute entity which must first exist so that all the individual relations of its members—super- and sub-ordination, cohesion, imitation, division of labour, exchange, common attack and defence, religious community, party formations and many others—can develop within its framework or be represented by it: it is only the synthesis or the general term for the totality of these specific interactions. (1990, 175)[6]

Money and Human Agency

How does money affect human autonomy, psychology, association, and personality? Money is psychologically significant since it directly *shapes the conditions of human freedom and human personality.* Money becomes a necessary means one must use to attain one's in-

tended purposes. Money is the perfected tool, an essential means
that mediates human-to-human and human-to-world interaction. In
short: "The tremendous importance of money for understanding the
basic motives of life lies in the fact that money embodies and subli-
mates the practical relation of man to the objects of his will, his
power and his impotence; one might say, paradoxically, that man is
an indirect being" (1990, 211).

Simmel illustrates the tool-like nature of money in his fascinating
discussions of money's psychological relevance, of the correlations
between degrees of wealth and specific personality attributes, and
also of the peculiar role of money for pariah ethnoreligious groups,
for example, Jews and Armenians. The prevalence of a money-based
social order produces notable changes in human psychology and personality. There is an overwhelming tendency for money to become an
absolute end instead of a conditional means to valued ends. Money
assumes a God-like status, and reduces all possible cultural values
to the mere fact of possession for possession's sake. It is a fetish
whose peculiar power consists in transferring relativity into ab-
soluteness and human independence into human merging with the
possession of an absolute. Questions of value are radically circumscribed, finally, in this worshipful attitude toward money. In a society governed in this way by money, certain personality types and
characteristic attitudes are also made possible: for example, avarice,
extravagance, cynicism, and a blasé attitude may be traceable to the
unique power of money to corrupt the process of human valuation.
Even the ascetic renunciation of materialistic culture, whether by a
priest or member of the counterculture, is explicable only in relation
to this crisis of values. In a world where possession of money has become an end-in-itself, money fails to furnish a meaningful conception
of life.[7]

Simmel identifies transformations in the *quality* of social interaction accompanying differences in wealth among individuals. Money
is unique in that *what* money is, its qualitative existence, is intrin-
sically related to *how much* money one has. Variations in an individual's wealth effect one's orientation toward risk-taking, sensitivity toward social and economic stimuli, the likelihood of expressing
emotional reactions such as anger and resentment, and one's overall
feeling of power. These qualitative changes in human personality
correlate with an individual's degree of wealth and are eventually expressed in the sphere of culture. *How much,* rather than why, how,
or what for, prevails as a generalized cultural norm.

Finally, because money can accrue independently of recognized and officially sanctioned status privilege, it is portable and therefore easily circulates, and is a universal completely abstract means of exchange. Money empowers certain groups who have been otherwise denied access to social rank, privilege, and access to landed estates. For outcast peoples money "provides chances . . . that are open to fully entitled persons or to the indigenous people by specific concrete channels and [only] by personal relationships" (Simmel, 1990, 224).

Money as Positive Force for Freedom

Based on the above account of Simmel's detailing of money's distorting powers, one may be tempted to conclude that Simmel condemns money, that he seeks to minimize its role in culture or that he advocates an alternative social system that would abolish money. That is to misunderstand his intent, however. Simmel seeks to show that negative *and* positive consequences are immanent in money, particularly in relation to the prospects of realizing genuine human freedom and autonomy. His appreciation of money's duality—its extraordinary capacity for enhancing human freedom, but also its negative potential, particularly in relation to traditionalistic social groups that are disadvantaged by the potential liberties associated with money—ensure Simmel's status as one of the outstanding classical theorists of the modern ethical predicament. Unlike reactionary thinkers seeking the return of a premodern, premonetary order, or utopian laissez-faire advocates envisioning the emancipated libertarian society based on freedom and money, Simmel theorized the positive *and* negative dimensions of freedom associated with money.

Freedom is a cardinal value for Simmel, and it demands that one commit to "the development of individuality, the conviction to unfold the core of our being with all its individual desires and feelings" (1990, 298). How, then, does money promote the realization of this freedom? Money payment for the use of one's services, unlike previous patterns of obligatory service like slavery or serfdom, emancipates one from a lifelong bondage to a specific task, location, and vocational one-sidedness. In previous nonmonetized societies a given individual was valued for the unique qualities he or she possessed, and these qualities were obtained during the individual's lifetime. Money's very abstractness and impersonality, however, allows an individual to engage in a broad array of pursuits; since the individual can be compensated for any expenditure of labor, one is free to explore and engage in a greater variety of potentially satisfying expressions of one's life energies. In place of lifetime servitude, individuals may examine many aspects of their personality, and this is due in great measure to money's indifference to the specific features of concrete labor:

> Money is the ideal representative of such a condition since it makes possible relationships between people but leaves them personally undisturbed; it is the exact measure of material achievements, but is very inadequate for the particular and the personal. (1990, 303)

Money also allows a more intensive relationship to objects one may wish to possess, and therefore, a deeper sense of selfhood. For Simmel possessing objects in the world is not a merely passive phenomenon; we do not simply "hold" or "have" or "gain" an object. Rather, possession is an active process through which one projects one's personality, values, and desires into the world and deliberately seeks ownership and a confirmation of selfhood through self-mastery. Ownership of objects confirms to a self that it is effective in this world, and this sense of power produces an assertive, world-making attitude. Human autonomy is based in active possession and self-mastery, and it is Simmel's belief that money greatly enhances the intensity and extensivity of this process. Moreover, because of the modern industrial capitalist class system that separates laboring from ownership and control of the means of production and products of labor—what Simmel refers to as separating "being" from "having"—a society-wide potential for active possession has now been created.

Simmel celebrates the value of individuation, but he is adamant that this is only possible within a given social division of labor. Human personality arises within this sphere of mutual interdependence, and therefore authentic freedom can never turn on the notion of an isolated individual; rather, freedom turns on precise relations between forms of association and individual psychic life. The size of groups, forms of association, social and technical division of labor, the importance of capitalism as a form of work organization, all directly shape the nature of psychological life, and vice versa. In fact, money is instrumental for allowing one to pursue common objectives, while still retaining one's personal noninvolvement.

> Here we have one of the most effective cultural formations, namely the possibility of the individual participating in associations, the objective purpose of which he wants to promote and enjoy, without that connection implying any commitment on his part. Money has made it possible for peo-

ple to join a group without having to give up any personal freedom and reserve.

. . . Only money could bring about such associations which in no way prejudiced the individual member; only money could create, in its pure form, the association of particular purposes—a type of organization that united individuals' non-personal elements in a project. Money has provided us with the sole possibility for uniting people while excluding everything personal and specific. (1990, 345)

Money and the Negation of Freedom

Money discloses striking new personal vistas; however, a money-based social order can also undermine human freedom. One may comprehend this potential for negativity by examining the relationship between personal value and money value. The monetary fine for criminal acts—including murder—is a key example of equating a fundamental human value, that is, the dignity of human life, with money. Today, insurance companies, tort lawyers, and the courts routinely calculate losses associated with loss of one's life, limb(s), or hardships caused thereby, in monetary terms. In many congregations, tithing, besides supporting a church, replaces more ancient sacrificial rites, for example, the sacrificing of a first-born son, a beast of burden, or source of sustenance. These intrinsic, absolute values are now for us moderns, expressible in terms of price or money. The absolute value of a woman, though circumscribed by a patriarchal order, came also to be expressed in terms of "bride-price." The equating of the value of women with money persists in the ritual of purchasing flowers and "priceless" jewelry; these ultimate expressions of the absolute value a person is deemed to hold for another. One is not bought for money, and thereby cheapened. Simmel's point is quite the opposite: No matter how abstract money appears to be, and no matter its apparent indifference to the specific properties of people and things, money still expresses absolute, intrinsic values.

But under what conditions might this transformation of personal into money value undermine rather than support human freedom? Simmel is explicit:

. . . if the obligated person cannot simply be paid off with a concrete return [i.e., a sum of money] but if he has acquired a right, an influence, a personal importance through this relationship; and this is precisely because he contributes such a definite personal relationship. Under such circumstances, the objectification of the relationship brought about by changing to the money form of payment will have unfavorable results. (1990, 395)

Simmel illustrates this point by describing the process of "proletarianization": the process through which persons bound by traditional relations of labor service, for example, a subsistence peasant owning his own plot of land or sharing a commons, a serf tied to her owner's estate, or a slave functioning as the private property of his owner, are dispossessed of their personal, specific relations and transformed into landless wage-laborers. They are cut adrift to fend for themselves. Traditional forms of labor servitude are incompatible with modern notions of liberty, but *at least* these specific titles and duties in general guaranteed individuals a subsistence right. Dislodged from this traditional system of reciprocal rights and obligations, these newly created wage laborers are now unable to guarantee subsistence without exchanging labor-power for a wage.

> Thus the extreme danger for the peasant of being 'liberated' by cash payments is part of the general pattern of human freedom. It is true he gained freedom, but only freedom *from* something, not liberty *to do* something. . . . Because the freedom that money offers is only a potential, formal, and negative freedom, to receive money in exchange for the positive contents of life implies the selling of personal values (1990, 402–403).

Simmel is distressed by proletarianization, but his criticisms are more far-ranging: the transformation of absolute, particular existence for mere potentiality inaugurated through the money-form ramifies throughout culture and societal relations generally. Simmel insists that one recognize this two-sidedness to modern freedom: whether freedom is a positive, defined, specific entitlement or obligation, or is mere potential vested in possession of the abstract, indifferent symbolic equivalent—money.[8]

Money and Culture

Simmel concludes *The Philosophy of Money* by examining money's effects on modern culture. His discussion begins with an examination of money's effects on mental life and mental conception; he then discusses money's effects on culture generally; finally, Simmel examines how money shapes distinct styles of life, and thereby, distinct relations of distance between the self and its object world. Simmel views mental life within the terms of a dualistic notion of the human self.

On one side lies the irrational vital elements of one's nature—sensuous, impulse-driven, particular, instinctual bodily drives, and on the other lies one's intellect, understood by Simmel to be a distinctly rational faculty, that is, one's mind. One's rational mind, unlike one's irrational will, has a transpersonal, objective, and social nature. By its very constitution this human mind is formed as a social phenomenon, irreducible to the subjective desires or thoughts of an individual. Mind is basic for Simmel since, following a hermeneutic tradition that emphasizes human reason in guiding human behavior, he believes that shared objective culture is produced by mind, and that in his words, the mind *objectifies* or gives reality to the world.

> The objectification of the mind provides the form that makes the conservation and accumulation of mental labour possible; it is the most significant and most far-reaching of the historical categories of mankind ... the objectification of the mind in words and works, organizations and traditions is the basis for this distinction by which man takes possession of his world, or even of any world at all. (1990, 453)[9]

As objective culture develops, Simmel states, intellect is forced into a direction of greater objectivity and relates to the world of particular values in the same way that money relates to the particularity of values. This ever-increasing depersonalizing, abstract human intellect is the vehicle through which each individual can share in generalized cultural products, and therefore facilitates a higher degree of individuation. For example, though no particular individual is responsible for instituting the arts, culture, journalism, science, or technology, each is able to appropriate and use these cultural products: a complex division of labor creates them but each individual may consume them. Supra-personalness, abstractness, and objectivity are also manifest in other cultural products, for example, logical reasoning, statutory law, and the widespread existence of calculation and calculability evident in society, including the modern invention of time-clocks. In Simmel's estimation, this universalization of formal rationality, evident in the emptying out of cultural contents in support of a purely formal or abstract existence, was becoming ever-prevalent in the culture of his time.

The modern, complex division of labor and the capitalist organization of industrial production were key phenomena associated with this rise of formal rationality in society. Simmel believed, like Spencer and Durkheim, that the modern division of labor was a necessary and historically inevitable fact of life. The modern functional differentiation of tasks demands a social division of labor involving the combined energies of all society's participants. Moreover, modern forms of individuation, personal identity, and freedom, were inconceivable without the increased productivity of labor, availability of cultural products, and potential for social mobility accompanying the relatively open system of social class stratification. Nonetheless, Simmel also identifies those genuine dangers (to human freedom) associated with the modern capitalist division of labor, as for example: the narrowing of one's personality due to the detailed, repetitive character of factory work; the estrangement workers experience when separated from their means of laboring and labor-process; elimination of older forms of solidarity accompanying artisanship, such as a tailor's personal relation to his customer; and heightening estrangement from one's surroundings, since one is surrounded by products one did not create, under conditions one does not control. Even fashion may betray its potential for freedom, since the very essence of fashion is to eliminate stability in one's identity in favor of an ever-changing cycle of innovation.[10]

The modern industrial capitalist division of labor produces estrangement, but Simmel is at pains to point out that extremely important positive phenomena also arise. The creation of a relatively cultured lay public, the possibility of scientific work and achievements, new forms of interdependency among people, and a deepened awareness of one's own individuality, make the modern form of the division of labor inescapable and, indeed, desirable.

Finally, money affects our experience of temporal and spatial distance. Modern art both attracts and repels the public. Symbolist painting for example, aims at an abstracted, mediated sense of reality, whereas modern notions of subjectivist taste and judgment celebrate the immediate, unmediated artistic experience. Widespread availability of money credit extends the quantity and range of circulating goods and people, and because credit varies according to a given individual's credit worthiness, it enhances our ability to distinguish among persons based on matters of trust, risk, and honesty. Extensive availability of electricity, communication, and transportation creates a ceaseless, restless, 24-hour day, and as a consequence, traditional rhythms and symmetries of life based on seasonal natural cycles are no longer observed. However, in place of ancient seasonal regularities, new regularities govern modern life, such as a standardized workday, and the cyclical boom-bust capitalist business cycle.

Money itself assumes a pivotal role in modern culture; overabundance of money leads to inflationary expectations and declines in consumer and worker confidence, as well as to an acceleration or deceleration of consumer purchasing. And money's very abstractness ensures that it can be centrally concentrated in great banks and financial institutions. The quantitative features of money discussed earlier allow for an increase in the velocity at which money may circulate, allowing a mobilization of values for practically any purpose, and in defiance of any spatial and temporal limitation.

CONCLUSION

For much of the twentieth century Simmel's *The Philosophy of Money* has been a relatively neglected work in the English-speaking world. This neglect contributes to a highly circumscribed interpretation of Simmel's sociological contributions and to an underestimation of Simmel's force as a classical German social theorist. In this great work Simmel first explores the relations of value, exchange, and money, and then guides us through his analysis of the many consequences money holds for modern social life. Money is a basic social institution. It is a necessary means for attaining personal goals, and the freedom that a money-based society contains is positive—it allows for genuine individualism and promotes an all-rounded individual. But such freedom is also negative—for example, in the potential freedom that is wasted owing to one's loss of subsistence and loss of attachment to a guaranteed order of responsibilities and duties. No matter how relative money appears, however, Simmel assures us that the basis for all value resides in one's psychological and metaphysical quest to render the world meaningful and to attain more value from this world than one had before one entered it. Modern culture, for Simmel, and for us, remains a contradictory, dualistic, divided phenomenon; it opens up prospects for a radical new sense of modern individualism, yet it also presents opportunities for estrangement from this project of accomplished, fulfilled personality. Modernity also has a tragic structure for Simmel since the attempt by individuals to fully realize their total personality can only be frustrated by the overwhelming and inexorable logic of the growth of suprapersonal, formalistic, rationalistic, objective culture.

But tragedy admits of both good and evil, of affirmation and negation. Simmel's genius, and perhaps the chief reason for the contemporary renaissance in Simmel scholarship, consists precisely in the sheer depth of his portrayal of modernity's two faces—of its good *and* evil. Future accounts of Simmel may regard *The Philosophy of Money* as *the* most comprehensive statement of his overall vision. In any

event, it is an enduring analysis of the nature of modernity, modern
selfhood, and the quest for individual freedom.

NOTES

1. A handful of sociologists translated and published important selections from some of Simmel's most important works. For the most influential
edited volumes of Simmel's work, see Wolff (1950), Levine (1971), Etzkorn
(1968), and Oakes (1984). For important recent commentary on aspects of
Simmel's work, or overviews of his entire project, see Levine (1981;1985, chs.
5, 6, 9; 1989) and Frisby (1981, 1984).

2. See Levine (1976) for an assessment of Simmel's influence on American sociology.

3. Several important essays were translated for the first time in Etzkorn
(1968), Oakes (1984), Levine (1971) and Wolff (1950). Four of Simmel's books
have also been translated: *The Philosophy of Money* (1900/trans. 1978), *The
Problems of the Philosophy of History* ([1892–1907]/trans. 1977), *Schopenhauer and Nietzsche* (1907/trans. 1986), and *Sociology* (1908/trans. in Wolff
[1950], Wolff and Bendix [1955], and Levine [1971]).

4. David Frisby, (ed.) *The Philosophy of Money* [*Philosophie des Geldes*
[1900/1907]. 2nd enlarged ed. Trans. by Tom Bottomore and David Frisby.
London and New York: Routledge, 1990. First published in English translation in 1978.

5. Marx (1976 [1845–46], 19–93; 1982 [1846], 95–106; 1987 [1859],
261–65).

6. See Frisby (1984b) and Köhnke (1990) for important discussions of
Simmel's uniquely social-psychological conception of society.

7. Simmel's discussion of fetishism has many parallels to Marx's discussion in *Capital* (1967 [1867], 76–87). Marx's and Simmel's critique of the cor-
rupting power of money is evident in their earliest writings: see for example, Marx (1975 [1844], 322–326) and Simmel (1968 [1896], 79–80).

8. See Paul Gomberg's essay in this volume for amplification of this
point in the writings of Hegel and Marx.

9. See Ron Schultz's essay in this volume for the origins of this conception of mind-objectified culture in Dilthey's and Hegel's notions of objective
spirit (*Objektiver Geist*).

10. Simmel's discussion of alienation and estrangement is remarkable.
Not only does it parallel in significant ways the very famous discussion of
alienation Marx produced in his now-classic *Economic and Philosophic
Manuscripts of 1844*, but Simmel was completely unaware of Marx's work,
since it was first made available to the reading public in 1932, fourteen years
after Simmel's death.

REFERENCES

Etzkorn, P. (ed. and trans). 1968. *Georg Simmel: The Conflict in Mod-
        ern Culture and Other Essays.* New York: Teachers College
        Press.

Frisby, D. 1981. *Sociological Impressionism: A Reassessment of Georg Simmel's Social Theory.* London: Heinemann.

———. 1984a. *Georg Simmel.* Chichester, Eng.: Ellis Horwood.

———. 1984b. "Georg Simmel and Social Psychology." *Journal of the History of the Behavioral Sciences,* 20(2):107–27.

Köhnke, K. 1990. "Four concepts of Social Science at Berlin University: Dilthey, Lazarus, Schmoller and Simmel." In M. Kaern et al. (eds.) *Georg Simmel and Contemporary Sociology.* Dordrecht/Boston/London: Kluwer.

Levine, D. (ed.). 1971. *George Simmel: On Individuality and Social Forms.* Chicago: University of Chicago Press.

———. 1981. "Sociology's Quest for the Classics: The Case of Simmel." 60–80, in *The Future of the Sociological Classics.* Ed. Buford Rhea. London: Allen Unwin.

———. 1985. *The Flight from Ambiguity: Essays in Social and Cultural Theory.* Chicago: University of Chicago Press.

———. 1989. "Simmel as a Resource for Sociological Metatheory." *Sociological Theory,* 7(2), Fall:161–74.

Levine, D., E. B. Carter and E. M. Gorman. 1976. "Simmel's Influence on American Sociology, I & II." *American Journal of Sociology,* 81 (4 & 5), 813–845, 112–132.

Marx, K. 1975 [1844]. "Economic and Philosophic Manuscripts of 1844." In *Collected Works,* vol. 3. Moscow: Progress Publishers.

———. 1976 [1845–46]. "The German Ideology: Part I." In *Collected Works,* vol. 5. Moscow: Progress Publishers.

———. 1982 [1846]. "Marx's Letter to Annenkov, 28 December 1846." In *Collected Works,* vol. 38. Moscow: Progress Publishers.

———. 1987 [1859]. "Preface to *Contribution to the Critique of Political Economy.*" In *Collected Works,* vol. 29. New York: International Publishers.

———. 1967 [1867]. *Capital.* New York: International Publishers.

Oakes, G. (ed. and trans). 1984. *Georg Simmel on Women, Sexuality and Love.* New Haven, CT: Yale University Press.

Simmel, Georg. 1977 [1892/1905/1907]. *The Problems of the Philosophy of History.* [orig. *Die Probleme der Geschichtsphilosophie*]. trans. and ed. with Introduction by Guy Oakes. New York: Free Press.

———. 1968 [1896]. "Sociological Aesthetics." In P. Etzkorn (ed.) *Georg Simmel: The Conflict in Modern Culture and Other Essays.* New York: Teacher's College Press; Teacher's College, Columbia University.

———. 1990 [1900/1907a]. *The Philosophy of Money* [orig. *Die*

Philosophie des Geldes]. 2nd enlarged ed. Ed. David Frisby; trans. T. Bottomore and D. Frisby. New York and London: Routledge.

————. 1986 [1907b]. *Schopenhauer and Nietzsche.* [orig. *Schopenhauer und Nietzsche*]. trans. Helmut Loiskandl, Deena Weinstein, and Michael Weinstein. Amherst: University of Massachussetts Press.

Wolff, Kurt H.(ed. and trans). 1950 [1908]. *The Sociology of Georg Simmel.* New York: Free Press.

Wolff, Kurt H., and R. Bendix (eds. and trans.). 1955. *Conflict* and *The Web of Group Affliliations.* New York: Free Press.

10

THE HISTORICAL AND BIOGRAPHICAL CONTEXT OF MAX WEBER'S METHODOLOGY

Randall Halle

INTRODUCTION

Max Weber contributed central definitions to modern sociological theory. Despite this fact, his influence and reputation in Germany differs significantly from his perception in American sociology. The difference has many sources, but the main one is the distinct separation, in the American scholarly context, between Weber's methodological work and his political work. In Germany, Weber's political writings were as well known as his theoretical ones. Given that the focus of these writings was the political situation in Germany, the reception of Weber in America has tended to overlook the political writings, concentrating on what then appears to be purely theoretical works. The failure to draw out the connections between the two creates an uneven framework for American students of Weber who seek to assess fully Weber's work and to approach critically the pervasive sociological dictum—now commonplace—of value-neutrality that originated with Weber.[1]

In an attempt to examine these connections and deepen the readers' appreciation for Weber, I want to explore Weber's social and historical context. First, I will give an overview of the political development of Germany during Weber's lifetime, along with a parallel development in Weber's own biography. I will then acquaint the reader with the key terms of Weber's methodology and then finally examine how the concept of value-neutrality sought to respond to the problems of this period.

WEBER'S HISTORICAL CONTEXT

The politically and socially volatile era stretching from the German *Kaiserreich* to the immediate aftermath of World War I covers

169

the lifespan of Max Weber, serving as the historical setting for his work. What this section will seek to do is to provide both a brief overview of significant events from 1871–1923 as well as some conceptual frameworks for understanding this period and its impact on Weber. This section will supply the reader with a necessary context as well as an organizing principle for the rest of the chapter. I hope the reader will recognize this as an invitation to further study of a complex period.

The year 1871 marks the foundation of the Second German Reich. The bourgeois revolution of 1848 had failed to form a nation-state out of the myriad of independent German kingdoms, principalities, duchies, bishopherics, and city-states left-over from the Holy Roman Empire. But what the revolutionary politics of the bourgeoisie could not accomplish, eventually came about from the economic pressures of industrialization and the hegemony of Prussia under the leadership of Prince Otto Von Bismarck. Bismarck staged a series of wars that had the effect of forging a union of the various states and polities, excluding the weakened multinational Austro-Hungarian empire, and constructing a complicated system of alliances on the continent that provided the new state with a central and relatively stable role in European politics.

The date 1871, however, should not be viewed as marking the culmination of a national awakening, the achievement of some Hegelian *Volksgeist*. Rather in this year there began a process of nation-building under the direction of Bismarck.[2] Perhaps the most significant achievement of 1871 was the resulting reformulation of the public sphere. The nation-state allowed for new forms of communication and political interaction. Separate parties, unions, and interest groups from Munich to Hamburg could unite into larger mass movements. National media directed attention beyond limited borders to distant centers of government. Redrawn borders created a new sense of inside and outside, domestic and foreign.

The new parameters of the public sphere allowed three basic political postures: nationalist *Realpolitik,* antinationalist, and national idealist. The phrase *Realpolitik* emerged in the period after 1848 and its use expanded after 1871 as a means to designate a politics of compromise and conformity to existing conditions. Members of the nobility, seeking to maintain their dominant role in the government, had to accept limited constitutional controls. Bourgeois liberals accepted favorable economic conditions without equivalent political influence. They hoped this influence would follow. Both groups were willing to accept the given conditions of the new state based on the immediate gains such a compromise provided.

In this political position lay perhaps the best example of what Weber would describe as action based on instrumental reason. The willingness to conform is based primarily on a rational assessment of the positive possibilities for the expansion of self-interest. As Weber pointed out, however, such *Realpolitik* only recognizes the legitimacy of the state in a limited fashion. It provides no emotional, traditional, or value-based allegiance. I will return to these points later in the discussion of Weber's methodology.

An *antinationalist* posture rejected the nation-state entirely. It was a position forced upon (and to a certain extent adopted by) both the Catholics and the socialists. These were groups who recognized governmental legitimacy not in the new nation-state, but elsewhere in what Weber described as value-rational or affectual bonds. Bismarck utilized this antinationalist position in his nation-building process by identifying the Catholics and socialists as the empire's inner enemies and making them objects of persecution. From 1871–1878 the *Kulturkampf* [Culture War] unleashed a wave of oppression on Catholics, the majority in the regions along the Rhine and in the South. The depression of the 1870s resulted in Bismarck withdrawing support from the liberal parties in favor of protectionist economics. The end of the liberal era brought a shift in the persecution away from Catholics. From 1878–1890 the government upheld the antisocialist laws which attacked socialist and left-liberal organizations. Accordingly, liberal representation in the *Reichstag* all but disappeared and support for a national idealist stance rose.

The *national idealists* emerged slowly in the Reich and can be characterized as highly critical of the existing conditions. For the national idealists, 1871 marked at best the *political* formation of the nation. They now sought the *cultural* transformation into a national community (*Volksgemeinschaft.*) Whereas the antinationalists opposed the state with a distinct value system, national idealists criticized the state through the very language of nationalism promoted by the state. They wanted to create a truly German state and the egalitarian aspect of a national "brotherhood" appealed to many national liberals. National idealism offered them a way to influence the state from within the terms of its own rhetoric. The dismissal in 1890 of Bismarck by the new Kaiser, Wilhelm II, and the expansion of the nation-building process as a response to the antinationalists helped spur the rise of the national idealists.[3] Instead of parliamentary par-

ties, they organized into special interest groups. The parliament had
been kept purposefully weak and ineffectual during Bismarck's reign,
and it continued to be hemmed in under Wilhelm II who instead expanded the influence of the military and bureaucratic agencies that
were directly answerable to him. The national idealist special interest groups stood farthest on the right of the political spectrum and
acted as jingoist chauvinist critics of the state. They directly encouraged the Kaiser and bureaucracy in anti-Semitic, imperialist, and
social-Darwinist policies.

In his methodology Weber concentrated extensively on providing
definitions that helped analyze interest groups, their social and political structures, and their goals. We will see that although Weber
presented his terms as having a universal analytic potential for sociological research, the amount of consideration devoted to such social forms as interest groups indicates clearly how well suited these
terms were to analyzing Weber's own era. Along with exhibiting concern for special interest groups, Weber's work paid a great deal of attention to the role of bureaucracy in the functioning of the modern
state. Because Bismarck had purposefully kept the parliamentary
parties weak and easily divided, the bureaucracy became the institution through which the state increasingly functioned. In the period
following his dismissal and up to World War I, the role of the civil
servants was strengthened and expanded.

Bureaucracy is common to all modern states, yet in Germany it
took on a specific significance.[4] With the failure of the bourgeois revolution of 1848, the formation from the top down of the German
nation-state in 1871, and the relatively minor role accorded the
Reichstag in the constitution, the bourgeoisie experienced a form of
increasing disenfranchisement from the direction of government. Yet
simultaneously they were invited to assume civil servant positions
through which they could be integrated into the process of government as loyal agents of an aristocratic will. In opposition to loyalist
subservience, Weber recognized a need for a bureaucracy based on
impartial voices that could be relied upon to inform the government
of harsh as well as favorable realities and assist in the making of policy decisions. Such voices could not come from a bureaucracy which
was by definition subservient to the king. And it certainly could not
come from the special interests.[5]

Such conditions particularly suited the young monarch. His ambitions to lead government resulted in Bismarck's dismissal. Wilhelm II was, however, ill-equipped to replace the elder statesman.
The Kaiser tended to make policy decisions based more on whim and

personality than on the basis of a long-range vision. The Kaiser's main motivation was a dilettante interest in the military. He had an open ear for the jingoism of the special interest groups and succeeded in a very short time in alienating most of Germany's former allies. His frequent changes in policy decisions resulted in equally frequent appointment and dismissal of chancellors. They contributed dramatically to the European entente of the era and made almost inevitable the outbreak of World War I. Such conditions relied on a large bureaucracy and strong military subservient to the Kaiser's will.

In 1914 the assassination of Archduke Franz Ferdinand of Austria served as the spark that ignited the war. The system of alliances that had replaced those crafted by Bismarck drew one major European power after another into war against each other. Germany lacked strong allies and had to rely significantly on the strength of its military-industrial output and the total mobilization of the homefront. Accounts of the first days and months of the war universally report a united spirit among the people. For many this was seen as an achievement of the German *Volksgeist* in the face of national peril. The initial German successes in battle furthered this sense and validated the uncompromising chauvinism of the national idealists. As the war dragged on, however, the initial jubilation gave way to the hardships of a wartime economy and the enormous loss of life. An attitude of "endure until the end" set in, but the end goals defined by the unrealistic expectations of the far right, the military, and the special interest groups continued to recede into the horizon. Unwillingness to compromise and blindness to the real social conditions forced a total collapse of both warfront and homefront in 1918.

From November 1918 to 1923 a state of civil war and economic crisis existed in Germany. In Weberian terms, the successor government led by the socialists lacked value-rational legitimacy among vast portions of the people and it was unable to provide the economic stability necessary for broad instrumental support. Militias ruled large areas and fostered frequent attempts from both the right and the left to overthrow the government. The system entered into a phase of relative stability only after economic reforms in 1923 put an end to the runaway inflation that robbed many middle class citizens of their savings. Unfortunately during the next six years of relative stability the government failed to establish legitimacy or hegemony, so that in 1929 when the Great Depression broke out the government collapsed with the economy.

WEBER'S BIOGRAPHY

The Weber family consisted of significant figures in the historical setting described above. From his earliest days on, Max Jr. was exposed to and involved in the significant questions posed to the new nation-state. Max Weber, Sr. was an official within the National Liberal Party which played a significant role in the formation of the Second Reich and the promotion of *Realpolitik* as a stance. The Weber household welcomed many of the leading political and academic *intellectuals* of the time. As an adult Max Jr. married one of the leading figures in the bourgeois women's movement. Both Marianne and Max were well respected in Germany and, like his childhood home, their household continued to welcome many of the influential figures of their era.

With his move to attend university in 1882 Weber moved away from his father's politics and towards a more conservative position. He was influenced in the move by his military service in what was then the Eastern Prussian territories, which are now part of Poland. There he witnessed first hand the conditions and the successes of the state's "germanization" attempts in the region. Weber became outspoken on the Polish question, supporting the expansion of German influence in the region by advocating the development of modern industrial farming techniques. According to Weber such techniques could replace the old estate system, which had come to rely on cheap migrant Polish labor and thus free the border regions from the Polish presence. In 1893 Weber joined the Pan-German League, one of the most significant proponents of a national idealist stance, and went on lectures on their behalf. In those lectures he discussed the colonization of these territories.

Weber held his most significant lecture on the topic in 1894 with his inaugural address at the University of Freiburg. The address moved between both a *Realpolitik* and a national idealist position; this ambivalence is exemplified best perhaps by the statement: "such are the circumstances, that our state form is a nation-state, which gives us the right to make these demands" (1958, 11). The demands he made in this lecture were extremely significant for Germany. In fact this lecture is often cited as the point at which the language and goals of national imperialism were made acceptable to the general German public and especially to the (liberal) middle class.

Using the "Polish question" as the focus of his speech, Weber advocated an imperialist expansionism that would (1) secure Germany's position among the great nations, (2) rationalize agrarian production and strengthen the economic and political position of the middle class, and (3) solve the social questions of the proletariat that rapid industrialization had precipitated. Weber distinguished between the economic interests of the ruling classes and the interests of the nation, arguing that the two are not always the same. The disparity of interest between nation and business required that the state adopt a national economic policy that would foster imperialism. Weber employed phrases from the farthest right in his speech, like "struggle for existence" (*Kampf ums Dasein*), and "power politics" (*Machtpolitik*). Such phrases were "calling cards" of the proto-fascist special interest groups.

Yet it should be kept in mind that what Weber was advocating differed little from the policies of any of the world powers of the time. English and French colonial expansion was fostered by similar arguments. The Monroe Doctrine, the Spanish-American War, or the speeches of the great American orator Henry Cabot Lodge were all cut from similar rhetorical cloth. Expansionist language was part of the era. It is important to keep this in mind so that Weber is not simplistically identified as a proto-fascist. Rather we should be able to see Weber as participating in the significant and recurring debates of modernity. Indeed, Weber's description of the threat of the Polish migrant workers stealing the good jobs and driving down wages differs little from current perceptions in the United States and in Europe concerning the threats to national economies from migrant labor. An awareness of such positions only enhances the ongoing study and application of Weber's work.

Weber would eventually distance himself from the "Polish question," in part because the government adopted an economic course that made impossible the policies he had advocated. The government instituted tariffs that allowed the Junkers[6] to maintain their power without having to modernize or give up their reliance on cheap Polish laborers. His departure from the Pan-German League in 1900 signaled not only a change on the "Polish question," but also a related reanalysis of the function of nationalism. Weber never turned his back on national imperialism, in fact if anything he only became a more fervent advocate. However, he distanced himself from the increasingly vociferous national idealists, openly rejecting the notion that the nation was an essential genetic or linguistic community. Weber came to describe the nation as originating "from a common political fate, membership in the same political community and not from any objective anthropological kinship" (Mommsen 1984, 51). In

this, historian Wolfgang Mommsen points out, Weber came to re-
semble closely Ernest Renan's formulation of the nation as a daily
plebiscite. In Weberian terms the nation is a communal association
(*Vergemeinschaftung*), based on the value-rational actions that unite
its citizens. Weber would elaborate in detail on this political base of
the nation in *Economy and Society*.

With much foresight, Weber focused his attention on political developments that only became more urgent during the reign of Wilhelm
II: the crisis of parliamentary representation, the need for democratic
reforms, and the threat posed by the expansion of the bureaucracy.
The previous section discussed briefly the interconnectedness of these
three points and the reasons behind them. As solutions to the crisis of
governance Weber advocated a democratization of political culture to
meet these challenges and to transform the Germans into a *Herren-
volk* [master race] (Mommsen 1984, 392). Weber's notion of democracy
differed, however, from that employed typically in the United States
Weber was wary of the rule of the majority over the minority.[7] Democratization meant for Weber a form of consensus building through
politics; a unified public political will formed the center of Weber's conception of the nation. This concept of democratization sought to
strengthen the role of the weakened parliament, yet Weber did not advocate an expansion of the legislative powers of the Reichstag. In response to the threat that bureaucratic expansion posed to the function
of parliament, he advocated for the Reichstag a simple right of inquiry
into the functioning of the bureaucracy. He hoped to imbue the parliament with a policing function viz-a-viz the bureaucracy.

The war presented a number of serious challenges to Weber's political stance. Initially Weber opposed the war. He felt that the weak
system of alliances German diplomats since Bismarck had maintained would guarantee military defeat. However, the experience of
mobilization, the unification into collective will, led him to change
his mind, albeit with some reservations. Weber advocated a short
war that would consolidate the initial territorial gains without later
eliciting a general European desire for revenge, like the wars that
had consolidated the German Reich in 1871.

Political conditions on the homefront presented little opportunity
for Weber to be heard. His plans for reform were not instituted until
Weber had the opportunity to work on the drafting of the Weimar
Constitution in the aftermath of World War I. At the outbreak of the
war the Kaiser had called on the political parties in the time of national crisis to put aside their differences and support the war effort.
In effect this silenced any opposition and strengthened the influence

of the special interest groups and the military which pushed for ever-more far-reaching, expansionist war aims. In numerous articles Weber sought to point out the danger of total collapse that such policies presented. And thus he devoted his attention to the reform efforts that would be required after the war.

METHODOLOGY

Weber's final work *Economy and Society* (1910–14, 1918–20) represents the most mature expression of his methodology. The two volumes were written in two periods, 1910–14 and 1918–20. In the current form of publication, the second volume actually preceded the first in the chronology of writing. The opening goal of the first volume of the work was to bring clarity to the role of the discipline of sociology. The importance of this work is incalculable for the discipline because it was during Weber's lifetime, and in part due to his work, that sociology emerged as a distinct field of study. It drew practitioners from the traditional fields of philosophy, history, and, to a certain extent law, but lacked a unifying terminology.

A comparison of the text of *Economy and Society* to the writings of Kant and Hegel reveals that its style is typical of German social philosophical writings. Definitional statements are followed by distinct points of elaboration and refinement. In this manner, the first chapter sets forth the basic terms through which sociological investigation can take place. It establishes a common language of practice for sociologist. However, although its form may be typical, its content is not. Central to the emergence of this discipline, and a key contribution of Weber, was a shift away from the traditional activity of moral and ethical philosophy: the description of how ideal society should be organized, toward a description of how real society is organized. From the opening sentence, Weber makes this intention clear: "Sociology is a science concerning itself with the interpretive understanding of social action and thereby with a causal explanation of its course and consequences" (1978 [1923], 4).

By defining social action as the object of sociological inquiry, Weber focuses on activity that is related to other individuals. He distinguishes social action from simple behavior by virtue of the meaning actors attach to their actions. This distinction separates sociology from a purely descriptive behaviorism or determinism. Sociology should not conduct a search for laws that govern human behavior, rather it should concern itself with interpreting the meaning attached to human action.

The precision with which Weber chose the terms of these definitions cannot be overlooked. In the opening statement he uses the
German word *Handeln,* translated here generally as action. The use
of this word indicates clearly the broad field Weber intends as the object of sociology. *Handeln* denotes a type of intersubjective economy
of behavior. Exchange, trade, intercourse could perhaps serve as better translations than simple action or activity. The choice of *Handeln*
also defined sociology as an ongoing project. Because forms of exchange change over time, new meanings are continually being produced, giving rise to new objects of study.

Weber focused the study of social action on individuals. The individual is the producer of subjectively understandable behavior. What
distinguished Weber dramatically from other sociologists of the period was his complete insistence on this point. Weber insists that
even when groups, like societies, nations, guilds, etc, are being discussed, they should be treated as individuals. In general Weber's colleagues proceeded from the thesis that the community or society is a
meaningful body, and they viewed the individual as a dependent or-
gan in that body.[8] Weber's orientation toward the individual subject
did not suggest, however, the assertion of an inexhaustible heterogeneity of human behavior. Individuals do not exist in an endless
state of unique variation. At the center of the interpretive project of
sociology is the description of ideal types. In defining the activity of
sociology, Weber separates it from history whose object is similar.
History for Weber is the discipline that is oriented towards an "explanation of individual action" (Ibid., 19), while sociology turns to the
actions of the individual as typical. The definition of what is typical
is developed in the course of Weber's discussion of the various modes
of social action.

Weber distinguished four types of social action that have since become classic to sociological inquiry. *Traditional action* is "determined
by ingrained habituations," (Ibid., 25) and as such hovers at the border between reactive or initiative behaviors and meaningful action.
Affectual action lingers at the same borders; it is action that is "determined by the actor's specific affects and feeling states" (Ibid., 25).
Value-rational action, however, is "determined by a conscious belief
in the value for its own sake of some ethical, aesthetic, religious, or
other form of behavior independently of its prospects of success"
(Ibid., 25). *Instrumentally rational action* is "determined by expectations as to the behavior of objects in the environment and of other
human beings: these expectations are used as 'conditions' or 'means'
for the attainment of the actor's own rationally pursued and calcu-

lated ends" (Ibid., 24). The final category is also determined by self-conscious action.

In this schema the types of individual social action can in turn give rise to consistent patterns of greater social action; for example, traditional action gives rise to customs, value-rational action gives rise to mores, and instrumentally rational action can give rise to a market-based conduct derived from identical economic expectations. For instance, merchants may choose to forego any of the benefits of cheating because they realize a good reputation will draw in more customers. And as a further development the types of social action can lead to individuals recognizing the existence of a legitimate order as a guide for actions. For instance, affectual orientation can result in an emotional commitment to an order's legitimacy as in nationalist or tribal connections. Or value-rational orientation can lead an individual to recognize an order as supremely ethical or as a provider of religious salvation.

The last of the main issues that motivated Weber's work is his discussion of legitimacy. As the recognition of the legitimacy of a social order by individuals emanates from a certain type of communal behavior, this ideational activity also creates material governmental forms, for example, traditional tribal units, religious organizations, or rational bureaucratic states. The one exception is instrumental reason. Instrumental reason does not confer legitimacy because of its grounding in self-interest. It cannot guarantee communal bonds. It directs an individual to act in conformity with an order but does not elicit the same validation that the other types of action confer.

Weber suggested that legitimacy substantiates an order better than activity motivated by instrumental rationality. Thus he advised the state to base itself on legitimacy in order to guarantee social cohesion. He strongly espoused German nationalist and imperialist ambitions as values that could create this legitimacy. Only in such an order could one create peace.[9]

Weber dealt extensively with questions of conflict and disharmony. Unlike his contemporary, Georg Simmel, Weber did not recognize conflict as a fundamental factor of all social action. He concerned himself instead primarily with defining intentional conflict which he accorded a key role in human organization. In this view Weber separated sociology further from the moral/ethical basis of earlier social philosophy. Such philosophical work, driven by the desire to define what ought to be the ideal social formation—a formation in which universally disharmony and conflict did not exist—neglected to analyze what actually was. The purpose of the Weberian terminology, to the contrary, was to provide a means for the sociologist to interpret and describe the real existing world as it is. Recognizing the existence of conflict, Weber provided the social analyst with definitions of power and hegemony as a means to define the structure of conflict.

Weber sought definitions based on ideal types, yet he clearly recognized individuals and societies as being motivated by a variety of social actions and forms. He wrote that "it would be very unusual to find concrete cases . . . which were oriented *only* in one or another of these ways" (Ibid., 26). Society, in his view a place of competing and conflictual interests, does not have a single coherent form, but rather consists of various tendencies. However, Weber felt that clear terminology would allow the sociologist to bring some analytical order to these tendencies. Thus Weber was careful to define his terms accordingly.

Weber's success in developing a flexible set of terms can be illustrated by examining the difference between him and his contemporary, Ferdinand Tönnies. Tönnies's major work, *Community and Society* [*Gemeinschaft und Gesellschaft*], differentiated between two types of social organization, the community and the society. This book was highly influential and fueled a nostalgic conservative attack on the "society" of the modern era that had lost all traces of "community." The ideal type of the community had been lost to the new industrialized urban centers. Explicit in Tönnies's work is a moral imperative of how society should be. Weber, on the other hand, transformed these ideas into the terms 'communal' and 'associative' relationships (*Vergemeinschaftung* and *Vergesellschaftung*). The first form of relationship (families, nations, brotherhoods) is based on affectual or traditional action, whereas the second (economic interest groups, voluntary associations) tends more toward value or instrumental rational reasoning. This transformation of Tönnies's terms allowed for a more fluid analysis as opposed to the one-dimensional description of the types of society. It also did away with the "should" implicit in Tönnies's work.

The final set of terms put forth by Weber concerned the description of various group and party formations. We will return to the significance of these formations later. In the remainder of the two volumes of *Economy and Society* Weber employed and elaborated these terms through a discussion of historical and contemporary economies and power arrangements, for example, bureaucracy, religious groups, charisma, and the city. The first chapter, however, functioned primarily as an exposition of certain key terms for sociology. Although this chapter remained void of historical analysis, in its historical context we can see how it created an apparatus particularly appropriate for the description of the conflicts of Weber's own period.

POLITICS AND SOCIOLOGY

Given the extent of Weber's involvement in the political life of his era, why do the terms of his methodology outlined above seem so apolitical or ahistorical? While as we have seen, they were well tailored for an analysis of Weber's contemporary conditions, it is also clear that they avoided direct confrontation with those conditions. This is an important disjunction to examine, because outside of Germany sociological interest in Weber has fostered an apolitical understanding of his work, passing over his more overtly political writings for this.

There are a number of reasons. The rate and choice of texts translated focused primarily on what were identified as methodological writings and overlooked the other works. The division of Weber's writing into political and methodological rests in part on a lack of knowledge of contexts of production without which the reader could not understand the highly polemical nature of all of Weber's writings. But most important Weber supported and sought to actualize a *value-neutral* political position for sociologists. His own proposition of value-neutrality has served as a justification to overlook Weber's political work. Thus a number of questions are raised that serve as points of consideration in the last section of this discussion. Is such a division into political and methodological writings possible? Or is it possible to reconcile these two sides of Weber? Was his insistence on value-neutrality an act of bad faith, a standard he advocated but did not adhere to in his own work? Or should we be satisfied with a division of Weber's works into these two distinct categories?

Weber's understanding of value-neutrality rejected the political allegiance and crass ideological promotion that passed for teaching in the classrooms of many colleagues and former professors.[10] It also rejected a more general position, following Hegel, of the role of education as fostering the moral/ethical framework that distinguished a nation. There were many who argued that science should foster the specific values of a nation.[11] Such an organic understanding of society, Weber could not accept. In the ideal terms and types of *Economy and Society,* Weber sought to realize value-neutral sociology as he had defined it. The necessity of value-neutrality can be comprehended by noting how foundational was his insistence on the individual subject as being the agent of action. Weber saw the subjects who comprise society as in a constant state of development and unending variation, effecting changes in their social order. In such a state of variation, to achieve an objective judgment or decision, science must agree on a certain common language that can encompass variation. Otherwise judgments are meted out as part of the expansion of power of single individuals or groups. The terms of Weber's methodology were envisioned as the beginnings of that common language.

Weber, in his national imperialism, was not opposed to the hegemony of certain groups, nor did he adhere to a pacifism that sought to remove all conflict from society. Weber believed struggle and conflict to be a central aspect of social interaction. However, he did not believe it to be the role of science to foster one side in a power struggle over another. That was the role of politics.[12] The objective judgments of science enabled the politicians to arrive at their decisions and they therefore needed to interpret the wide variety of subjective actions and rationales as clearly and objectively as possible. Thus already in his inaugural address from 1894, we can see the beginning of a value-neutrality in the statement "Such are the circumstances, that our state form is a nation-state." Thus, he does not question the parameters of the state, but rather proceeds from its self-definition. Within these parameters sociology can put forth an analysis designed to serve the interests of that state not by telling it what it *wants* to hear, but by telling it what it *needs* to hear.

Perhaps one of the most illustrative examples of Weber's understanding of value-neutrality and the role of politics can be found in the related essays "Politics as Vocation" and "Science as Vocation." Both of these articles were written in the "Revolution Winter" of 1918/1919 as lectures for the Free Students' Federation. Given the total capitulation of Germany, the collapse of civil government, the devastation to the economy as well as a myriad of other pressing immediate political events, the opening of "Politics as Vocation" must have come as a shock, if not disappointment to his audience. Weber refused directly to discuss the politics of the day and chose instead to discuss on a more theoretical and terminological level the function of politics and science. However, the surface refusal of the quotidian politics belies the fact that the lecture was a powerful and insightful analysis of the forces at work in his contemporary political situation.

In "Politics as Vocation," we can identify certain key ideas and constructions that would be incorporated into *Economy and Society*. His discussion of the overinflated use of the word "politics" appears almost verbatim in section 17.2 of *Economy and Society*. And in "Politics as Vocation" we can find the well-known and pointed formulation that "the state is that human community that within a certain territory successfully claims a monopoly on legitimate physical force." The anarchic conditions of 1918/1919 were the exact opposite of this definition. A modified version of this statement was incorporated into section 17.3. Pointing out these connections is not to suggest that there is some hidden agenda in *Economy and Society*, but rather to indicate the relation of the two. Ultimately, "Politics as Vocation" can be understood as an example of how the typologies being developed in *Economy and Society* were intended to be applied in sociological analysis.

Weber identified the origins of the modern state in the confrontation between aristocracy and bureaucracy. He described how bureaucrats, historically themselves aristocrats, had to serve the interests of the king *and* their own interests. Then as the aristocratic individuals were replaced by functionary office holders from the middle classes, they came to serve the interests of the bureaucracy itself. The new bureaucrats controlled money and power which was not their own but rather an aspect of the office they held, leading them to strengthen the office. Such conditions threaten the state, since such functionaries, acting on the basis of instrumental rationality, are in no position to direct the values of the state. These conditions of modern politics lead Weber to identify the need for a new type of politician who does not live *from* his office but *for* it, whose profession is not bound to the fulfillment of a function, but rather to the realization of certain values. Such a politician would have to rely on what Weber called charisma, in order to attract the unified will of the people to give their support to his values and his leadership. The institutions of parliament should provide the atmosphere out of which the charismatic leader could emerge. There, in the midst of debates and the battle of political wills, politicians should learn not how to form consensus, but rather how to lead the people.

Weber's death in 1923 prevented him from witnessing the rise to power of the National Socialists. Although Hitler might appear to have been the embodiment of the charismatic leader Weber advocated, it is highly unlikely that Weber would have approved. Weber's authoritarianism was based on an elitist democratic commitment that would have resisted the imposition of complete dictatorship. However Wolfgang Mommsen has suggested that "Weber's theory of charismatic leadership combined with the radical formalization of the meaning of democratic institutions [by his contemporaries] helped, if only marginally, to make the German people receptive to support a leader, and to that extent to Adolf Hitler" (1984, 410).

Such historical, political, and ideological relationships are necessary for the continuing critical reception of Weber by his students. In the German tradition of philosophy, *Kritik* is not an act of dismissal but rather an ongoing process of reevaluating legacies in order to distinguish what is viable and current. And much in Weber's legacy continues to compel modern sociology. The scientific understanding of sociology, the role of sociologists as advisors to the state, and the value-neutral position of sociological inquiry became commonplaces even as the state conception for which they were constructed was repudiated.

NOTES

1. Value-neutral work is commonly understood in U.S. sociology to be nonideological work. This bears only a superficial resemblance to Weber's original idea which we will examine later.

2. For a discussion of the rise of nationalism see Anderson, B. 1983. *Imagined Communities: Reflections on the Origin and Spread of Nationalism.* London: Verso; Hobsbawm, E. 1990. *Nations and Nationalism since 1780: Programme, Myth, Reality.* Cambridge: Cambridge University Press. Mosse, G. 1981. *The Crisis of German Ideology: Intellectual Origins of the Third Reich.* New York: Schocken Books.

3. Bismarck was dismissed because he was entertaining plans to lead a coup in order to rid Germany of the socialist threat. The new Kaiser, desiring to rule as more than a figurehead for Bismarck, rejected Bismarck's revolutionary plans. He sought instead to solve the antinationalist problem through his own policies of social and political reform.

4. See Kocka, J. 1993. *Bourgeois Society in Nineteenth-Century Europe.* Oxford: Berg.

5. In the absence of a functioning democratic consensus to provide decisions of state with legitimacy, governments require some means to gather the information necessary to reach decisions. This is the role that Weber accorded his own contemporary bureaucratic institutions.

6. *Junker* is the title for the large estate owners from the nobility in Eastern Prussia. Their existence perilously dependent on the continuation of a conservative economic policy, they became one of the centers of proto-fascist organization in Germany.

7. Social theorists from the Enlightenment onwards had been concerned with this situation. Especially in Germany, from Kant onwards, the idea of consensual democracy where the minority must abide by the vote of the majority, was rejected. In its place figures like Fichte, Hegel, and Herder advanced the idea of the nation as a unified body lacking a dissenting minority will. They put forth moral/ethical education and socialization as the means to bring about and enforce this unified will of the people.

8. See for example, Tönnies (1988 [1887]).

9. Such a position rejects the proposition that Immanuel Kant made in *Perpetual Peace* (1795) that free market trade would naturally lead to the

formation of a peaceful world order. Weber felt that not commerce but the state must act as a cohesive force through the espousal of certain unifying values.

10. There are a number of important figures of the era who openly advocated nationalist political positions in their classrooms, such as the historian Heinrich von Treitschke (1834–1896). Also telling in this matter is the fact that although the Pan-German League was never a large group, it did have as members a disproportionate number of educators, allowing them to influence a very significant portion of the German public with their political position.

11. The German word *"Wissenschaft"* is translated into English as science, however science is too often equated solely with natural science. *"Wissenschaft"* means literally something more like knowledge-craft. It is science only in the sense of the human, social, *and* natural sciences.

12. This distinction is a variation on a position taken by Kant in his article "An Answer to the Question 'What is Enlightenment?'" (1784). Kant differentiated between the public and the private role of an individual. In a public role, that is, at work, the subject must obey the demands of his superior and his profession. In private, however, he is answerable only to himself and is called to speak out on greater social issues.

REFERENCES

Anderson, B. 1983. *Imagined Communities: Reflections on the Origin and Spread of Nationalism.* London: Verso.

Hobsbawm, E. 1990. *Nations and Nationalism since 1780: Programme, Myth, Reality.* Cambridge: Cambridge University Press.

Kocka, J. 1993. *Bourgeois Society in Nineteenth-Century Europe.* Oxford: Berg.

Mommsen, W. 1984. *Max Weber and German Politics 1890–1920.* Chicago: University of Chicago Press.

Mosse, G. 1981. *The Crisis of German Ideology: Intellectual Origins of the Third Reich.* New York: Schocken Books.

Tönnies, F. 1988 [1887]. *Community and Society.* New Brunswick: Transaction Books.

Weber, Max. 1978 [1923]. *Economy and Society.* 2 vols. Berkeley: University of California Press.

———. 1958. *Gesammelte Politische Schriften.* Tübingen: Paul Siebeck.

———. 1967 [1922]. *Wissenschaft als Beruf.* Berlin: Duncker & Humbolt.

11

MAX WEBER: ON FREEDOM, RATIONALITY, AND VALUE JUDGMENTS IN EDUCATIONAL DISCOURSE

Felecia M. Briscoe

INTRODUCTION

Max Weber's writings on education reveal the dilemma inherent in the values of the Enlightenment, specifically, the values of freedom and pure rationality. These two Enlightenment ideals are pregnant with the question of how one rationally supports a value that espouses a freedom from value judgments. Weber encounters this contradiction which is later explored in depth by postmodern scholars. Weber's writings on the role of value judgments in the sociological analysis of education and in his own sociological, philosophical, and political analyses of education are fraught with this quandary. Weber's discourses on education are found in *The Protestant Ethic and the Spirit of Capitalism,*[1] and in three widely used edited volumes of Weber's writings. These titles are not Weber's but are provided by each of the editors: "Bureaucracy,"[2] "On Universities,"[3] and finally, in Runciman ed. (1984), "The Nature of Social Actions," "Value-judgements in Social Science," and "The Logic of Historical Explanation."

Before examining Weber's thoughts on education, I briefly outline the role of value judgments in sociological research. My examination of Weber's thoughts on education begins with a summary of Weber's sociological method, which includes his debt to Georg Simmel, and continues with Weber's unique contributions. I then summarize Weber's description of education as a sociological phenomenon. I pay particular attention to Weber's description and implicit critique of the role that education plays and is increasingly likely to play in the modern bureaucratic nation-state. My analysis of Weber's writing on this issue delineates his Enlightenment values of freedom of thought and rationality that frame his sociology, philosophy and politics of education. Weber's views on education in general, and particularly his discourse concerning the German university system reveal a commitment to these Enlightenment values. Indeed, Weber consistently advocated the values of freedom of thought, rationality, human dignity, and intellectual integrity.

VALUE JUDGMENTS IN SCHOLARLY EDUCATIONAL DISCOURSE

In scholarly discourse there are two fundamental positions from which the nature of educational research and role of value judgment may be understood: essentialist and relativist. The essentialist position maintains that there is an *essential nature* to a good education. Such essentialist positions may differ as to whether education is a process (for example, bringing out what is in a person), a product (for example, producing a critical thinker), or a combination of both (for example, a socialization process that produces a survivor), but they are alike in their insistence that education has an essential nature or purpose. If one takes any of these essentialist positions, it becomes possible to critique or make absolute value judgments about any educational system—to make prescriptive statements about the way that education ought to be or proscriptive statements about what education ought not be. Essentialism generally begins with an absolute value foundation (such as freedom and human dignity) that provides the criteria for determining what constitutes a good education.

Relativists, on the other hand, take the position that a particular educational system and the values by which we judge that educational system are historically and socially contingent. By contingent I mean that these values are not the result of some transcendental, ahistorical process and therefore must not be conceived as being the result of pure reasoning—hence must not be conceived as absolute. Rather, value judgments are grounded and subject to historical and social forces. Under a relativistic position, one may attempt to simply describe education without making value judgments, recognizing that any value judgments about education are contingent and thus susceptible to revision.

I say the relativist might "attempt to describe," because many theorists claim that due to the theory-ladenness of observation, facts, and descriptions, one can never simply observe and describe the facts, but always describes from within the confines of a normative theoretical framework or paradigm.[4] Therefore, according to this position, no fact or description can ever be completely objective and free from implicit value judgments. This second relativistic position claims that even though we realize that value judgments are always contingent, it is nevertheless impossible to eliminate all value judgments—the best that one can do is to try to identify the value framework from within which one writes and explicitly recognize the contingencies of these values.

In examining educational discourse then, one can discriminate between essentialist discourse that is intentionally and explicitly valuative and relativistic discourse which attempts to eliminate value judgments. Alternatively, one can combine a relativist and essentialist position. As an essentialist, the researcher can explicitly identify the value framework from within which one makes observations, descriptions, and judgments. As a relativist the researcher can also explicitly recognize that the value framework used is contingent and subject to revision. The foregoing positions regarding the nature and role of value judgments in scholarly discourse have historical antecedents, one of which is found in the work of Max Weber.

Weber defined value judgments as the "practical evaluations of a phenomenon which is capable of being influenced by our actions as worthy of either condemnations or approval," (Weber 1994, 69). Weber wrote about education from both a relativist and an essentialist position. As a sociologist, Weber took a relativist discursive position, noting the contingent nature of values and asserting that such value judgments should be eliminated in sociological analyses. Despite Weber's relativistic stand on values in sociological discourse, an implicit critique framed by Enlightenment values pervades Weber's sociological description of education. Furthermore, Weber clearly brackets (disregards for the purpose of a present analysis) his understanding of the contingent nature of value judgments when elaborating upon his ideas concerning the nature of a good education. As a philosopher and political writer, Weber made explicit and at times "cutting" value judgments about education in general and about the German university system in which he taught. These value judgments he saw as nonetheless contingent.

WEBER'S SOCIOLOGICAL METHODOLOGY[5]

Influences of the German Tradition

Like Georg Simmel, Weber embraced the Enlightenment ideals of freedom of thought and pure rationality. In accordance with these values, both thinkers sought to avoid imposing their or anyone else's ideas or values, especially in the name of ration-al knowledge. Simmel and later Weber maintained that social norms (and forms) are always partly a matter of historical and social contingency. According to Simmel, when discussing sociological phenomena, " . . . no objective content is realized by its own logic alone, but only through the cooperation of historical and psychological forces. .," (Simmel 1950, 16;cf. 99–104). And later in speaking about the forms of sociation, Simmel claims that " . . . [forms] do not flow like our inner development does, but always remain fixed over a certain period of time. For this reason , it is [their] nature sometimes to be ahead of inner reality and sometimes to lag behind it. . . . [m]ore specifically, when the life, which pulsates beneath these outlived forms, breaks these forms . . . " (1950, 386). Accordingly, for Simmel sociological phenomena should simply be described and not evaluated by societal values which were always contingent and subject to change.

Weber agreed with Simmel's claim that a different epistemological approach was needed for sociology—sociology's purpose entails a unique value-free method. According to Simmel, the purpose of sociology was to gain an " . . . understanding [of] the unique structure which we call society, its nature, its forms and its development" (Simmel 1950). According to both Simmel and Weber, human interactions do follow general causal laws and at least one purpose of sociology is to discover these general laws by elucidating the forms of human interaction. Consequently, claimed Simmel and Weber, the laws concerning human interaction should be studied and reported objectively like a natural science.

Yet Simmel allowed that not just value judgments, but indeed all knowledge, is produced within social and historical forms that go through periodic transformations. Therefore all knowledge, not just values, are partly contingent. Indeed, both Simmel and Weber agreed that a scholar's values and interests would determine the particular problems or aspects of issues the sociologist selects to study. Neither theorist explicitly addressed the dilemma posed by making value judgments in any scholarly area, especially the dilemma this posed for distinguishing between that which counted as objective knowledge and that which was "subjective" or subject to historical or psychological contingencies. Nonetheless both maintained that the study of any sociological phenomena (irrespective of the values that went into picking out the phenomenon) was to be value-neutral and objectively described in order to develop scientific, sociological, causal explanations.

Weber's Unique Contributions

Weber's unique ideas concerning the interaction of culture and sociology, especially the importance of cultural meanings for describing social actions, have contributed to the science of sociology in five ways.

1. Weber thought that Simmel's characterization of sociology as the study of human interactions was incomplete and ambiguous. Weber developed his own definition of sociology: "a science concerning itself with the *interpretive* [italics added] understanding of social action and thereby with causal explanation of its course and consequences," (Weber 1994, 3). In this instance Weber went a step further than Simmel toward noting the necessity of including the subjective aspect of interpreting the social actor's intentions and meaning when performing an action. Weber maintained that neglecting the actors' understanding of their own action would render the description of the action incomplete. This assertion led Weber to include a further step in sociological methodology.

2. Simmel claimed that *verstehen* (the empathetic understanding of actions as an expression of human intentions) should only be used in historical research—hence it should be kept out of the science of sociology. However, Weber maintained that the objective content of social action could not be considered apart from the content (subjective meaning) of social action. Weber contended that the subjective content of social action *was* the defining criterion of social action, not just the forms that social action took. Accordingly, Weber claimed that one should include the content of interactions as well as the forms in order to discover the general causal laws of sociology. Content could only be grasped by using the *verstehen* method. Thus, for Weber *verstehen* should be part of sociological methodology.

3. Accordingly, in order to correctly understand social action, Weber maintained that we must also begin to understand social phenomena by knowing their history. Thus, history becomes a part of sociology.

4. Weber also questioned the validity of Simmel's use of analogies (appealing to non-sociological, nonempirical understandings) to support his claims about sociological matters. Rather, Weber maintained, a sociological research program should be comparative—for example, should compare empirical sociological data—and be interpretive in nature.

5. Consequently, Weber's unit of sociological analysis was the "ideal type" (Weber 1994, 23–26) which was embedded in history, not Simmel's ahistorical "form." According to Weber, when seeking to understand a sociological phenomenon, one should gather as many dif-

ferent examples as possible and from those different examples derive
an "ideal type." Weber used this method in analyzing the role of education in the modern bureaucratic state.

WEBER'S SOCIOLOGICAL ANALYSIS OF EDUCATION

The Historical Development

The problems that Weber identifies in his sociological analysis of
education are picked out by his Enlightenment values of freedom
and full rationality. He begins his analysis with a description and critique of the "ideal type" of bureaucratic state. In compiling his research on the modern bureaucratic state, Weber focused on his own
nation state of Germany and on the United States of America. Part
of his research program entailed tracing the historical development
of the modern bureaucratic state, as seen in the *Protestant Ethic and
the Spirit of Capitalism.* In this history Weber delineated how the
Protestant world view gave rise to a particular sort of capitalism, one
that encompassed democracy, bureaucracy and an increasing use of
instrumental rationality. Instrumental rationality is reasoning that
is limited to determining the efficiency of means and fails to evaluate other aspects of the means or the ends to which the means are
directed. Weber's history also indicates that democracies, in order to
function, need bureaucracy. Yet, in conjunction with the increased
use of instrumental rationality, the bureaucratic machine threatens
to dominate the democratic system. Thus, though democracies and
bureaucratic systems need each other initially, they can eventually
become pitted against each other through the extreme application of
instrumental rationality. Weber's critique of the prevalence of instrumental rationality (what he saw as an incomplete rationality
that led to an eventual loss of freedom) continued in the comparative
component of his research program.

The Comparative Sociological Analysis

Weber's comparative sociological analysis of the educational system is couched within his sociology of the modern bureaucratic state.
His sociological analysis is a critique based upon the enlightenment
values of freedom and full rationality. In the comparative component
of his research program, Weber sought commonalities that would indicate the nature of the "ideal type," of the modern bureaucratic

state. Weber claimed that the modern bureaucratic state was impelling an ever-increasing rationalization that would lead to an "iron cage of rationality" that precluded human freedom. This over-rationalization of life tends "to turn individuals into robots" (Levine 1991, 99–117) as their lives become increasingly determined by instrumental rationality.

Weber maintained that societies' activities are increasingly arranged and carried out by bureaucratic positions rather than persons. In such cases, the position of a person determines the person's actions rather than vice versa. In the modern bureaucratic state, Weber maintained that the educational system would come to assume a particular role. The role of the educational system would become that of producing people who are absolutely obedient to the state. Such an educational system also promotes instrumental rationality in which the goodness of the end would not be considered. Instead, the sole measure of goodness becomes the efficiency with which the ends dictated by the state are achieved. In this regard, Weber was certainly prophetic about the course that the Nazis and their efficient disposal of "unwanted" persons would take in twentieth-century Germany.

Weber argued that the modern bureaucratic state also tends to produce an educational system of special examinations for certificates which become the key to positions of social prestige and respect. Moreover, access to these positions would become restricted to those who can afford the "education" that culminates in the award of the certificate. Finally, the intellectual effort and development needed to obtain one of these education certificates would decrease while the number of certificates would increase. In summary, Weber maintains that education in a bureaucratic state produces an elite corps of certified people obedient to their positions. This obedience to position influences the once democratic state to become a machine in which everyone is caught—a machine that can be taken over by any master. The human cogs in the bureaucratic machine have been educated to develop a social attitude of precise obedience that prevails even after a revolution intended to produce a more democratic state of affairs. At one point even the "master" of a bureaucratic state becomes dependent upon the machine of experts. The bureaucratic machine itself comes to control the state as even the position of the master comes to dictate the master's actions. This machine with its human cogs functions without regard to the goodness of the ends to which it is directed, as efficiency becomes the sole measure of goodness.

The values (freedom, judgment, human dignity, intellectual integrity, and thoughtful actions) that frame Weber's sociological analysis of education are implicit. As both Simmel and Weber indicated, they are evident in the particular sociological aspects that Weber chose to consider in his analysis of education in the modern bureaucratic state. Although Weber never openly makes a negative value judgment about the educational trends he finds in the modern bureaucratic state, his analysis is certainly a critique. Weber's negative judgment of these educational trends is abundantly clear in his philosophy of education and in his political actions.

Weber's Philosophy and Politics of Education

Weber's sociology, philosophy and politics of education were interwoven. Weber's political thought and action crystallized in his educational philosophy found in "Science as a Vocation" (Weber 1946). In this lecture, Weber made explicit value judgments concerning the educational system in a modern state. "Science as a Vocation" delineates how the educational system even in a modern state can actively oppose the direction in which bureaucracy impels it. His strategy for opposition is composed of three prohibitions and a primary directive.

Weber's primary directive is that educators should teach students intelligently to confront "inconvenient facts" and make judgments that lead to thoughtful actions. The teacher's role in teaching this confrontation and judgment, according to Weber, is to provide facts, but not to provide *ersatz* leadership. Educators, maintains Weber, should confront students with choices and help them deduce the possible consequences of actions based upon those choices. Weber suggests that students be taught to question the inner consistency of their judgments and to ask themselves about the ultimate meaning of their conduct. Levine (1991) summarizes Weber's educational remedies for the ills of modern bureaucratic society: One should educate for judgment, help people to think critically, and encourage people to become reflective about social decisions rather than merely swayed by conventional practice and habit.

Along with his primary directive, Weber places three prohibitions upon the educator. First, just as the sociologist should avoid making value judgments as they analyze society, so too should educators refrain from making value judgments as they present "the facts." Perhaps more important, Weber claims that the educator should take great pains to avoid presenting only her side of an issue—especially presenting it as though it were the uncontested truth. And educators should not mix in religion or make "*ersatz* prophecies." Second, Weber advises that the "devil" of intellectualization found in an increasingly rationalized society should not be "flown from." Instead, the educational system should seek to produce understanding of the increasing store of knowledge and the effects of increasing rationalization. Third, Weber states that because of the educator's position of power, students are not in a position to openly and even perhaps covertly to reject the educator's politics. Therefore, educators should never bring their personal politics into the classroom.

Weber's prescriptions about the proper forum for an educator's politics were reflected in his own political actions. *Max Weber: On Universities* (Weber, 1974) contains numerous letters and rebuttals in which Weber actively pursued the political actions in his university system that his philosophy advocated.[6] According to Shils, "most of Weber's writings on the problems of the German University in the face of political and bureaucratic authority were published in the *Frankfurter Zeitun*" (Weber 1974, 2). Weber's other political writing appeared as short journal articles.

Most of his political writings were concerned with preserving the autonomy, academic freedom, and hence intellectual integrity of the German university system. In these letters and articles Weber argues against the appointment of university administrators and professors due to the "correctness" of their politics or religion. He feared that such a policy would encourage men to become mere "operators" without ethics. These operators would become the mouthpieces and *factota* of whatever party was currently in power. In other words, such a policy produces educators and administrators who were blindly obedient to the state and who engaged primarily in instrumental rationality. He felt that the hiring of such operators on grounds other than academic and scientific would lead to the disintegration of academic standards. He also adamantly opposed state support of religiously affiliated institutions of higher education. If educators and administrators were hired on the basis of their religion or political contacts, such educators would probably be expected to expound certain value judgments and censor other types of value judgments. Weber was concerned that the autonomy and intellectual integrity of his university system was becoming compromised by the policy of hiring administrators and professors due to political or religious affiliations rather than expertise. His politics of education found in letters and short articles opposed this policy. Thus, his pol-

itics were in accordance with his philosophy of education both of
which supported the Enlightenment values of freedom, intellectual
integrity, informed value judgments, and thoughtful actions.

Weber's (Enlightenment) Value Judgments in Education

The philosophy of education that Weber delineated clearly advocates the Enlightenment values that were only implicit in his sociological analysis. Weber's philosophy of education presents a strategy
designed to preserve certain values against the encroachment of the
bureaucratic state. His philosophy seeks to protect human freedom to
individually form and act upon value judgments, to promote intellectual development, and to preserve human dignity. His analysis includes the means of fighting against blind obedience and its atten-
dant instrumental rationality that tends to occur in a bureaucratic
system. His strategy also seeks to encourage thoughtful human judgments and action by presenting students with several options and by
helping them to develop their abilities to make intelligent, informed
value judgments. Weber's educational philosophy attempts to enable
individuals to retain their autonomy in a society that is increasingly
governed by "certified" positions; in so doing it seeks to preserve the
intellectual integrity of the educational system. He does not want the
educator's position to determine the judgments of the students.

The Contingency Dilemma of Enlightenment Values

Weber ended his lecture on "Science as a Vocation" by asking about
the relationship between value judgments and science. While Weber
believes that value judgments have no place in science, he clearly
sees the need for value judgments. It is here that we see him come
closest to facing the dilemma posed by his acknowledgment of the extreme importance of value judgments which, nonetheless, can never
be certain because of their historical and social contingency. Weber
makes and acts on value judgments while knowing that the norms
that produce the values and hence the values themselves are matters of historical and social contingency. In the educational prohibitions found in Weber's philosophy and politics of education we see an
indication of the manner in which Max Weber resolved this "value
contingency dilemma." Educators, Weber maintains, should not air
their value judgments in the class for the benefit of the students. Nor

should the classroom be a forum in which the current political leaders' value judgments are fed to the students by the educator. If Weber had believed that some values were absolute and not simply a matter of contingency, then he might have accepted the role of a prophet or leader—a role evidently assumed by his colleagues speaking either for themselves or for their administrators. Nonetheless, even making and acting upon the judgment that educators should not impose their views upon students is in itself a value judgment. Additionally, given Weber's stand on the proper way to educate, it is obvious that he would be extremely uncomfortable with asserting that he or any others (students in this case) ought to refrain from making value judgments despite their contingent nature. His whole educational philosophy is designed to produce people who are capable of making their *own* value judgments.

Likewise, Weber expected educators to form, hold, and express their value judgments, for Weber did allow an arena for educators' value judgments and political action. That place, however, is outside the classroom. The educator's value judgments and political acts should not take place with implicit public governmental backing. Especially, educators should not use their position to censor other possible value judgments. Rather, educators should place their value judgments in a venue which is open to contestation and perform their political acts as private individuals.

Weber's implicit resolution of the contingency dilemma—accepting that value judgments are a matter of social and historical contingency—foreshadows that of current postmodern social scientists. Several postmodern social scientists, for example, Michel Foucault, have deconstructed or otherwise argued for the contingent nature of values and social institutions. Like Weber's sociological analysis of the modern bureaucratic state, many of these deconstructions are nonetheless framed within a critique. In searching for some values that are not contingent, other social scientists—for example, Nancy Fraser (1981)—have pointed out the dilemma that Weber and current postmodern scholars find themselves in when they make critiques from a relativistic discursive position. Weber's implicit solution to the dilemma foreshadows the solution that some current postmodern scholars have come upon.

Michel Foucault deconstructs some modern humanist values to demonstrate their links to efficient strategies of social control. Like Weber's sociological analysis of education, Foucault's deconstruction of humanist values is framed within a critique of current social institutions (prisons, schools, and clinics). Again, like Weber, Foucault formed, held, and acted upon his value judgments while maintaining the contingent nature of value judgments. Foucault, too, never explicitly addresses the dilemma posed by the understanding of values as contingent.

Richard Rorty in *Contingency, Irony, and Solidarity* (1990) explicitly delineates this dilemma of forming, holding, and acting upon value judgments that are at the same time understood as contingent. Rorty also explicitly proposes a solution to this dilemma. His solution resembles Weber's implicit solution. Rorty maintains that, like Weber's educator in the classroom, those holding several viewpoints, including those to which one is opposed, should be encouraged to participate in a public discussion. Rorty, like Weber, recognizes that once all viewpoints have been considered, one nevertheless needs to form a value judgment upon which one is willing to act. Rorty explicitly expounds the position that Weber embraced in his writings on universities. One should act whole-heartedly according to the value judgments that one forms even while ironically recognizing the contingency of those value judgments. Rorty maintains that " . . . a belief can still regulate action, can still be thought worth dying for, among people who are quite aware that this belief is caused by nothing deeper than contingent historical circumstance," (1990, 189).

CONCLUSION

Weber's stand on value judgments in educational discourse was complex. As a sociologist he maintained that value judgments were a matter of social and historical contingency and as such had no place in scientific sociological analyses. Yet Weber did recognize that despite the sociologist's best intentions, values could not be left entirely out of sociological analysis. Moreover, Weber's sociology of education was framed by the Enlightenment values of freedom, human dignity, intellectual integrity, and thoughtful actions. Furthermore, Weber completely dropped his relativistic position on values in his philosophy and politics of education. In these two spheres, Weber clearly supported the Enlightenment values of freedom, intellectual integrity, and the importance of each individual making and acting upon value judgments. Therefore, Weber at times eschewed value judgments in educational discourse and at other times actively made value judgments about education.

Weber was caught in a dilemma that is currently faced by many social scientists and his implicit solution has provided guidance to others faced with the dilemma. Weber never explicitly addressed the dilemma posed by his inconsistency on value judgments in educational discourse. However Weber's philosophy and politics of education indirectly suggest a solution to the value judgment contingency dilemma. The solution suggested by his philosophy and politics of education advocates the creation of a public sphere in which all viewpoints and value judgments should be heard, but at the same time encourages students to form authentic value judgments that provide the ground for their actions.

NOTES

1. Weber, Max. [1930] 1992. The Protestant Ethic and the Spirit of Capitalism. Trans. Parsons: New York and London: Routledge.

2. Runciman, Walter, ed. 1994. *Max Weber: Selections in Translation.* Cambridge: Cambridge University Press.

3. In Weber 1974.

4. See for example, Kuhn, T., *The Structure of the Scientific Revolutions,* (Chicago: University of Chicago Press, 1962); Harris, K., *Education and Knowledge,* (London: Routledge & Kegan Paul, 1979); Feyerabend, P., *Against Method.* (London: New Left books, 1975); Mulkay, M., *Science Observed: Perspectives in the social studies of Science,* (London: Sage, 1983).

5. This description of Weber's sociological method is not intended to be complete. It concentrates mainly on Simmel's influence and those parts that would affect the understanding and descriptions of education. For a more detailed explanation of his method see the preceding chapter by Randall Halle.

6. For Weber's philosophy of education see "Science as a Vocation" (Weber 1946).

REFERENCES

Fraser, Nancy. 1981. "Foucault on Modern Power: Empirical Insights and Normative Confusions," *Praxis International* (vol. 1, pp. 272–287).

Levine, Donald N. 1991. "Simmel as an Educator," in *Theory, Culture, and Society.* London: Sage, vol. 18, 99–117.

Rorty, Richard. 1990. *Contingency, Irony, and Solidarity.* Cambridge: Cambridge University Press.

Simmel, Georg. 1950. *The Sociology of Georg Simmel,* trans. Kurt Wolff. New York: Free Press, Macmillan.

Weber, Max. 1946. *From Max Weber: Essays in Sociology,* trans. and ed. H. Gerth and C. Wright Mills. New York: Oxford University Press.

———. 1974. *Max Weber: On Universities; The Power of the State and the Dignity of the Academic Calling in Imperial Germany,* trans. and ed. Edward Shils. Chicago: University of Chicago Press.

————. 1992 [1904–05]. *The Protestant Ethic and the Spirit of Capitalism*. New York: Routledge.

————. 1994. *Selections in Translation,* (ed.). W. G. Runciman, trans. Eric Matthews, New York: Cambridge University Press.

INDEX